Elder Flowering

Elder Flowering

Lived Experiences of Growing Older

Edited by

Signe Eklund Schaefer

&

Karen Gierlach

SteinerBooks | 2024

2024
STEINERBOOKS
An imprint of Anthroposophic Press/SteinerBooks
834 Main Street, PO Box 358
Spencertown, New York 12165
www.steinerbooks.org

LIBRARY OF CONGRESS CONTROL NUMBER: 2024948448

ISBN: 978-1-62148-377-9

Printed in the United States of America
by Integrated Books International

Contents

Preface   ix

Onward from Sixty-three: Helpful Concepts and Personal Stories

From Seven to Twelve: A New View
Patricia Rubano
                                                                                   3

Opening and Choosing
Anne Kollender
                                                                                  26

Sixty-three and Beyond
Victoria Seeley
                                                                                  33

Born on a Saturday
Martha Loving Orgain
                                                                                  41

Eldering Exploration in My Pluto Time
Linda Bergh
                                                                                  58

Tracing the Arc of Life: Gifts of Aging

Following a Thread
Karen Gierlach
                                                                                  83

Croneology
Davina Muse
                                                                                  94

Somebodies and Nobodies
Christopher Schaefer
                                                                                 111

Coming of Sage
Mary Bowen
                                                                                 121

The Gift of Aging: The Beauty in Getting Older
Joseph Rubano
                                                                                 129

"There Is So Much to Admire, to Weep Over"
Alex Reid
                                                                                 149

Health Questions

New Perspectives on Health, Aging, and Biography Work
Douglas Garrett and Renee Meyer, MD   167

The Paradox of Aging
Ann Sawyer   184

Death Is Part of the Story

Death as a Process of Grace and a Doorway into Light
Karen Nani Apana, PhD   201

Memories of the Future
Christa Hornor   213

Loss and Transformation
Lorna Kohler   219

Ways of Working: Ongoing Reflection

Researching the Later Years
Betty Staley   245

Biographical Questions: Sharing Our Stories
Signe Eklund Schaefer   252

Why Not (a) Play?

Heart and Soul: A One-Act Play
Kathi Ciskowski   275

Bibliography   284

The Elder Flower is symbolic of endings and rebirth...

"*Love of wisdom acquired from life may be compared to the flowering of a plant at the proper stage of maturity.*"
—RUDOLF STEINER, *Love and Its Meaning in the World*

"*If humans learn to become older consciously with every day, then this really means a meeting with spiritual beings, just as being born and possessing inherited qualities means a descent from physical beings.*"
—RUDOLF STEINER, *Ancient Myths and the New Isis Mystery*

PREFACE

N ot too long ago, as editors of this book, we sent out a call to colleagues active in the development of biography and social art activities. We were seeking articles about aging. Biography and social art is a new field of work based on the ideas of Rudolf Steiner, the early 20th-century philosopher, spiritual scientist and founder of Anthroposophy. For people interested in Steiner's ideas about human development and the course of life, there is not much written material in English dealing with the post-63 years. But many of us active in the work are now well into these later years. So our invitation went out to our colleagues over seventy.

Very soon we began receiving proposals from people we knew and some we knew about but had never met. Recognizing that this would not be a project on which to spend many years, we set the deadline for chapters within a few months. Amazingly, the offerings began to arrive—nineteen of them!

As editors we had imagined that people would consider some of the foundational ideas about aging that have arisen from Steiner's indications, would explore recognizable landmarks of growing older and clues to deeper understanding. And indeed we received rich and varied offerings. For example, some chapters extend the idea of the connections between the evolutionary planets and the seven year life phases leading up to age 63, by exploring the post-63 years in relation to the planets Uranus, Neptune and Pluto. These latter were comets before moving into orbit in our solar system, thereby furthering imaginations of earth evolution, even as the later decades of life move beyond earlier expectations of longevity.

Working from a different imagination, another writer considers the post-63 years as an opening into the starry world, into the realm of the Zodiac. These different pictures can be seen as paradoxical; we have welcomed varied perspectives as a way of deepening our understanding of aging.

As chapters began to come in, it was very interesting to see the book take on a life of its own. What people have written is very individual, often surprisingly personal. We came to value the variety of voices and reflections. One person's story would become an unexpected illumination of an idea articulated by someone else. The honesty with which people have written is profoundly moving, and deeply inspiring. There are contradictory pictures, for example about retirement, because that is how life is. There is no one "right way" to grow old. These are the stories and reflections of real people, still very involved in their ongoing lives.

Many of our contributors were comfortable exploring ideas through writing, but several had never considered themselves to be writers and found the process very challenging. And yet, again and again we heard variations on "writing this was so important for me." There were significant experiences of resolution—coming to a new peace, ownership, acceptance of lingering life themes.

The intention to write about the later decades of one's life meant for some the reemergence of memories from childhood. Inevitably, many of these personal stories look back into earlier years, exploring the foundations of what led the writers to their current insights and experiences. Editing these very individual reflections was not easy: how do you make "cuts" into another's life?

A very recognizable quality of aging is how ever-freer people can feel in relation to guidelines or instructions, and this is part of how the book moved beyond our initial intentions. Our writers have very individual styles of expressing themselves. Living ever more in the now of life, people wrote what came to them, often sharing what presented itself in the moment. One writer turned her observations into a one-act play! And why not?

The book is divided into several sections. The sections are somewhat arbitrary, and definitely overlapping. For example, some of the personal stories could equally well have been put together with others looking at health, or at death and dying. The gifts of aging are addressed in all the chapters, not only in the section bearing that title. With the variety of offerings, it is our hope that every reader will find words that speak directly to their own questions or observations.

Several writers make reference to Sophia—she who is known as the wisdom of the world. This is not surprising since we all share an interest in Anthroposophy (*Anthropo-Sophia*). Many of us have felt an evolving relationship to this being throughout our lives. As editors, we would like to think that Sophia has inspired and embraces this work, this book, this effort to articulate the complexity—the beauty, challenge, heartache and hope—of the eldering years.

Signe Eklund Schaefer & Karen Gierlach
May 2024

ONWARD FROM SIXTY-THREE:
HELPFUL CONCEPTS AND PERSONAL STORIES

FROM SEVEN TO TWELVE: A NEW VIEW

PATRICIA RUBANO

I would like to offer an Imagination to this topic of life beyond 63. It is a picture I have been living with for some time now. It adds another level to other ideas I have worked with, and I can only say that it inspires me to strive toward a more selfless existence. An Imagination for me is a picture that moves me—and in itself, it is a "moving picture" in that it can change along with my understanding. It is important that you realize I am sharing something that is still in movement as I write this. As I live with it, I continue to find more to add to the picture so that it continues to grow and bring added meaning and depth to my experiences as I age.

I will begin with a brief overview of what is familiar from most of the books written about biography work before adding this other movement that I have not found in books.

Threefold Human Being

Most people will be familiar with, or can recognize, three principal aspects to the human being. The essential or eternal part of us that we call *Spirit* is born into a physical *Body* in which we dwell between birth and death. The third aspect, called *Soul,* mediates our spiritual and earthly experiences through the faculties of thinking, feeling and willing.

The *Body* grows and develops until the life forces peak and then decline—an ascent and then a descent. The *Spirit* gradually enters or incarnates into this physical, earthly existence and then gradually excarnates—a descent and then an ascent. What we experience as we take in all the ups and downs, the contractions and expansions of life, inwardly fills out our *Soul* and is the journey that we call our life or biography.

Every movement possible is contained in this journey, but because we are in a body and a world of time and space, we mostly think of this in terms of a chronological and forward movement—our life is thought of as existing on a timeline. This timeline can be worked with in various ways. Making a life-chart—whether it be on a straight line, a U-chart, or various other forms—can be a wonderful resource to look at themes, patterns, rhythms, etc. The most typical rhythm used to divide life into stages is that of seven years for each phase. Why seven?

Rhythms of Life

It is easy to see seven as a number related to development when we think of the seven notes of a scale that progress or climb until they reach the octave, which is the "same" note that we started with but now on another level. And when we look at a rainbow or see light passing through a prism, we see seven bands of color. They blend one into another; and if we are lucky enough to see a double rainbow, we will see the colors repeat, but in reverse order. Something progresses or repeats, but is changed.

Therefore, we use the rhythm of seven in looking at life as a process of development and changing consciousness as we mature. The number seven also holds correlations with the seven classical or evolutionary planets that Rudolf Steiner speaks of. They each hold qualities and characteristics that have been ascribed to them since Greek times and that can be recognized as soul qualities in human life.

Thus, we move first through the inner planetary spheres of Moon (birth–7), Mercury (7–14) and Venus (14–21). The Sun reigns for twenty-one years over the middle of life (three phases—21–28, 28–35, 35–42), and then we journey through the outer planetary spheres of Mars (42–49), Jupiter (49–56) and Saturn (56–63).

Rudolf Steiner speaks about the planetary influences that work upon the earth and into our souls, not only while we are living but also during the journey we make between death and rebirth. Here we pass through the different planetary spheres as we leave the earthly realm to gain what can be added to our being and offered to the spiritual world from our life on earth, and to see where we have missed the mark and need to make compensation.

Eventually we reach the realm of the zodiac, and ultimately the point at which we decide to make a return journey. This decision is made with other souls and spiritual helpers, in order to gather what we will need to continue our own evolution and contribute to the evolution of humanity. As we travel back, the zodiac gives us our human form and the planets help create our organs.

At last, we enter a new life through the gateway of the Moon, to begin again the work of body, soul and spirit through our willing, feeling and thinking.

Another Imagination

In the picture just given there is life before birth and life after death. The journey upon earth passes through the nine seven-year phases, moving through the planetary spheres (with the Sun shining over 21–42), bringing us to 63. What happens after sixty-three? This question has been addressed in various ways. Now that there are enough of us who have been working in the field of biography to be of an age to look back and reflect, we can begin to bring more research to this question out of actual experience.

Given that I have only now turned 71, I am hardly qualified to speak authoritatively, so I will simply share the following Imagination as it has grown in me as something to consider; and I will try to share how it informs my own life experience thus far. I hope that others will take it up if it is worthy of further investigation.

In its simplest form, this Imagination is one in which the individual journeys along the path of life comprised of the various phases and their planetary influences up to the age of 63. Then—perhaps—there is the potential to enter into the realm of the Zodiac, the fixed stars, which stand "above" the circling planets. How, or even if, we experience this may well depend upon the development that we have undergone thus far.

This is not original to me and I must give credit to Christopher Bee as the source of inspiration for this Imagination, which I encountered during a workshop he facilitated at a Worldwide Biography Conference at Emerson College in England, in 2013. Christopher, in his own way, has developed it much farther, into the depths of the twelve Zodiacal signs and all that is associated with them: virtues, perspectives, etc.[1] It has served me to live with a more general picture of entering a new sphere within the realm of the twelve in the years beyond 63, and to discover the meaning this has for me.

I am still interested in other approaches to this question. Beredene Jocelyn works with the qualities of Uranus, Neptune and Pluto in the post-63 years and I can easily see the correlations that are spoken of there.[2] The O'Neil's view is one of spiraling back into the U-Chart so that we are now moving between both the inner and outer planets once again, on our way in the end, to the Sun Sphere.[3]

I do not see these pictures as mutually exclusive or contradictory. I am beginning to see this picture of stepping into the Zodiacal realm to be a parallel path that may potentially be simultaneous as we can begin to wake up to it. Just as the Zodiac is seen to be "above" the planets, it may be that it is a sphere we can be aspiring to enter, to more consciously connect with our *spirit,* or "*I,*" as we continue on our *soul* journey through the planetary spheres—even as we are still in our *physical bodies.* Each of these is a unique realm of experience that works along with and interpenetrates the others, as do thinking, feeling and willing, and body, soul and spirit. It is possible that new realms become accessible as we age.

---

1 Christopher Bee; see his writings at https://www.christophori.com/; https://www.biographaea.com/.

2 Beredene Jocelyn, *Citizens of the Cosmos.*

3 George O'Neil and Gisela O'Neil, *The Human Life.*

From Seven to Twelve?

What is it about this number 12 that evokes a sense of wholeness? Is it only the result of all the pictures that we have taken in as we were growing up? There are 12 wise women (fairy godmothers ala Disney), 12 Knights of the Round Table, 12 tribes of Israel, 12 disciples of Christ, 12 months to the year, 12 hours in a day and night, 12 animals in the Chinese Calendar, 12 signs of the Zodiac, etc. Or is there something behind all these pictures that gave birth to them in the first place?

Twelve indicates a completeness in contrast to the developmental process of the seven, where each has its own orbit. I find that entertaining the circle of 12 as a primary focus gives a different mood and gesture to the years after 63. Here we would surely have to cross a threshold; and our lifeline would take on the nature of a circle in this realm, requiring of us a whole new gesture and a new entry point.

The realm of the Zodiac is present all the time, but our potential "entry" is dependent on our spiritual development. If we are developing the provisional soul states of Sentient Soul, Intellectual/Mind Soul, and Spiritual/Consciousness Soul in the middle years of life (21 to 42) in the way Rudolf Steiner outlines, these may begin their transformation to becoming Imaginative, Inspirational and Intuitional Soul states in the years between 42 and 63.

As this occurs, it should become increasingly possible in our later years to enter and "be" in the center of this circle of the Zodiac, with a strongly established "I" organization, even as we move freely into and between the twelve perspectives that surround us—*while* maintaining our individual "I."

Perhaps this could be a reflection of the idea that we return full circle to "become, Again, as a little child," so that after building up our unique individuality during all the years along the archetypal human journey we call life, we begin to let go into the circle and, again, allow ourselves to be permeated by all the people and surroundings in our environment, as we did when we first entered this earthly realm. Unlike the child, however, this time we enter the circle with consciousness and with a developed and individuated "I" or ego.

With the idea of simultaneity, I can imagine that one aspect of myself is always moving forward, so to speak, toward the point when I will depart this earthly life. At the same time, I can imagine that another aspect of myself is not dwelling in the linear movement of past to future, but rather in a circular and interweaving movement that is continuous and therefore timeless. Doesn't this sound like the realm of spirit and the natural home of the eternal "I"?

One way I find something of this in my life is when I have entered into an "other" so fully (be that a thought or action or person) that I am interwoven with it/them and have lost all sense of time. Or in those moments when I feel an invisible tap on my shoulder—or head—or heart that lifts me out of the moment and says, "This moment is important only in so far as you are present and awake in consciousness." In other words, "Don't get caught in the *what* of it, but attend to the *how* of it—*now.*" And it is always "now."

Moving into the Great Round

This illustration of entering the circle of the fixed stars at age 63, shows the developed human "I" standing at the center after journeying through the planetary spheres. This image, created by Vera G. Klein, appears with Christopher Bee's 2011 article, "The Temple of Life," and also in their new publication, *Edition Biographaea.*[4]

Free movement among and between the various points on the periphery of the circle would necessitate an "I" that is unencumbered by the egotistically motivated views that typically limit and obscure our vision.

In practice, this means that I must leave my own particular preferences, opinions, values, etc., to stand in another's place on the

---

4   Vera G. Klein, Veráce: illustrator, biographical coach, and life artist (www.veragklein.nl). Also, see Bee, Christopher, op. cit.

"The Temple of Life"

circle to see the world from that standpoint. I can always pick up my former thoughts again, but if I have fully taken in the other's perspective, my view will have changed to include new and different elements than were there before. In such an ideal and far-reaching imagination, my picture of the "I" at the center would have to be empty to a certain extent and more like a strong and beautiful vessel. A vessel that is continually emptying to make space for the incoming flow, as a fountain does.

I recognize I have a long way to go to approach this ideal. However, I can see in myself, and in some others, that this practice becomes more possible with age. With a strong enough interest in the world and in the "other," along with the impulse to continue learning and growing throughout life, I am more willing to move from my favorite, comfortable spots on the circle to visit ever more foreign lands—*and*—it is not easy! As I am willing and able, I find opportunities and encounters with others who say things that give rise in me to a reaction of, "How in the world can they see the world or that issue in that way!?" And yet, I find I have more desire and capacity not to stop at that initial reaction but to move to a different question, "How in the world can I find a way to enter into their thinking and see through the window they are looking through?"

I have found that when I can step away from my own window and listen with true interest—and even amazement—I get at least a glimpse of a different view than I have seen before. My viewpoint is expanded, and I am changed. For example, the only way I can talk about politics with some of my family members is to listen to their very different view of how things are. I still may not agree with what they say, but I understand more; and I find things in my own view to think about and question that were unseen before. During the Covid pandemic I had friends on both ends of the spectrum in their views around the vaccinations. I found that speaking with them and listening to their choices and considerations informed my thoughts and helped me to stay in the middle without rejecting either side. I made it a point to have the difficult conversations instead of avoiding them. We could always find understanding, if not agreement, and so we could continue to respect one another's choices.

Like drawing a teapot from twelve angles, each of which shows only a partial view, there is a greater chance with all twelve to come to a true picture. No view is complete and none is wholly untrue just like the blind man who felt the elephant's leg and said the elephant is like a tree—and the one who felt the trunk said it is like a snake—neither was wholly "wrong"—and neither was wholly "right."

With the imagination of needing the full circle to find a true picture, I find that I am far less attached to the idea of right and wrong. I am more interested in being open and interested than I am in being right. I am more inclined to see that we all have a piece of that fuller picture. I find that as I relax my hold on the notion of right and wrong, conversations deepen and open in ways that they did not when I was trying to persuade someone to see my point of view, or when I simply shut the conversation down because I would speak with such assurance that no opening could be found. Nowadays, I may or may not even share my perspective, as I try to be more attentive to whether it is wanted or not. However, I will listen and at least I have heard the other's point of view.

The imagination of being within the circle of 12 has less a feeling of "somewhere to get to!" Rather, it feels more "centered" even if I cannot always maintain connection to that center. When I am not connected to that center, which is both mine and everyone else's, I am caught and cannot let go of my point of view. I am neither centered nor can I move to any other point on the circle. It is only later that I see this. I am humbled and pained to see my inability to open or find common ground. I see that I stopped listening and/or shut down. I am stuck and *nothing* moves.

This is ever a work in progress and though I might prefer to keep them outside, I meet the beasts of the abyss that separates us from the spiritual and the natural worlds in my own being! The beasts of fear, doubt and hatred that surround us—and that are being continually fed to us—are also in us, in me. However, I feel more ready than before to bear the reality that I am part of everything that is happening in the world. The last stanza of what is called "The Destiny Verse" ("I find my star, my star finds me...) by Rudolf Steiner describes how I often feel quite well.

> ...Life grows more radiant about me
> Life grows more arduous for me
> Life grows more abundant within me.

We may have been working to develop many of these capacities for years and yet it seems to be true that as the life forces are leaving the body, they become available in new ways—ways that make it possible to build not physical, but spiritual capacities. As I write these words, I see again a picture of emptying and filling as the fountain does. Stepping into this new gesture surely brings us to a Threshold that will be challenging, as we are asked to face ourselves. Maybe this is the most difficult part of aging: we come face to face with our own mortality and what our life has been. This crossing and stepping into the circle of the fixed stars is where we might find something more true and real *if* we can face ourselves as we are.

It seems, with age, that I can increasingly recognize my own Double: all that has been taken in from my surroundings and lives in me unconsciously—behaviors, thoughts, ideas, etc. (This concept is somewhat related to the Shadow in Jungian terms.) Though I may cringe at the truth of what I see, by recognizing and trying to own these parts of myself I can then see how difficult it must be for others to live with me. A very humbling experience! I also see that things my near and dear ones do that irritate me, are also a reflection or a different version of things that I, myself, do. I try to see all of this, take responsibility for my part, and bear the pain of my own unconsciousness without either excusing or blaming myself. Out of this comes far more compassion and acceptance of both myself and others.

I sense and hear the questions of the Guardian who asks: "How well do you know yourself? Are you able to look at your unconscious bias and prejudice; or at the sympathies and antipathies that have accompanied you through life—the ones that have not yet been transformed? Can you reverse the direction of your will, which has always been occupied with taking care of yourself, to one devoted to taking care of others? Can you let go of old ways of thinking, feeling and acting to make way for new ones—allowing the ideas of others to enter and change you? Can you allow others the freedom to create the world as you once did? Can you allow others to take care of you as you have cared for others?" (And of course, this "you" is "me"!)

What can we do? A part of the St. Francis Prayer that is a companion to me helps to remind me of my striving. *"Lord, grant that I may not so much seek to be loved as to love—that I may not so much seek to be consoled as to console—that I may not so much seek to be understood as to understand."* I, for one, need regular reminding.

Oh, these are hard questions and demanding work! I think we can only approach them little by little, but doing so actually seems to build strength. To enter the circle where I can "be" in the center and yet move freely around it, is a continual test. Can I leave my precious standpoint to stand in the center—and then step away into another point—and another—and another—and weave wonderful patterns through these movements? This is a helpful quote by Rudolf Steiner from *The Younger Generation*:

> Nowadays, you continually hear, "That is my standpoint."
> Everyone has a standpoint. As if the standpoint itself really
> matters! The stand-point in spiritual life is just as fleeting as
> it is in the physical. Yesterday I stood in Dornach, today I am
> standing here. These are two different standpoints in physi-
> cal life. What matters is that a person should have a sound
> will and a sound heart in order to look at the world *from
> every standpoint*. But people today do not want what they
> can glean from different standpoints. The egoistic assertions
> of their own particular standpoints are more important to
> them. Yet, they thus shut themselves off in the most rigorous
> way from others.[5]

Only by putting aside my own personal opinion and standpoint can I open the possibility to look from various standpoints, until eventually a picture containing all parts can be brought into whole-ness. I find when I hold this picture of freedom to move between points, it is a relief to drop my precious beliefs and entertain oth-ers—not needing to feel attached to any.

There are numerous places where Steiner speaks of the circling planets, connecting them to the Soul and the astral aspect of the human being, while the Zodiac and fixed stars/twelve constella-tions are the realm of the Spirit and the "I." Things I have read before but had nothing to connect them with have found a place

---

5   Rudolf Steiner, *Becoming the Archangel Michael's Companions*, p. 5.

in this Imagination, continually expanding the picture. Like this quote from *Macrocosm and Microcosm,* for example, with its intriguing description of what happens when we pass the Guardian of the Threshold to the spiritual world—if we are prepared to do so in a healthy way:

> On passing the Guardian of the Threshold, the Ego is objectively before us. But we may look at this Ego once, twice, three times, four times, and each time obtain different pictures. According to conditions prevailing in the physical world we might say to ourselves, Now I have seen what I am in the higher world. And the second time: Now I have found myself again and am something different. And the third time again we find something different. When through the training described we enter the Imaginative world and see a picture of our Ego, it is essential to know that twelve different pictures of the Ego can be seen. There are twelve different pictures of every single Ego, and only after contemplating it from twelve different standpoints have we a complete picture. This view of the Ego from outside corresponds exactly to what is reflected in the relationship of the twelve constellations of the Zodiac to the Sun. Just as the Sun passes through the twelve constellations and has in each a different power, just as it illumines our Earth through the course of the year and even the day, from twelve different stations, so the human Ego is illumined from twelve different stations in the higher world. Therefore, in rising into the higher worlds we must realize the necessity of not being satisfied with one standpoint only. We must train ourselves in order to escape confusion.[6]

This may relate to repeated earth lives and incarnating under different constellations. I see it as an ever-present reality not bound by time.

What could it mean that I am one and I am twelve? And if this is true for me, then it must be true for everyone! Entering into this Imagination as a "moving picture," I see an amazing weaving of "I

---

6   Rudolf Steiner, *Macrocosm and Microcosm,* lect. 9.

and Thou"—where I meet myself at every point. A picture where the world and every other person are an expression of my very own "I"—as my own "I" is an expression of world-processes. Is some intuition of this why many older people *feel* the world and all that is happening so much more intensely than they ever did before?

By practicing biography and social art for so many years—looking at my own life in the company of others who are doing the same, and sharing what we find—I continually recognize my own life in someone else's story, and I see theirs in mine. I have a growing sense of looking at my life from the outside, as if watching a movie. I feel less attached to my life, as it has played out, as the one and only version possible. I feel more like this is the way it unfolded this time because of choices that I made—that it might have been different and yet the one that "I am" in essence would have remained the same. It even becomes possible, as I meet others, to see them as another version of myself, and I am another version of them. "There but for the grace of God go I" becomes more of a reality than a wise saying. I don't know if this makes sense to others, but if you have some real experience of what I am trying to say, then you are probably an older individual.

Life itself is an initiation in the times we are living in. We meet trials and thresholds daily; and if we have lived an intentional life (within Anthroposophy or not) devoted to truth and consciousness, life itself prepares us and brings us to some kind of actual knowledge that we are not separate from the world or each other.

I can no longer put what happens in the world "out there," but have to recognize that it happens also in me. This actually empowers each of us to take responsibility at a much deeper level, as we know that how we live our own life impacts the whole world.

I recall some of the older individuals I have known, when I was younger, who had a radiant quality about them. They were real representatives of true humanity for me. Though their bodies appeared frail, their skin was almost translucent. I could easily imagine that they had found their way into the Sun sphere and were traveling among the stars. They seemed somehow mysteriously nourished by a spiritual substance streaming into them so that they radiated warmth and light, and thus brought blessing to others. What rayed into them invisibly, rayed out into the world in ways that were perceptible if you could perceive it.

Another Picture of Twelve

Rudolf Steiner enumerated twelve senses before the scientific community had settled on five. These additional senses include gateways through which we perceive the world beyond the merely physical. He often placed them into three groups, relating four to *Body,* four to *Soul,* and four to *Spirit.* I will try to show a relationship between the four foundational or *Bodily* senses and the four higher or *Spiritual* senses, and I will speak of the middle or *Soul* senses as central to a process of development or transformation that can occur.

It would seem impossible to understand any process of transformation or metamorphosis without taking into consideration the supersensible realm—what cannot be weighed and measured in the physical realm. I have tried for years to make out what this transformation of the senses might mean in a practical, experiential way in terms of becoming truly human. Considering this question through the lens of "eldering" and the phenomena of aging has brought new substance of experience to what were thoughts and theory before.

I begin to see a way in which the senses that are turned inward as children, telling us about ourselves, are turning outward as we age, and those that are outward directed, telling us about the other, are experienced more inwardly as we grow older. The wisdom of language can provide an entry into some ideas as we see how we use the same words for both physical and soul/spiritual experiences. Through this, some of the more ephemeral ideas can take on form. As I allow this approach, I experience new connections appearing in an imaginative way. I find this similar to the way a fairytale opens to me when I have lived with it for a long time, and I listen to what comes. I hope that what follows sparks some thoughts and questions for your own research. Rudolf Steiner spoke of the first four senses as related to the Body. Through these we learn about ourselves as beings embodied in space. These foundational senses are *Touch, Life, Self-Movement* and *Balance.*

The middle senses related to the Soul are *Smell, Taste, Sight* and *Warmth,* through which we learn about the interplay between self and world; we take in the world through these portals and respond with the sympathies and antipathies of the soul. The senses related to the Spirit are *Hearing, Language, Concept,* and finally, *the Sense of the "I" of the Other.* Through these we learn to know what is not our self.

The foundational, *Bodily* senses give us a healthy grounding in the body and serve the incarnating spirit for its life on earth. The *Soul* senses are central to our lives in the process of realizing our humanity. What we do here will determine how deeply we live into the realm of the *Spiritual* senses, as we learn to hear behind the sound to the true nature of what sounds; where we recognize language as the medium of speech that carries meaning vs. sound itself; where we see behind and beyond the words to the concept; and where we can recognize the being behind the concept that received and communicated the thought.

Steiner eventually settled on the sense of *Touch* as the first sense. Although we typically think that touch tells us about the thing we are touching, in fact it is only the boundary of our own body that is experienced. Other senses such as movement and warmth, must be added to know more than our own boundary.

The sense of *Touch* gives us the fundamental experience and knowledge that we are separate beings in our physical body while simultaneously giving rise to the longing for the oneness we experienced in the spiritual world.

TWELVE SENSES

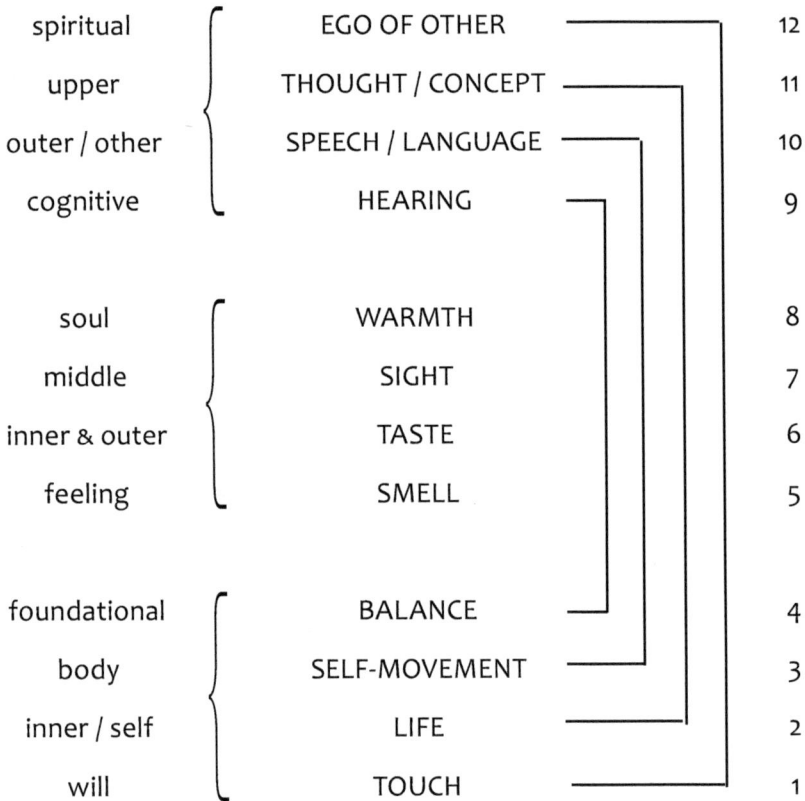

spiritual	EGO OF OTHER	12
upper	THOUGHT / CONCEPT	11
outer / other	SPEECH / LANGUAGE	10
cognitive	HEARING	9
soul	WARMTH	8
middle	SIGHT	7
inner & outer	TASTE	6
feeling	SMELL	5
foundational	BALANCE	4
body	SELF-MOVEMENT	3
inner / self	LIFE	2
will	TOUCH	1

My father, as he got older, noted how songs or poems or even the sight of a kind deed could bring tears; and I see this in my husband, myself and many others. In recalling this, I can feel how what *touches* me most deeply in these things is the commonality and universality of human experience and within this, that longing for unity in our separateness.

This first sense of *Touch* is related to the twelfth and highest sense—the *sense of the "I" of the Other.* Just as touch is spread over our whole body, Steiner says that the organ for the sense of the *"I" of the Other* is found throughout our entire body/being. Could we see a transformation from an organ of boundary to what becomes a more subtle and permeable membrane in order to allow another to enter into us and we into them? Wouldn't this be the inverse of our first learnings through touch?

The sense of *Life* lets us know if all is in order in our body. Pain is the messenger that tells us when something is out of whack and needs attention. I am not at ease if there is dis-ease and my sense of *Life* lets me know this. Nowadays I feel pain in my heart as I sense the life of the world, and this tells me that there are things that are out of whack and that need attention for the health and well-being of the earth and its inhabitants.

The *Life-sense* can be related to the sense of *Concept or Thought*. I must have a certain level of ease in my body in order to grasp and/or follow a train of thought. This is true even for a child. As an elder, am I now able to see beyond the surface understanding of climate change to the reality of the *concept* of the earth as a living being and know that the Lakota phrase "Mitakuye Oyasin" (all my relations) is truth? We are all related, and if one part is ill then so is the whole. Here again, it may be pain that is the messenger.

With *Self-movement* we sense our own movement, and in fact, Steiner points out that out of healthy movement we experience a sense of freedom and independence. We are not *entirely* bound in a body but can run, jump, skip as we sense the spirit moving in and through us, especially as children. With age, the loss of outer flexibility and freedom of movement may bring a sense of being bound in the body, and yet there is often a newfound freedom in many elders to try through artistic means to express the inner movements of the soul.

The sense of *Self-movement* is transformed in the sense of *Language* or *Word*. Free movement of the limbs is connected to the development of speech, which is focused in the area of the mouth and jaws—the moving "limbs" of the head. We first enter language through its movement and music as we coo and babble. This universal "singing" then comes to rest in single words as "naming" occurs, and thus the world is created—again. *Movement* is required for writing and reading symbols, and yet we still our bodies to learn and to truly understand what is being spoken—especially if it is something complex or deeply meaningful. There is something about the moving spirit of *Language* and of bringing something to rest, that once again describes an inverse activity that speaks of metamorphosis to me.

If we slow down and become more still outwardly as we age, and yet are still moving inwardly so we can follow the moving spirit of *Language*—maybe we grow closer to the realm of the Logos—the Living *Word*. Might we then hear the wisdom that whispers under the surface, and thus reawaken to what the child once knew?

The sense of *Balance,* which is totally related to the earth and gravity, helps us to orient ourselves in space, allowing us to become upright and to walk. This is still a Bodily sense and yet after we stop supporting ourselves with physical objects, we must actually extend out with our life-body and our sight to "lean" on, anchor and support ourselves with all that surrounds us. We become less stable on our feet as we age. Now, perhaps an inner orientation is necessary—a moral sense that helps us maintain our uprightness in spirit, providing a true orientation in the spiritual realm.

The sense of *Balance* is related to the sense of *Hearing*, both centered in the ear. The Sense of *Hearing* brings sound right into us and allows us to perceive the true nature of what is sounding, be it bird, bell or a baby. *Balance* is totally dependent on the earth and gravity. On the other hand, in order to hear matter sound, we must free it from the earth and create a hollow space for earthly substance, such as wood or metal, to sing or ring rather than simply thud or clang. It is the hollowed or "hallowed" space that allows spirit to sound.

The ear itself is hollowed out of the bony structure of our head. While we must extend out into space to keep our bodily *Balance,* we must take deeply into ourselves the sounds of the world, even as we screen out "noise" to sense something essential. Does it become easier, as our outer hearing becomes weaker, to re-orient ourselves to the "still, small voice within" that is so easily missed amidst the noise of the world? The capacities for deep listening and focused attention are gifts for both the recipient and the giver. We can practice ever more consciously if we realize that the true nature of what we orient ourselves toward can be revealed to us.

The middle or *Soul* senses are where much of the real work occurs, and should begin earlier than later. These senses are given to humans in the same form that the animals have them, though less acute. They are *Smell, Taste, Sight* and *Warmth* and they have a strong instinctual nature to them. Unadulterated they hold great wisdom. For example, the young child has an appestat that tells them what foods their body needs and which to reject—and we react with flight, fight or freeze mechanisms when danger is sensed via these messengers. Our work is to humanize them—to lift them out of the instinctual into the moral realm so that we can choose how we respond rather than merely reacting.

Our reactions to *Smell,* especially smells of rot and death, are particularly strong. Fortunately, olfactory fatigue sets in and we cease to be conscious of it. Nevertheless, the doctors and nurses who work with disease and decay must rise above the natural reaction in order to see the human being before them. Even outside the physical realm, do we give in to an instinctive reaction and wrinkle our nose when we don't agree with someone, as if the idea or the person is offensive to us? Do we see and treat people as objects or as individuals?

We are born with a healthy sense of *Taste,* but we quickly take on the particular tastes of our family and culture. We develop preferences for salt or sweet, sour or bitter. It is quite a task to return to the point where we can discern, before even eating it, how our body will respond to a certain food. However, it can be done. It is interesting that we are more willing to allow others to have their own taste when it comes to food, but many are the arguments that arise because of differing aesthetic tastes.

Consider that our eyes grow out directly from our brain and are primarily receptors for color. Other senses come into play to observe form, etc. *Sight* shows us the surface of things and perhaps that is why it is the easiest sense to fool. (Think of optical illusions.) We see the apparent reality, but it takes years of experience and a different kind of insight to question first impressions and what the mind tells us is real. "There is more to life than meets the eye." We must work to develop the capacity to see what lies behind appearances, as well as behind our assumptions and prejudices, to *see* what is true.

The last of the *Soul* senses is the sense of *Warmth*. Through this process of ennobling these senses, the kind of *Warmth* that will take us through the gateway from the *Soul* senses to the *Spiritual* senses is created. (We have already visited the *Spiritual* senses in their relationship to the *Bodily* senses.)

Warmth is at the heart of everything. Even with bodily *warmth*, we can only live within a small range in temperature. Further, it is the human quality of warmth extended to the infant that determines whether it thrives or even dies. Although it is true that we also need the *warmth* of others as we age, the quality of our life is also enhanced according to the *warmth* that we extend to others—the *warmth* of our interest and caring. This is a blessing that can be bestowed by elders.

I hope it is clear how important it is that we transform the instinctual senses so that they also live in us as moral faculties. Our language is filled with references that speak of these senses in a moral "sense." It is complimentary to say someone is a "warm" individual, a "hot number," or really "cool." It is not nice to give someone the "cold shoulder" or to be "burned" by another. We may call someone "rotten to the core" or say they are a "real stinker." There is "good taste" and "bad taste," not only aesthetically but also referring to actions taken. Someone is a "sweetheart," a "sourpuss," a "sight for sore eyes," or an "eyesore." I'm sure you can think of many more.

Final Thoughts

We like to focus on gains in modern Western culture. We focus on the gains of the child as they learn to read and write, and on high performance in academic terms. We do not look at what is lost alongside these gains—such as a global awareness or the capacity to wonder. These are especially at risk when academics are begun too early. And we focus on the losses of old age without looking to see what might be gained.

What else might be happening here that is less obvious? Is it possible that with the diminishment of our outer, sensory experience of the world other capacities are enhanced?

Can insight/inner sight improve with dimmed vision and a softer gaze? Can we look in new directions and "see" connections in new ways? How many people with macular degeneration find ways to compensate and make do with their peripheral vision? Are there things at the edges they may have missed before, as they focused on what was in front of them? Is it a new and needed capacity to place the life that surrounds us into the periphery of our awareness, and to make our inner life a central and primary focus? There is, in fact, a Tibetan Buddhist practice that is exactly this—to soften and expand our vision of the periphery while placing our attention on an inner sense of spaciousness—on the place of awareness itself.

Do smell and taste diminish as we age so that we can begin to let go of satisfying our bodily desires and learn to sense what is good for us, or not—also morally? Can we generate warmth of interest and enthusiasm for what others are doing? What new insights might we encounter if we let go of some of the old pictures? Who doesn't wonder about dementia? What pictures can we bring to this?

My mother, even with dementia, still appreciated the beauty of a flower or a sunset even more than before, when there was always something to do. She delighted in the clothes in her closet, sure she had "never seen that before"; and she could still make someone smile by being her genuine, kind self. She maintained these capacities even as she lost, or let go of, more and more of herself. However, she lived with trust, and when I would tell her that these things held meaning and purpose enough to still be living into her 90s, she believed and trusted me.

Could even something like dementia be a physical manifestation of our inability to be selfless? Could this be an extreme outcome of an extreme culture of Me-My-Mine with our iPhones, iPods, iPads, etc.? This is a harsh picture that has just occurred to me: a version of selflessness, forcefully pressed all the way into the body.

In another way, dementia can also be seen as a natural reflection of the two ends of life. None of us hold the memories of our first years of life. We must ask those who knew us as young children—family or friends who hold those memories for us. Could it also be that we need to learn to hold our elders in the same way—warmly care and hold for them the memories of their life? Without thinking of them as diminished? Allowing them (and/or ourselves?) to let go. Is this part of the picture?

What kind of Imagination can we form for this other realm of twelve? It could be one that again sees connections and weaving between them. One that includes a metamorphosis of the sense organs that tell us about ourselves as physical beings into the organs that tell us about the inner nature of the "other" and the changes that can occur in our own soul if we take up the task of transformation.

This work of conscious soul development can help us to overcome and override our "natural" reactions based on sympathies and antipathies; to cultivate the *Spiritual* senses; to respond on the basis of what is good for us, for the other and for the world. In this way, we can move toward the development of a moral intuition.

> We have lived our lives by the assumption that what was good for us would be good for the world. We have been wrong. We must change our lives so that it will be possible to live by the contrary assumption, that what is good for the world will be good for us. And that requires that we make the effort to know the world and learn what is good for it.[7]

The fact that we can rise above survival instincts to serve another, perhaps even to sacrifice our life, is what makes us unique

---

7   Wendell Berry, *The Long-Legged House.*

as human beings. When we respond to anyone or anything that is unknown or different from what we are accustomed to with fixed ideas and prejudices—with fear—it is the primitive brain, or our unconscious Double, that is calling the shots. The newest part of our brain houses our newest capacities, those of judgment and compassion. These are still young and developing. I believe that this Wendell Berry quote indicates what Rudolf Steiner refers to as a reversal of the will. I am only now beginning to understand this, and yet it seems obvious that this is the only way forward. To lay down (put aside) one's own "life" (ideas, beliefs, opinions) for another is actually a deed that we can practice on a daily basis! As we get older and hopefully wiser, I believe we can help develop these young capacities and, in this way, contribute to the future.

This is what I wanted to offer. I realize that you may well find yourself with more questions than answers at this point. In that case, please join me in the quest toward finding ever richer and deeper understandings for what it means to be human. I hope there are seeds here for you to plant and see if they sprout for you. If not, there will be many other seeds in the chapters that follow.

Patricia Rubano found Anthroposophy and her first career as a Waldorf early childhood educator at twenty-one. Her second career found her at her second moon-node in England, where she studied Biographical counseling, extending her understanding of child development to phases of adulthood. Joining Signe Schaefer in the Biography and Social Art training expanded her view of development to include all life within the cosmos in exciting and practical terms. She is currently director and faculty member for the Biography and Social Art Certificate Program and its representative on the International Trainers Forum. She lives with her husband and extended family in San Diego.

OPENING AND CHOOSING

ANNE KOLLENDER

I love the form of the lemniscate, because it is a continuity, an unbroken wholeness—though there comes the transition point, the "thin" point, as we move from one side of the form to the other. Visually this form communicates to me the sense of life without end or beginning. If one draws it, one may leave the pencil on the paper and just trace the form in a continuous flow, passing through the "thin" point and back again. It speaks to me of the infinite and the recurring, the past and the present, and their weaving as one whole cloth. We come from the cosmos with our pre-birth intentions, pass through the thin point of earthly birth, and begin to live into our destiny and intentions until at last we pass through the thin point again, rejoining the cosmos in new form.

Both the present and the distant reaches of time live within the lemniscate through its lens of continuous flow. Destiny, choice and the act of responsibility are contained in that flow across time, space and dimensions. If we take the view that all creation is One, and we are each part of and present with the One, then how we choose to live out of our free will matters—not only for us individually—but for all, and in all times, because we touch the All in all, the One as a continuity. Then the question of where we place attention, the weight and grace of consciousness, comes naturally to the fore as essential, at all points and periods of life, and on either side of the lemniscate's "thin" point. This, I feel, is the essential question before me personally as I journey with and through my 75th year on the planet! How shall I walk and choose now? The image of eurythmy's threefold walking, of the lift, carry and placement of the foot, slowly, and in conscious awareness, comes to mind as metaphor.

I find that at a certain point, one cannot reasonably assume that there will be more temporal time and life…there may be…one minute, one hour, one day, ten years or more… and there may not! Grace begins to be seen to play a greater role than statistics would indicate. Modern health technologies allow for possibilities, not certainties, of physical life extension or quality of life in that extension. Gone are my assumptions of earlier years that life will continue; and gradually, I find that many of my friends and family have moved beyond the threshold of death.

Given this, for me the question of where to place attention, precious time and life energy has become ever more acute. This urgency may be softened (it doesn't all have to be done now!) if one takes the long view of multiple incarnations. I have wondered, what if, at 63, I have the opportunity to exercise my power of choice out of my most true self, *and* out of my sense of the needs of our world, to create future possibilities for good that may come to fruition far into the future of humanity—"that good may become."

Where meeting the karmic moment coming from the past had been the focus earlier in life, it seems that I am now free to envision and bring something of value for the future out of my free attention and initiative, creating something new that enters the karmic stream. This perspective gives a certain heft and excitement to choices about where to put sustained effort and attention after 63. Clearly, this is not the leisure world model, but play is still essential in engaging our truest self! When I live playfully, what is most true for me may appear! In play I am more open to myself and to the voice of the cosmos as it moves through me. I am returned to joy and discovery. For me, engaging playfulness at 74 comes through engaging with artistic process in the making of paintings, poetry, relationship with the natural world, and the practice of "biography and social art," which I like to think of and visualize as one word! There I find a place to listen to myself, to other human beings, to the natural world, and to what lives in the liminal and manifests through artistic practice.

But the act of listening deeply has a new character now. My entire adult life has been oriented toward listening inwardly and intuiting my own unique pathway through life. Truly all of the major choices and doings have been out of a pattern of first listening, hearing, and then acting, employing logic as a useful tool in service of the direction that came through inner listening.

Coming along with this process there has been a strongly felt sense of *being impelled* to take up certain work for humanity and the world. The phrases, "this is mine to do" and "look neither to the left nor the right" come to mind; such was the sense of direction and urgency that came to me through this inner listening! Although I knew that I was free to refuse what came, I never did or would have because I knew that what I have called my "Golden Thread" lay there, on the path Divine Love gave me to walk, and truly I did not want to let that go! Most of the time I found that I had not been prepared through direct, specific training or life experience for what the path asked of me, and instead was required to apply myself to learn and find my way. This called up my inner fire, and became a life practice: listening, trusting, and taking one step at a time, as well as some major leaps into the unknown when called for! This began in earnest at 19 and continued in my biography right through to 63 plus.

Then There Was a Distinct Change!

At around the age of 63, much to my wonderment and delight, I felt a lifting of something invisible that had been with me all along—as if I had been wearing an invisible cloak—and when it lifted, I felt the lightening. This happened over a year or two, and was a direct, discernible felt experience at and around 63. Some years before, in my early 40s I had encountered the writing and thought of George and Gisela O'Neil through their book, "The Human Life." I remembered that they had spoken of a time when karma lifts around 63, and we are freer in our choices for a time before we cross the threshold. I had noted this at the time, and thought "How interesting!," and then let it sink down into consciousness, going on about my life, saying to myself, "Is this true? We'll see when the time comes." In the spirit of research, I have been open to consider new ideas and perceptions expressed by others, but need to see whether or not they are confirmed in my own direct experience. Sixty-three still seemed distant at 43!

When, some 20 years later, I had the direct experience of that sense of lightening, what they had written appeared in fact, and I recognized it as the shift at 63, when the *relationship* to karma changes. I felt this in my body, mind, soul and spirit as a definite lightening, lifting and freeing. I felt as though I were released a bit from the gravity of the earth and what I had carried as karma to be worked with, and I could now look around from a new vantage point! I remember that in my Biography and Social Art training we talked at one point about what one takes on or assumes as one passes through the realms preceding birth. Whatever this is, it felt as though it had fallen away or been lifted. My guess is that this process was occurring before I was actually able to discern it. It has been accompanied with a feeling of joy and gratitude that keeps growing, like a silent glowing or warmth within that continues to emerge, along with the questions of what to do, how to be and how to live in this time of possibility, before the crossing of physical death, whenever that will be.

My personal story is that the years between 63 and 70 were a time of freely choosing to contribute and develop through acts of service that included Waldorf early childhood mentoring, site visits for AWSNA and WECAN, work as a training director with LifeWays North America, and board work for The Center for Biography and Social Art. I also opened a portion of my home to an artist who created a studio there called Rose Well, where I and others began to practice veil painting.

I had long had a love of biography but had never been able to pursue a training due to family and work commitments. At 63, The

Center for Biography and Social Art came into my life; and I said "yes" to her, first as a participant in the training, and later as board member and board President. I had no formal training in board work, but felt as though I had been preparing my whole life for this specific work with the Center. It felt as though I had been presented with the opportunity to bring everything that I had learned previously in the social realm to bear at a delicate time for the then seven-year old Center. I also felt as though I deeply knew my fellow board members at a core level, though I did not know any of them well personally! Yet, here we all were together to help the Center find her way from her gracious founding to her next iteration as a tiny, but mighty and growing nonprofit whose origin story began in the stars! Notably, the opportunity to join with this work presented itself gently, *without an accompanying feeling of necessity*. I was able to freely choose this time of service in the new way that I have described, though it was clear that there were karmic connections and threads among the human beings, and with the being incarnating as the Center for Biography and Social Art!

And now at 74, I ask again, and will keep asking, where do I place attention/consciousness? To me, attention/consciousness is like a ray that has the power to illuminate and help to grow what it falls upon. It has deep value for the world and its workings. To me, it seems to be a wholly non-physical, yet perceptible illumination that has the power to nourish one's surroundings—people, animals, plants and elementals, the seen and the unseen world, near and far. After 70, it seems possible to consciously bring what has been developed and worked with in the biography up to that point, to that new raying forth into the world in a creative, non-physical, non-linear way. There is again a freeing and giving, this time of forces, so that light within may be perceived as shining on the outside, surrounding the physical body, and touching the world round about in blessing. I think the only thing that could stand in the way of this phenomenon of elder blessing is a closed or chilled heart, and I suspect that even that condition would yield as the essential human spirit emerges at the threshold—such is the glory and magnitude of the human spirit of each one of us! Most of us can directly experience this glory and magnitude in the presence of the newly born as it is all around them, and it is also potentially there as we move toward the thin place at the close of earthly life. We are no more confined to the density of matter, but begin to be visible as light around ourselves! I remember the first time I perceived this "light" around my mother. She was in her 80s, and it was a felt perception of her as living in the space around her body while still inhabiting it! It felt like a kind of very gentle sharing of herself. At this time, she had fully entered into living in the being space, while still carrying her life in the physical. I would describe it as living large in the truest sense!

Between 63 and 70, my own balance of activity shifted noticeably from the earlier time of doing in the physical, to a time of "being" with the world and myself. I have realized that "being with" is also active, though not physical! What does that mean? How is this expressed in real time and experience? I imagine that it means different things to different people. Since 70, my experience is that the time of "being with" keeps expanding. I have become less and less willing to fill my days with the business and busyness of life. Instead, I have sought and been able to step into "being with" in ways large and small, with gratitude and a deepening sense of its graciousness. Working with the arts of poetry and painting as well as deepening my practice of gardening, earth and animal care have helped me open into this time.

Many poets have spoken of the liminal space, a place of fertility and growing openness to the cosmos. During the day I will lie for an hour or more on the earth, looking up at the giant conifers that grow here in the Pacific Northwest, smelling the healing pine aerosols they release, watching them move in the breeze, listening to the songs of birds in their branches—letting myself be *with them*, swaying and yet rooted, together on this earth. At night, I go to the stars and planets with my naked eye, opening out to reach toward them with my heart, soul and spirit in the being space, speaking to them inwardly and listening for what they may speak to me. What I hear is that we are all longing for love, for reciprocity, giving and receiving. The stars are, too! Didn't Steiner remind us that the stars once spoke to mankind and that now they are listening for what we might speak to them? I want to learn and speak words of Love from my heart to the stars!

Anne Kollender is a poet and visual artist who has pursued her lifelong interest in human becoming in many ways through the years: as a counselor working in trauma recovery, Waldorf early childhood teacher and mentor, and LifeWays training director and mentor. And yet, her most profound learning and experience of human becoming has been as the devoted parent of two! She holds an ALB in Humanities from Harvard University, an MS in Counseling Psychology, and a Certificate in Early Childhood Education from Rudolf Steiner College. Most recently, Anne has trained in the practice of biography and social art with the Center for Biography and Social Art, and served for six years on the Center's board as member and Chair.

SIXTY-THREE AND BEYOND

VICTORIA SEELEY

Around the age of 63, I experienced a turning point in my own life. I felt a rebirth or an awakening of something totally new. This emergence into something totally new was gradual rather than sudden. Birth might be an accurate metaphor. Birth happens gradually, over time; pregnancy, then labor, then transition, then a new life.

In the past I had an understanding of the developmental cycles of life from a conceptual point of view. The concept was more intellectual; abstract. Then, at 63, I was beginning to live these concepts. This understanding did not come from an intellectual knowledge but rather a lived knowing. As I lived these cycles of life, I realized the truth of these concepts. Much of my adult life had been, as I imagine many others' lives have been, focused on building an outer life. An inkling of how to deepen my life came in my mid-40s. I returned to school to obtain a Master's degree in psychology. This return to school became a 10-year process to acquire my license as a Marriage and Family Therapist. Actually, it was more like a 15-year process of building my new life. At 63, I felt a new found freedom. Both a freedom from and a freedom to.

My freedom from meant I no longer struggled to make ends meet. My children were adults making their own ends meet. My career, which was also my vocation, was established on a solid footing. It gave me satisfaction and a sense of purpose. I had developed friendships over the years that were comforting and supportive.

The most persistent inner conflict that had been with me for decades was also loosening its grip on my soul. I had felt a split between my physical/material/outer life and my soul/spiritual/inner life. The awareness of this split had been with me since my early 20s. That awareness, however, was not able to mend the split. This tug and pull caused me great consternation. I often felt at odds with myself, and I actually was at odds with myself.

At about the age of 63, I began to build a bridge. This bridge was a connection between my outer life and my inner life. To offer an image, the split would look like two separate circles whereas the connection would look like an infinity symbol. This joining together of the two lives, outer and inner, was a great comfort. No longer was I conflicted but rather connected to these different aspects of my life. I was free from this battle; the two had become woven as weft and warp in the weaving of my life. They could then work in harmony with one another. By this time, I was also free to be more of who I knew I was meant to become and free to do what was needed in order to follow my karmic path.

As I look back on those earlier years, I realize my focus was still more on the material world aspect of these endeavors. I was getting things done. This "getting things done" was filled with ups and downs, pain and struggle, grief and loss, joy and sorrow. As a person of will I meet each challenge with a "can do it" attitude. That, however, was not always the case. Sometimes, I could not do it. Health difficulties stopped me in my tracks. These chronic health issues put me in my place, so to speak. My world was very small; raising three teenagers after divorce and establishing a new career was the extent of my life for several years.

I had made a career change during midlife; my 40s. I was licensed as a Marriage and Family Therapist at the age of 50. Since that time, I have been gradually and continually shaping my vocation with my inner knowing. This meant I needed to break some of the clinical rules of my profession—rules that would compromise my knowing.

Some examples of this rule breaking: don't take insurance, don't advertise, discern when self-disclosure is therapeutic, answer questions from a client without interpretation, don't pathologize, don't advocate medication, join with my clients in their struggle to grow and develop, and last but most important LOVE my clients.

These "rule breaking rules" did not come all at once but over the ensuing decade. They went against the norm and the socially correct methods of being a psychotherapist. It took me a while to realize rule breaking for the right reasons has been a part of my life since my early 20s. By my mid 60s I felt free to be fully congruent with my long-standing professional values. I was free to contribute without the restraints of conflicting loyalties.

I was also free to fulfill a 35-year dream of purchasing rural, off the grid land. This dream had been set aside for years as I raised my three children and provided them with a Waldorf education on a very small income. Eventually, I found the land. As with many dreams in my life, the land I found was much more than I had imagined. It had an unfinished cabin, a well, and a pristine river running right through the middle of the property.

These 40 acres have been so much more than just a piece of remote land. For 17 years Turtle Rock Valley has provided a sanctuary for my children, my grandchildren, my friends, and my children's and grandchildren's friends. It has been a gathering place for one adventure after another. I have taken women there for 3-day retreats; focused on getting in touch with the great, wild outdoors (of nature) and the great indoors (of the self). I have also been free to be more available to my spiritual practice. I had been a single mother since my mid 40s. I was raising three teenagers on my own. Making ends meet financially and keeping track of my children's growing pains kept me preoccupied with the fundamentals of survival in the suburbs.

At 50 years of age three life changing events occurred; my mother died, I filed for divorce, and I passed my licensing exam. During my early 50s I also acquired an autoimmune illness, and my life became extremely limited. Fatigue met me each day for five years, after which my body began to recalibrate. With some exceptions, I began to feel physically strong once again. The more life I live the more I realize that every step, every action, every occurrence, every situation and every event in my life has had a purpose, guiding me to the next step, action, etc.

Since my mid 60s, my energy levels have been high and my enthusiasm for doing the good is stronger than ever. I have more space—physical, psychological, and spiritual—to contribute and give back to the world.

At age 66, two things occurred that would, once again, change my life. The first one was my diagnosis with breast cancer. My mother was 75 when she died of pancreatic cancer, so I had my own personal experience with this disease. I did a lot of soul-searching and had many questions. As I considered my options for treatment, I made decisions that I knew were the right ones for me. These decisions went against conventional medical advice. I chose NOT to have chemotherapy. I chose a radiation protocol that required minimal treatment over a short amount of time. After the surgery I searched for lymph drainage trained therapists. My choices for continuing care were based in natural treatments and anthroposophical medicine. I continue to inject myself with mistletoe treatment to this day.

The second event was a fire that burned my home. I was away at my office at the time. By the time I returned home all my children were there. My home did not burn to the ground but the whole house needed to be gutted. Because I had a dog door in my home my dog and cat were saved from smoke inhalation. I called the fire a disaster but not a tragedy because my dog and cat lived.

The rebuild took over a year, and I purchased a 35-foot trailer to live in. My two sons took charge of rebuilding my home. The day of the fire, my youngest son said to me, "Mom, you are going to be a phoenix that rises from the ashes." That image of death and rebirth carried me through the following months. In fact, that image lives with me enduringly.

I think life brings us situations and struggles as opportunities to grow. It is strange how often, when we look back on these events, we are able to see the blessing in the pain. My experience with cancer taught me the truth of the axiom: what doesn't kill you makes you stronger. It was not just the cancer itself that made me stronger. It was the strength to make decisions that disagreed with the authority figures. It was the strength to drive myself each morning to radiation treatments and then drive to work for the rest of each day. It was the strength to face mortality, up close and personal.

I learned so much from the fire and I am grateful for the lessons. I learned what it is like to be homeless. I learned what it is like to have only the clothes on your back. I learned how unimportant my belongings were (they were gone, and I didn't miss them). Although I lived in the trailer for 14 months, I learned I could have lived there happily for the rest of my life. Outside my trailer door hung a sign that said, "Happy Camper." It was true; I was.

These two events, my cancer and my house fire, helped me to grow in my faith and trust. Neither of these events had predicable outcomes. I did not know what would be on the other side of these, almost simultaneous, events. Twelve years later both these situations continue to be lessons for me on how to make difficult, often unpopular, choices. In fact, for me, to make the right choice is also, often, to make the unpopular one.

During my early 70s, another long-held dream was realized: I was able to purchase a small house within the city limits of Mt. Shasta. I travel there each month and reconnect with the land and the mountain. In my late 20s I had moved to Mt. Shasta, and I thought this would be my permanent home. It was there I met Anthroposophy, my spiritual path. That meeting meant I had to leave Mt. Shasta to study this new path. I returned often but my focus was caring for the life I had made away from Mt. Shasta. Now I am able to be home once again.

For the past several years I have reflected more on my life, looking back at my intimate, personal, and professional relationships. I have done much connecting the dots. I see my life as a type of tapestry; a weft and warp of interconnectivity. I am often awed and amazed as I realize how so many of the people in my life have been there to help me, guide me, teach me to be more and more of who I am becoming.

I think about my great grandmother, my grandmother, my mother and the housekeeper my family had for decades. These older women all had a great influence on me during my formative years. They each were role models of how to be a competent and capable person. As I think about each of them, I can say with confidence, they were women ahead of their times. All of these women are a part of my past. They all crossed the threshold many years ago. And yet, I carry each of them within me. I give thanks to them as teachers who offered great wisdom.

When I turned 70, I celebrated with a destination birthday. Twenty-five people—family and friends—accompanied me to my favorite village in central Mexico. My gift to those present was Things I Have Learned by Seventy:

1. I need to start following my own advice.
2. I am loved because of who I am AND in spite of who I am.
3. My totem animal is a turtle: a) they are not slow; b) they win the race; c) they pace; d) turtles are a "walking meditation"— consciously putting one foot in front of the other.
4. Generosity costs nothing; penny pinching comes at a great price.
5. Life is a gestalt; the whole is more than the sum of its parts: a) Clean up a wee bit more than you mess up. b) Give a wee bit more than you get. c) Laugh a bit more than you cry. d) Cry a lot.
6. Opposites do attract; in other words, say "no" more when you think you should say "yes." Say "yes" to everything else.

7. Hug some people; embrace all people.
8. Paradox—Failure is preferable to success; it is the only way we learn and grow. To learn and grow through failure is success.
9. Play is the work of the young child and the elder.
10. When your children, grandchildren, friends, loved ones come to visit, fling open the door, widen your arms, and run to greet them.
11. There are only three kinds of prayer: please God; thank you, God; and paying attention.
12. To most decisions in life ask these two questions, then decide: What brings me the most joy? What brings me the least regret?
13. To die is not the opposite of life; it is the opposite of birth. It will come soon enough, so my main task is to live life and be ready when I die.

I credit my children and grandchildren with being my finest teachers. They continue to this day to provide me with an understanding I would not have without their persistent nudge. This nudge gives me the opportunity to see into their world, the world of the future. Without these helping guides I would be nothing. They have each served me in the past, in the present, and this goes on into the future. All the people who have come into my life (and some who have gone out of my life) have brought gifts of discovery.

This discovery is ongoing. I do not think or expect there to be an end, even through death and beyond. At least, from my vantage point there is no end in sight. I relish these later years. At 79, I am not only looking back in reflection, but also looking forward in anticipation—an enthusiastic anticipation of what is to come. What's next! Time will tell. I am grateful for the time I have had, the time I have now and the time coming toward me from the future. Within the next few months, my oldest granddaughter will be giving birth. I will be a great grandmother. Another sure reminder of the eternal circle of life.

> *"Birth is God's opinion that the world should go on"*
> —Carl Sandburg

Victoria Seeley: My life is lived "hands on." I am mother, grandmother, great-grandmother, psychotherapist, gardener, poet and painter. Most of all, I am a seeker and all the above roles have allowed the seeker in me to move forward along this path of life.

BORN ON A SATURDAY

MARTHA LOVING ORGAIN

On a summer's day in August in the early 1950s, the hottest part of a Saturday afternoon, I was born with a twin brother three minutes after me, one day before a New Moon Solar Eclipse in Cancer, the Crab. Both of us have always known how to share. Forever compared to him, I knew I was different and wanted to be my own self. Raised in "small town Virginia," with an older and a younger brother and no sisters, I forged a path of self-determination. If it wasn't happening, you had to make it happen. A few years ago, my twin brother said, "Well, 'Maaahh-tha,' you've always done what you wanted." This birth on a Saturday (you will recall the verse...*Saturday's child works hard for a living*) before a Solar Eclipse has played out significantly in my life...death and rebirth, always starting over, letting go of the old, welcoming the new. Crash and burn...a Phoenix rising from the ashes; I was/am a force to be reckoned with.

There is definitely a Saturnian influence in my natal chart, and Saturn's placement is conjunct Neptune in the 10th house, the house of "mission in life." This conjunction in my destiny path this lifetime has to do with the healing arts and its placement in the tenth house shows what one is to give back to the world. Saturn is crystallization, manifestation, the past, tradition and contraction. Saturn brings focused attention, and responsibility—ability to respond. Saturn also can be associated with limitation. The Saturn phase in a person's biography is during ages 56 to 63.

Both Saturn and Neptune in my natal chart are nearly conjunct Spica, the brightest star in the Virgin, representing the Divine Feminine, Sophia. She is the uniting force/principle, Oneness, building community, and the future—where all creativity comes from out of the future...and Darkness. Darkness is not evil; Evil is evil. Darkness IS the Divine Feminine, Sophia, Wisdom of God. She is the World Soul, warmth, love, the archetypal mother, and unity. I'm ever TRUSTING in Her Guidance.

In Darkness we are incarnating through the lower pole of warmth into the metabolic system, relating to the color Magenta. This Magenta, a red violet, is a threshold color associated with birth, mothering, nurturing and learning to self-nurture, warmth and love. No one comes to Earth without coming through The Mother.

The Divine Masculine IS the Light, in our thinking, consciousness, our higher "I," spiritual ego, self-hood. Light is the forming principle, separating, and relating to Viridian Green. We are incarnating through the upper pole of our consciousness in the nerve/sense system. With these two colors, Magenta and Viridian, we have a color harmony. Johann Wolfgang von Goethe said, "Color is the dance between light and darkness." Out of the interplay between Darkness and Light the Angels bring us Color in our feeling life, the life of the human soul, and the cardiovascular system. Our world of Nature exists in Color, ever-changing between Light and Darkness. Nature is IN us, and we are THAT.

Steiner states it in this verse:

In my heart	The strength of the sun
Sun-strength shines	I will feel
In my soul	The warmth of the world.
World-warmth works.	Sun-strength fills me
I will breathe	World-warmth penetrates me

Rudolf Steiner, *Mantric Sayings* (CW 268)

As an Artist and a Visionary, I've always been on the cutting edge of the future, integrating and weaving together my interests. I am "sniffing out" next steps by "listening to Sophia." In undergraduate school I double majored in Textiles and Photography, photo-silk-screening my images of barns onto fabric, and making traditional quilts as my ancestors had made, yet with a "new twist." When I experienced technical difficulties, teachers could not help because I was doing something new that they had no experience of, and I had to figure it out for myself. I am a creative problem solver—and an image maker!

All my life I have been a pioneer, and it is no different now that I have reached the golden age of 70. This lifetime of joy, excitement, welcoming the future, TRUSTING IN SOPHIA and the ever-present help of the Spiritual World—suffering and sacrifice— is now in full bloom. All that I have prepared for is coming into focus now. What is it? Who are those welcoming my work in this stage of giving back?

Sacrifice is to make sacred.

What does it feel like to be in my elder years, continuing the destiny path I agreed to—my pre-birth intention? What does it mean to be an artist, visionary and pioneer?

"It's a sacrifice to be an artist." —Dennis Klocek

In meeting the work of Rudolf Steiner, I felt as if I had found "home." Introduced to anthroposophy at age 31, it has now been nearly 40 years. Finding myself on the edge of the future, again, I attended Dennis Klocek's Goethean Studies course, given at the time in the clay room at the Sacramento Waldorf School at 7 a.m. Monday mornings. It was our class that petitioned Rudolf Steiner College to have Dennis come up the hill and begin teaching on the RSC campus. Thus began a long relationship with Dennis and Consciousness Studies.

"Well, you're an artist!" —Dennis Klocek

When are we taught to follow our dreams? When are we taught *not* to believe in ourselves? When are we thwarted from doing what we love? How do we recognize what our true vocation really is?

Previously, when visiting an undergraduate school, a recruiter had said, "Why do you want to go into art? You'll never make any money in it." I resented that remark. Many years later Dennis was to say to me, "Well, you're an artist." That shifted something deep inside of me. I realized he was right, and I felt as if I had found myself again. I've always learned about myself *through* working with others.

In Goethe's Color Theory block, I found that I could answer questions that Dennis posed, and when he trailed off in the middle of a sentence, I knew what he was going to say. One day during this color block Dennis made mention of *his* wish that proceeded to change my life forever. He said that if he had his wish, he would study painting with Collot d'Herbois. At the time I had NO knowledge of who this person was, whether they were male or female, where they were, nor any information at all. Up until this time I'd had very little experience in painting, and yet somehow, *my ears got REALLY HOT!* I knew I was supposed to DO THIS.

It wasn't long before I found out that Liane Collot d'Herbois was a female Master Artist in veil painting, and with Ita Wegman, MD (a Dutch woman, first anthroposophical doctor) had developed a painting therapy method based on the Universal Laws of Light and Darkness—and Collot lived in The Netherlands. In September 1993 I was the first American living in the USA to attend courses in Den Haag. In meeting Liane Collot d'Herbois personally, and her work in Painting Therapy, a lifetime foundation and dedication to it commenced for me.

During years of training, I did all practicums in The Netherlands—in a Waldorf school with children, and with adults in anthroposophical medical clinics. Of my two published case studies, one was working with an adult, and the other was the first written about working with a child in this method. After my successful experience, Emerald Foundation training began to include courses in working with children out of Light and Darkness. In June 2003, I received my Diploma in Art (Painting) Therapy according to methods of Liane Collot d'Herbois, from the School of Spiritual Science, Medical Section, Goetheanum, Dornach, Switzerland. I was the first person in the USA to receive this distinction. Currently there are only seven of us in North America.

> *"One isn't necessarily born with courage, but one is born with potential. Without courage, we cannot practice any other virtue with consistency. We can't be kind, true, merciful, generous, or honest."* —Maya Angelou

To be a pioneer of something no one has yet heard of is a lonely path. One has to have dedication, commitment and courage. After thirty years of working in public and Waldorf schools, in private practice with doctors or alone, in Camphill communities with special needs children and adults, and with elders in assisted living facilities, it has been a great honor, privilege…and it's challenging. In working with elders with Dementia, I met the challenge of teaching myself to paint up-side-down and backward, standing behind a table easel to avoid the inevitable "Move out of the way, I can't see. You're in the way." What are we learning from elders who no longer have a "filter" yet who are, all the same, in need of support and our loving attention? They know, on a different level, what's going on. You must keep your eyes open for when someone dips an English muffin in Violet paint and eats it!

Another challenge of being a pioneer of this new revolutionary method of painting (art) therapy is that one cannot solicit work in schools or in doctors' practices. Another "factor" of my destiny path is that I have to wait for others to ask. I cannot push the river. This challenge is a hard one for a Vermillion (redheaded) choleric visionary. I've had to tame this in myself and wait for the world to "catch up with me," hoping, trusting that "the tree will grow under me."

Vermillion has to do with the Hebrew Cultural Period/Epoch—think of Moses and the burning bush, flames of fire and Wrath of God. You don't see many people wearing Vermillion—it's too much of a good thing and one can take it only in small doses.

> *"Vermillion is Spirit Fire, always moving. It is the movement back and forth between the ponderable and imponderable. Vermillion can be called the revelation of the Divine on the threshold of consciousness."* —Liane Collot d'Herbois

In many painting courses throughout North America, in both wet-on-wet and veil painting techniques, I've taught artistic applications following the Universal Laws of Light and Darkness. All these years work was slow and sporadic, yet it continued and I "stayed the course." When things were really slow after losing home and job, I went to The Netherlands and wrote my first book on the spiritual aspects of color, "soon to be published." It started as a huge "download from Heaven" when I was 63, just into the Uranus phase, ages 63 to 70. This phase brings in the new, what is revolutionary, unique, inventive, independent and freeing. For six weeks I glued myself to my friend's sofa and it was electrifying, like lightning. It was like downloading a work of art; and it came though me as I opened to spiritual worlds, expanding my consciousness. It was the opposite of slowing down, as I would do in painting veils, coming out of my connection to and conversation with spiritual worlds, a "feeling/listening" to Angels in the Color realm. This book about spiritual aspects of color includes simple painting exercises followed by color meditations. The Uranus phase is to be altruistic, reaching toward universality. It was my opportunity to give back what I had been given and to bring to the world the Universal Laws of Light, Darkness, and Color in a simple how-to process, to experience connecting to spirit, thereby developing supersensitive organs of perception and cognition.

I have always "known" that things would "take off" in my elder years. And here it comes! After struggling in Vermont for about 20 years to "make things happen," I was beginning to come out of the slowed-down-nothing-happening era after 2008 when I was invited to a Waldorf school down south. By this time, I was already into my "golden years," and at 65, any thought of "retirement" was a total fantasy. Why would I want to retire? My true vocation was rewarding, essential and so much fun! I was beginning, again, this time in service to a wider community.

The reason I was invited to this school was because of an absolute crisis, a critical event that took place right before Christmas. There is no way to put this mildly...a young child was murdered by the father who then took his own life. The whole community was in shock and totally devastated. I was asked to come to work with the children. Those who had been closest to this child were my "core group" of ten children, working twice weekly for six weeks. Expanding my usual practice of one-to-one work in the therapeutic model, during those six weeks I managed to paint with the child's mother, teacher and parents of the class, the whole faculty, and other members of the community. Throughout this experience I heard a lot about the biography of this child and family who had emigrated to the USA, classmates and friends, and the whole community. How can I possibly describe further how healing it was for these dear souls to do this therapeutic artwork?

Healing means coming back to wholeness.

We are spiritual beings living in a physical body. We are 75 to 95 percent water and our brains are floating in water. As soon as one touches a brush-load of watercolor to paper, it moves everything inside of us. Adding to this moving color are even greater forces of Light and Darkness, bringing balance, harmony and healing.

"We think with the head, and the heart feels the Light or Darkness of the thought." —Rudolf Steiner

The process of painting out of Light and Darkness is profound. I am grateful that this Waldorf community realized the power of healing through art and invited me back for three more blocks. At the very end of my fourth block in two years at this school, on March 13, 2020, all schools across the U.S. shut down due to the Covid-19 pandemic.

> *"Well, you never stopped long enough to reflect."*
> —Jane M. Orgain, when questioned about
> the childhood of her daughter, Martha

For three years I had next to no work. It was during this "quiet time" that I realized I was depressed and healing a very sore soul. Grateful to have temporary housing with The Christian Community of Greater Washington and Baltimore, I exhibited veil paintings and other artworks through the seasons, merging with liturgy of the Christian year, bringing something new, unique, inventive, and altruistic, commensurate with this Uranus phase. While in past years I was creating different workshops along themes of the seasons, during the three years of Covid, the challenge was to integrate exhibitions of artworks that spoke to the liturgy. I found this rather easy because my work is spiritually oriented and seemed to "fit right in."

I was in service to others yet having difficulty taking care of myself, knowing I had to "get back into circulation" out in the world. I heard about a new cohort of the Biography and Social Art (B&SA) training that was to begin; I was interested and joined this ninth cohort. Able and excited to be integrating this work into my life, I am finding new ways to weave it into my painting workshops, breathing new life into my practice.

While many other things are beginning anew, B&SA is giving me a new perspective on how to approach life in general, and specifically a reflection of my biography. As I am drawn to the work in order to know myself and connect more deeply with others, I am grateful for the myriad ways art is integrated into the whole experience. Art and expression are used in ways that harken back to my graduate professor's wisdom—Sonia said it is the process, not the product. Art making can be a process to "open the door" to something that lies deeper in the soul, rising up to be transformed. The only way we can change the past is to *change our thinking* about it. Proficiency in art isn't necessary. It feels totally fine when one can draw only stick figures. Drawing is just like anything else...it is a practice. As a pencil is a tool, so is a paint brush, not to be feared—yet played with! It is the process of making art that loosens memory and can bring deeper understanding of one's biography.

It wasn't until February and March 2023—"After Covid"—that my "true vocation" and next 6-week block in painting therapy came, when I was invited to Camphill Kimberton in Pennsylvania. In past years I had worked with differently abled children and this time I was tasked with painting with differently abled adults.

During the first block an invitation to exhibit artwork was offered and I hung 12 large veil paintings. Within two weeks I was invited to give the keynote address at a regional conference on the spiritual aspects of color, held October 2023, hosted by Camphill Kimberton. Knowing that attendees were coming from all over the USA, it was an opportunity to give them a "color experience" and I focused my keynote on Color Harmony. My lecture was well received, and I was asked to repeat it the following day. After my presentation I led 40+ people in a social painting exercise in Color Harmony. I created 12 painting "stations," each with two colors that were harmonious with one another, and asked the participants to take turns painting. Two to four people painted on one piece of paper, and my directives were to paint earth and sky, with earth being darker at the bottom getting lighter toward the middle of the paper. The sky was painted darker at the top getting lighter toward the middle of the paper. The brush stroke they were guided to use is called a "therapeutic stroke," going from the left side of the paper to the right without lifting the brush (no dab, dab, dab), connecting each new stroke with the previous one (leaving no gaps), and without making any "lines" on the paper...the more water, the more flow, the fewer lines. To paint in this way creates ever-so-subtle distance, depth, and appearance of space. All of these techniques create inner space and soul movement, peace, cooperation, and outer harmony between and with one another. Again, it isn't the product, it is the process and experience together that unites us.

In April 2023 I was invited to be adjunct faculty in Kairos, a program through Antioch University, one of two new 3-year anthroposophical art therapy courses started by my colleagues in summer 2022. Kairos is in New Hampshire on the east coast, and the other new program is Healing Through Art in California, through Bay Area Center for Waldorf Teacher Training. In both programs are my former students, and I tell them that I've waited 20 years for them to catch up with me.

What I really mean is that I've waited a long time to give back through teaching others this extraordinary gift of Liane Collot d'Herbois, painting therapy in Light, Darkness and Color. Within the first year of both programs, enrollment was busting! Already in 2017, the Surgeon General of the USA had pronounced that art therapy was of the utmost necessity to address isolation and depression, even before Covid isolated us. To make art is to heal death of the soul. It is particularly dangerous for us elders to be isolated, for we will slide down that slippery slope even faster. My answer to this is "The Time is at Hand."

Returning again to Camphill Kimberton in fall 2023, as part of the Color conference, I exhibited five artworks in a group showing of regional Camphill artisans at Penn State Great Valley Henry Gallery. Another 6-week block in painting therapy ensued following the conference and continued through mid-December, just in time to retrieve my artwork from the exhibition and head south to Nelson Co. for Christmas with family.

During these two 6-week blocks in 6 months it was amazing to find how deeply the work can go, also with people with cognitive limitations. Although the second block was a different season it was remarkable to see how much this population did retain. Because the work is given over a 40-day period, the work is IN them, and it's fascinating to see this over time and how the work can go deeper still each time one takes it up again. I find it poignant that I was asked to work mostly with people who were in their later years. In every case there were subtle yet marked improvements.

True to form since 2014, every summer I have headed back to The Netherlands for painting with colleagues and my own "continuing education" courses. After three years in temporary yet stable housing, then a horrible May of losing housing (again due to no fault of my own), I went back to the Netherlands and painted "Sophia, Divine Feminine, Rainbow Woman." This was incredibly healing for me, as well as deep preparation for next steps that would fall into place in January 2024, readying me for yet another new beginning.

"Sophia, Divine Feminine, Rainbow Woman"
original veil painting in full color, seen here in black and white,
by Martha Loving Orgain © August 2023, NL

Between January and February, I went on a long-distance road trip. In three days during mid-January, squeezed between two snow storms, I was over and out of the Blue Ridge Mountains in Virginia, heading to North Carolina. My cousin in Charlotte sent me on with a loaf of organic spelt bread, south to Jacksonville, Florida where I taught painting at a Waldorf school. While there, people came out of the woodwork for astrological chart readings. Without formally advertising this service I was amazed at the response from word-of-mouth. Never before had I done four readings in one day and eight charts in five days. This speaks to Neptune's phase—70 to 77—increasing compassion, empathy, Grace and self-bestowal. Thank you, God/dess, for the abundance of all good things.

On to Gainesville, FL where I taught painting to faculties and community members at two more Waldorf schools. During the two weeks in Gainesville I also created, facilitated, and mentored a Kairos student's art therapy practicum with two children in her kindergarten.

As a weaver from way back, I was able to integrate a short biography exercise into a painting workshop in Gainesville. Introducing the idea that we all have a pre-birth intention, we began with Rudolf Steiner's verse *"The Wishes of the Soul are Springing."*

The wishes of the soul are springing,
The deeds of the will are striving,
The fruits of life are maturing.

I feel my star, my star finds me.
I feel my destiny, my destiny finds me.
I feel my goals in life, my goals in life find me.

My soul and the great world are one.

Life grows more radiant about me.
Life grows more arduous for me.
Life grows more abundant within me.
—Rudolf Steiner

This verse, I have been told, is one that will "bring on your destiny" and speed up one's karmic processes. I have found that my relationship to this verse has changed since I learned it in my late 30s. Then, with more impatience, I used to struggle over the word *arduous*. Now I've realized and lived the true meaning of the word—*to do things with great care.*

Guiding participants in a short Biography exercise, I asked them to break into groups of two and spend about 10 minutes sharing what they imagined their pre-birth intentions to have been. Did you have a sense of what you came down here to Earth to do? Do you think you may have accomplished this intention? Are there things in your life that speak to this, or that you'd want to take up now, to fulfill your intention?

Did you have a deeper connection to this pre-birth intention around 18.5, 37, 55, 74, or 92 years of age? These ages are when we experience a Moon node, when the veils of the spiritual world are thinner and we might catch a glimpse of our pre-birth intention(s). Each Moon node has a different "flavor," and over a lifetime, different doors to spirit open to us. In different phases of our life's journey, Moon nodes will give a different impulse and may move us to change course.

In Gainesville, from this biographical exercise we moved into painting wet-on-wet. The exercise I introduced was "A Radiant Yellow Star in an Indigo Night Sky." Every time I demonstrate a painting exercise, guiding others through steps from beginning to end, it is fantastic to see so many different and beautiful paintings! Some people's "star" was far away and tiny in a vast Indigo night sky, and other people's star was close up and BIG!

My process of leading others in painting, both artistically and therapeutically, has continued for 30-plus years. Over this time period I have modified what I offer, trying to create things anew. I once did several workshops on "Art Farming," integrating Light and Darkness painting with Biodynamic Agriculture. Beginning with painting the metamorphosis of the plant in a wet-on-wet exercise, I then introduced the rhythms of cosmic dancing, of Heavenly Spheres (moving planets) against Fixed Constellations (Zodiac). I taught people how to read these movements as illustrated in the biodynamic calendar, *Stella Natura*. At the end of the art and science portion we went outside and did a stir and spray of the Biodynamic preparation 500 on the land.

Weaving together painting and a biography exercise is a natural progression for me in this regard.

The challenge for me to integrate these new practices is only difficult because…"Ain't nobody got time for that!" Painting is already quite foreign to most people, and it is a process that DOES slow you down, promoting balance and harmony. The biography work also takes much time. While we are learning these new techniques we are rushed through many exercises, "drinking from the firehose." However, with caution, we learn to S-L-O-W it all down once we start to practice, first within our cohort and then with others.

In this Neptune phase, years 70 to 77, I seem to be less concerned with having "to know" everything, and so "go with the flow," co-creating with the Spiritual World as I go.

> "What one has most to work and struggle for in painting is to do the work with a great amount of labor and sweat in such a way that it may afterward appear, however much it was labored upon, to have been done almost quickly and almost without any labor, and very easily, although it was not."

> —Michelangelo

I have been teaching painting for nearly 32 years, and though it feels simple and as if I can almost do this in my sleep, I cannot. To integrate the biography piece is a challenge, because people "don't have time." Within a painting workshop I will hope to bring in more as time goes on. Teaching this biography exercise again in the beginning of a 5-day veil-painting course in Chicago, as we finished the sharing in small groups, I asked for comments on how it was for them, and three people shouted out in unison, "Too short!" I am finding that folks are thirsty for this work!

> *May our feelings penetrate into the center of our heart*
> *And seek, in love, to unite with human beings*
> *Seeking the same goal,*
> *With spirit beings who*
> *Full of grace behold our earnest heartfelt striving*
> *And in beholding strengthen us from realms of light*
> *Illuminating our life in love.*
> —Rudolf Steiner

Finding new ways of working IS this next phase of life at 70, and it is related to the planet Neptune. Neptune's energy is somewhat psychic, nebulous, empathetic. There is an element of thinking about the past, recollecting what has come before. In my chart, Neptune being conjunct Saturn has to do with sensing spirit, being open to Cosmic Wisdom, and working in the Healing Arts. There is a distinct relaxing quality I feel, to *"trusting in the ever-present help of the Spiritual World."* As you can see, I'm still weaving what gifts I have received in the past into new possibilities for the future. With educating and mentoring I'm both online with students—the next generation—and teaching them in person. These are the people who are calling to me as I'm collaborating with colleagues, building a wider community. The arts and therapeutic work need to be done in person, yet on-going support and guidance can be communicated through online programs such as Zoom, anywhere at any time. This weaving of art, science, and technology comes back again in my life's story, now in service to many.

As of this writing while I am in The Netherlands again, I'm taking time to reflect on my life, and where the "cutting edge" has been, and where I am being "called into service" yet again. With a lifetime foundation and dedication to Collot's work, I am being met with next challenges to give it back. At every step of the way, I know that

I am guided, and I'm TRUSTING in Sophia and the ever-present help of the Spiritual World. What will the Spiritual World ask of me when I hit the next Moon node at 74/75?

You can see from this last half year that life grows in myriad ways; and I remain a vital, community-oriented, creative member of our human journey through time on this beautiful Blue-green planet Earth. Ever a weaver, I bring many people and things together. What is also interesting is that I find myself writing only while in The Netherlands. It is here that I find rest in my outer activities long enough to reflect.

For several years now I've had a dream of building a small, micro, tiny house to live in while traveling from pillar to post creating, weaving, and teaching. It is the "Emerald HeART Spot." With a GoFundMe already set up, perhaps someday a small traveling home on Earth will manifest.

> Saturday's child…working hard for a living, at 70…
> with no retirement in sight…and loving it…

BY THE GRACE OF THE DIVINE FEMININE, SOPHIA, WISDOM OF GOD!

A vision without a task is but a dream.

A task without a vision is a drudgery.

A vision and a task is the hope of the world.

Visionary Artist, **Martha Loving Orgain,** is responding to guidance from Spirit Worlds using painting, photography, weaving, and astrology. Creating beauty, she transforms spirit into matter and is lifting matter back into spirit. Studying the Universal Laws of Light, Darkness and Color in Nature and the Human Being, Martha is using methods she learned directly from Liane Collot d'Herbois in The Netherlands. As an arts educator for 40+ years, she is traveling and teaching throughout the USA, and is adjunct faculty at Kairos in New Hampshire, training students in anthroposophical art therapy. She lives part-time in The Netherlands regenerating, writing and painting. Have COLOR, will travel. www.lovingcolor.org

Eldering Exploration in My Pluto Time

Linda Bergh

Stonehenge is Light

I awoke with a dream
knowing how Stonehenge was raised
how the monoliths were moved
into sacred formation

I saw us in the dream
each a heavy weight
of grief or stories or pain
a monolith of life

then we are raising each other up
lifting each other as witness
carrying each other's pain
honoring each other's story

and in the dream
the monolith of each
became like a feather
with the love of the others

and we were each held up
in formations of circles
in the light of dawn
like Stonehenge

I awoke on a holy night morning
knowing love can lift the stones
community can hold the circle
and bring the new dawn

H ow do we find new ways of being with our soul and spirit as our bodies age? How do we stay connected with joy and love to this earth and our loved ones while we explore a closer connection to spirit? How do we honor our legacy and our closeness to the threshold of death? I will explore these questions about the Pluto years, ages 77 to 84, the 12th Life Phase, which is my current life phase. I will also share about the life of Jack Heckelman, my second husband, during this final phase of his life. The preceding Stonehenge poem encapsulates the essence of what still inspires and challenges me at age 81—striving for community and connection, listening to my truest inner voice, and choosing to stay awake to love rather than fear. In this phase, I have become more humble, more transparent, and more urgent about the importance of each moment and each interaction.

BEFRIENDING THE DRAGON

So often I wake to dreams of guidance—
being cared for and held
So often I go to nature, and see
and feel the beauty hidden there
and that is what my poems are about
Sending hope and promise and joy out into the world

In fact, it may be what my identity is to me.
That I have overcome, that I am in a state of peace,
That grace is with me at all points
But today a new sharing

I face a "Trauma"—small, not life-shattering like so many
of the things that have happened. Size doesn't matter.
The wall of deadness in my body does.
I am still frozen until I unravel it.
A simple thing—invitation to write a chapter for a
book—opened the deep chasm of failure and shame
about two other books which lie in my drawer and on my
computer—unfinished.

Not good enough? Not alive enough? Not believable
enough? Not enough?

This is an inner trauma of shame, of self-judgment, no matter what the world says.
This "invitation" at 81 is an opportunity to face that dragon
of disempowerment—
times when I gave away my power—to inner fear.

So—I call myself back to the place that says—I am worthy,
I am enough, I will do my best.
I say it now, not only to myself—but to you. I say it aloud:
I am going up the mountain to face the dragon, not to slay it,
but to befriend it.
My heart is pounding with terror and perhaps one more
ounce of courage than I had the last time I climbed this
mountain.
Now I have the courage to name it.

But let me not forget
I am not alone—even on this craggy mountainside
My guides accompany me—always
Let me feel them now—warming my back—with a hand
toward the future
and all of you hold me
My beloved friends on this warm earth
This warm earth beneath me. Why, even the cave and the
dragon welcome me with knowing

To bring me to the treasure of my unknowing
I will step forward

Eighty-one candles on the cake. "That's so many candles," I
say. "You must help me, I cannot do this alone!" "Okay, Oma,"
says the circle of young children gathered in the candlelight glow
around me. We blow them out. I look around as everyone eats their
cake. It is my birthday dance. The room, filled with soul community ages 5 to 81, is bursting with food, balloons, laughter, and
dancing. An evening of connection, of coming together during busy

lives to celebrate an elder. This night of joy, glowing far beyond the party, is my way of celebrating with the soul community that has supported me all these years.

Beredene Jocelyn writes in her book *Citizens of the Cosmos* about the Life Phases.[1] She calls Pluto the guiding "planet" for this 12th life phase: "The transcendent planet of Pluto is beyond the norm in terms of years—and carries one further beyond the usual limits." This is often how I feel in this current phase as when I work to fit 81 candles on a cake to celebrate age instead of hiding it. I initiated a birthday dance more than a decade ago. I now order special candles so they no longer get wax all over the cake!! But there is more to having a birthday dance than the candles. Before I share my life as an elder in these years, ages 77 to 84, I need to tell you about a time in my Jupiter Phase, ages 49 to 56, which informs everything I am living today. It is the fabric with which I meet these aging years.

Three decades ago, when I was 54 years old, my only child Kirsten died, just a year after the death of Paul, her father and my first husband. A car accident took her and her dear friend Nina when they were just teenagers. I was the sole survivor. My body was shattered and yet my soul was sustained by a love I didn't understand. It came in luminous figures holding me in the ICU room and in a community of people surrounding Nina and Kirsten in love during a home vigil. As I recovered from these losses, strong threads of continuous connection to the living and the "dead" formed the fabric of my life.

Three years after the accident two new threads helped further transform my recovery from loss. First, I fell in love with Jack Heckelman, 20 years my senior. Jack was just beginning his Pluto Phase, at 77, when we met. We married when he was 80. He died shortly before the age of 83. He became beloved to my community. Also, during this time with Jack, in my Saturn Phase, age 56 to 63, I began

1   Beredene Jocelyn, *Citizens of the Cosmos*, chap. 13, "The Pluto Time."

a new career of facilitating Biography and Social Art. After Jack's passing, when I was 63, I began serving in the Natural Death Care movement. These two threads of Biography and Natural Death Care deepened through my 60s and 70s, Uranus and Neptune Times.

I am now in my Pluto time, the years that Jack experienced during my life with him. Jocelyn calls Pluto an "arch extremist" and continues: "...this is because it can carry one to lofty heights of spirituality—or lead to depths of degradation....The greater the challenges, the greater the need to rise to higher spiritual capacities." She calls upon Pluto elders to shift priorities, transcend limits, refashion habits, face pain with patience and endurance, and meet death with transfiguration. I am challenged to live these qualities Jocelyn named, and I am more aware of how Jack lived them during his time with cancer until the day he died.

After his cancer diagnosis, Jack faced fear and found a new beginning. Each day he would rise and stand facing the sun with a salutation he created:

> I raise my arms in salutation to the dawn of a new day,
> the first day of the rest of my life,
> in gratitude for being alive, awake, alert,
> and in wonder as to what gifts the day may bring.

Then, during his day, he would say to someone, *"You are the gift of my day."* In that daily celebration of life, we all felt his love and joy, transfiguring his fear of death.

Spaciousness and Being

Almost on cue, the spring before I turned 77 and started this 12th Life Phase of Pluto, a new voice emerged. For most of my life I said "yes" to almost everything anyone had asked me to do, even if it meant transferring airplanes seventeen times on one biography training trip.

My new voice was saying "no" to these outer commitments and saying "yes" to an unknown inner invitation. I was yearning for spaciousness. "What are you going to do now?" people asked. My response was, "I have no idea!" I wondered if people thought I would disappear without my identity as a teacher. So began the release of a lifetime identity orchestrated by outside roles and responsibilities. I truly could not see what was coming toward me, calling me. A poem from that 77th birthday time illuminates my discoveries:

MIGRATING

Yesterday I saw three large V formations in the sky,
Along with noisy honking, just out of the edge of my eye,
Not in the center of my thoughts.
Questions began to come closer to the front of my thoughts.
Are they practicing? Getting stronger so they can make
    the long journey?

How do they know when to begin preparation?
Is it the angle of the sun? The heat of the day?
    The turning of the leaves?
An inside calling from somewhere far away?
Whatever it is, it angles inside of me,
    as my days are turning, too.
Is it a reminder of changes; the coming unknown?

How will I prepare to migrate? What will my formation be?
What formation am I a part of? Is something calling me?
How will I stay on purpose in unknown times?

The geese have awakened me to remember
that I know how to stay on purpose,
how to be in alignment with the present,
if I listen to the soft honking of my soul,
and strengthen my wings so I can fly the distance.

I met Jack when he was 77 years old, and he had written a personal mission statement that included "more being, less doing." His two other missions were meeting a new partner, which was me, and selling his 4-story house, which he did, moving to Minnesota. It took time to transition to "being." He was still completing out-side commitments, including his Earth Charter work, for which he headed a national conference at age 79. Still, he was committed to the shift to more spaciousness.

This movement toward spacious being and less doing did not come easily to me either. From ages 77 to 79, I worked to com-plete, celebrate, and pass on my responsibilities locally, nationally, and internationally. This poem, written when I had just turned 78, illustrates the shift:

BRIDGE TO NEW TIME

Shawl wrapped around me, I sit on my sunporch.
As the November morning sun rises in a pale cloud misted sky.
Today is a kind of turning of my sun,
the unveiling of more eldering and legacy.
I am wearing softer clothes,
letting aging be more comfortable.
These are small things, but choices nonetheless.
Finding more by doing less.
I notice I am allowing more time—in the moment—
     to hang out.
Finding even more preciousness in those close to me,
perhaps especially now in these "distancing" covid times.

Yesterday I handed over the last of the outside commitments
     to teach Biography Intensives, nervous at disappointing,
     and flinching at releasing that identity.
But after it was received with such warmth and understanding,
I am learning it is okay to change,
Listening equally for yes and no and unknown places
     in between.
Naming that I am a student again, and a mentor,
available for peership, in ways that feel nurturing,
     new, and life-giving.
There is everything to do in this new time.
Tears come behind my eyes.

The lark ascending by Ralph Vaughn Williams
    playing on my speakers
takes me to joy and aliveness,
like the new day.

Though I ended many roles and identities, I still had personal responsibilities, including my house, my health, and my day-to-day life. Now, I could attend to the sunroom collapsing from rot and the flooding in the basement. It was a substantial shift to a spaciousness I couldn't have imagined just two years earlier. I still say yes to requests from the world, but now it's a choice coming from listening to my elder self. This writing and drawing evokes a settling into a new harbor:

THE BUOY

I decided to draw a beautiful boat that I had seen at Lake
    Harriet.
The boat and the reflection were entrancing.
As I was drawing the buoy, I realized that I was feeling like
    that now.
When I had drawn an earlier boat, it was unmoored.

This boat is in the harbor, a new harbor,
not yet with sail up, but with comfort in its wake.
There is a gentle, ever so small turning toward being what I
    had envisioned.
A turning toward Being in Elder-hood and experiencing it,
not thinking about what it will be.
Noticing that my identity IS larger than teaching, or being a
    national leader.
I am home.
I am in harbor.
I can choose when to set sail,
and if to set sail.

I have a memory of being with my grandmother. She is peeling apples under the apple tree in the backyard of my family home. There is no hurry, there is no preoccupation with time at that moment. The apples will be peeled to make the pie. I realize now that she was in tune with my pace as a young child. She was present and joyous, and that nurtured me. My mother was always in a hurry, and soon enough I too learned to hurry though my activities, addicted to getting things done.

Now I have been learning to be a "Soul Grandmother." Young children open the screen door yelling, "We are here, Oma." We build worlds on the floor or sit by the fire. Time disappears as we share yummy snacks, run outside, play games, and draw pictures. After Kirsten died I made a commitment to stay in connection with Kirsten's friends and children. but until recently my time had often been over-scheduled. But now when I hear, "Can you come over for dinner Tuesday night?" I say, "Yes. Can I bring anything?" And when my soul granddaughter asks, "Can you come to my bike race on Saturday?" I get out my hiking boots. Former teaching time has become "being time." Oma time. My time habits are not gone, yet I feel more able to be spontaneous and present. I smile and thank my grandmother.

When I turned 79, I found myself longing for an inner spaciousness, a new rhythm, an uninterrupted time to start each day. This was in stark contrast to all my previous attempts to follow outer spiritual guidance about daily meditation. Now, I feel the day calling as I carry my coffee cup to the deck or couch, and this morning practice pulses with a life of its own, akin to a growing flower. At age 80, I listened to the call of my dreamer to write my dreams down every day. Each day I receive new insights and inspiration. This inner call extended to listening to Nature and Spirit, in and all around me.

for Holly
4/24/23 ƒB

SOPHIA—MOTHER DIVINE

You are in the falling rain, showering summer flowers
    with life.
You are in the eyes of a friend holding me with love.
You are in the dark night of dreams, as I wander
    unknown shores.
You are in the flicker of a candle, steady light by my side.
You are in my question: "How can I ease your pain?"
You are the blue mantle round me when I least expect
    your grace.
You are in the voice of the dying man who calls for his mama.

You are in the starkness of the desert, the grandeur of
    the redwoods,
the softness of the northern lakes through which
    the Mississippi flows.
You are in the bricks of city streets and the isolated
    country dwellings.

For you are wherever we are standing, or lying down to sleep.
You cannot bring us solace unless we stop and feel the pain.
Stop and feel the wetness of the grass beneath our feet.
Stop and let our breath fill us with the life we chose.
Stop and let the mantle round us unfold.

Just as we are.
Just as the dry earth takes in the rain.
Just as the mountain takes in the sky.
Just as a child takes in the mother's eyes.
Just as the darkness takes in the light.

Yes, this morning I heard your raindrops, and walked upon
    wet grass.
Yes, this morning I lit the candle in the grayness of the morn.
Yes, this morning I drank my coffee and found these
    words to write.
Yes, Sophia, Mother Divine,
I find you inside of me, and all around.

At age 79 Jack had a powerful experience the day before giving the keynote speech at a national Earth Charter Conference. We
were walking in a small wood near our home at the height of fall
colors. He went off by himself, and returned saying Gaia had spoken to him: "If we see her beauty, we will save her." He enlarged a
photo of the glowing leaves of our maple tree. The next day at the
conference, this scientific-type man in a crisp white shirt and tie,
held up the photo and shared his experience of Gaia, tears streaming down his cheeks. The room went silent.

Life Review

THE RED ROCK OF SEDONA

Hiking around the edges of the huge red rock,
feeling a solidness not only in its size and heft,
but in its wholeness.
At first, I thought:
This being is ever gathering itself upward toward the sky.
But then I wondered:
had it been whittled down from something more immense,
and stood now in its nakedness of weathering?
No matter.

It was a being with a presence beside me and beneath me
    as I climbed,
seeing ever new crevasses and edges,
granting me access to its history at every step.
Gratitude filled me for the chance to be in its presence.
It shared a few of its shadowed and sun-filled stories
as I touched the rugged layers with my hand.

Then I felt the very stone was taking me in,
including me in its essence,
my steps upon it adding to its beauty.
And as I walked away, sad to leave it,
I thought I heard a deep soft voice say:
"You are not leaving me, for I am with you now,
As you are ever now with me"

This poem about encountering the Red Rocks, touching the layered stone, evokes a life review. In our lives, review can happen at any age and is at the heart of Biography work. Perhaps like others living into these elder years, it has been compelling for me to view my story again. Yet, it has come in ways I could not have predicted.

Jocelyn, in *Citizens of the Cosmos*, writes that this life review work is a moral imperative, and that Pluto brings us to a deeper opportunity for inner transformation. "Pluto strengthens us to fulfill our moral responsibilities and obligations. It is our inner corrector." She reminds us that whatever we are able to review and heal during this lifetime, we will not take with us after death.

Recently my life as Kirsten's Mother has been reviewing me. During the years since she died, when I was 54 years old, I have worked not only to stay connected to her friends, but to keep her alive in our hearts. I remember her birth and death days, and share her poetry and art book, *She Would Draw Flowers.*[2] I get to be Kirsten's mother again when I see the light in the eyes of seventh grader students as Kirsten's work inspires them to find their muse. I thought I was doing all I could to honor her and to heal myself.

Meanwhile, all the family photo boxes lay silent on the basement shelves for decades, waiting patiently for me to take another step of remembrance. As I ended formal teaching and had more personal time, their voices became insistent: "Open us." It felt urgent. But, along with the invitation came a heaviness, perhaps an unstated fear of opening further pain of loss about a life that ended so abruptly. Then an inner voice gave me courage: "Please share Kirsten's life

2   Kirsten Bergh, *She Would Draw Flowers.*

with her community." With a friend by my side, I walked down the stairs and began unpacking, box by box and photo by photo. And in doing so, I have been given back the lives I lost instead of the grief and sadness I feared. I am taking in the smiles and hugs no longer possible at the physical level. As I take each photo and digitize it, my body fills with gratitude for the loving family Paul, Kirsten, and I created. While the original idea of making a book for her friends will happen, it is now clear that this is my life review. I will make a book for me, as well, as I heal my losses ever more deeply, and love this world even more fiercely.

A dream initiated another life review last summer. While viewing photos of Kirsten as a baby with my parents, I found a picture of my mother smiling warmly. I did not remember seeing her smile in photos. Shortly afterward, I received a powerful dream of a beautiful, soft peach room with flowing veils instead of walls. Wondering if it was a vigil room for me, I awoke asking, "Am I dying?" "No," a clear deep voice said. "This is for your parents."

My parents both died suddenly, without a chance to review their lives or receive proper goodbyes. This dream thrust me into a review of their lives. I traced their ancestry through documents and pictures, and their experiences unfurled before me. I sensed the rigors and joys of life on Iowa farms. I witnessed their struggles living through World War One, the depression, and deep personal losses. They married and began their family shortly before World War Two. I was born during this war. My father's service in the war brought more challenges for both of them. Viewing their story, I found a growing compassion for the suffering and unexpressed grief they carried in their bodies. I looked at my childhood—not only as a daughter now, but as a witness, seeing their struggles and their strengths. I put together a Zoom slide show and invited close friends to join the call on my mom's birthday. A week later, I held a small, in-person ceremony in my backyard honoring both parents. I made their favorite foods for dinner and placed colorful mushrooms in Kirsten's sacred rose garden, one representing my mom and one my dad.

This ancestral work honored them forty years after they died. But it was I who received the greatest gift. This was my life review, too. I had been working all my life to heal childhood secrets of angry fights and a loveless marriage, of a mother whose screaming voice silenced mine for years, of a father whose grief of losing his first wife was never spoken aloud. This ancestral unraveling opened their suffering and pain and made brighter the many gifts they brought me, including love of music, learning, and community engagement. The gifts of this life review have not stopped. New dreams keep coming, shifting the very ground of having this mother and father in this lifetime. I am not the same daughter I was nine months ago, and they are not the same parents. May I remain open to new insights that I cannot even imagine, that may release me further before I cross that final threshold.

In Jack's case, he was too busy with life to do any life review work, until he got the cancer diagnosis. Then he was conflicted. Sitting in his office, every surface stacked with papers and thousands of slides, he couldn't decide what to finish. I had an idea. I asked him, "What is it only you can do?" He quickly decided to spend the best hours of his day working on his story. One day he came down with tears in his eyes, remembering a colleague whom he had treated without compassion. With no way to contact the man, he didn't know what to do. I suggested that his intention of healing that past moment could be accomplished now, while he was alive, by writing the person a letter and sending it by spirit mail. He did, and it released that regret.

At the same time, he wrote and videotaped his Ethical Will, sharing his inspirational values. He agreed when his sister, Nancy, asked to videotape his life and death, which he named "my last great adventure." He shared his last days, not only with friends and family, but with a cheap video camera. After a life of service to others, his willingness to focus on himself became a service and gift to loved ones, and later to hundreds who watched the movie, *The Most Excellent Dying of Theodore Jack Heckelman.*

Peership and Reciprocity

In the Pluto Cycle chapter of *Citizens of the Cosmos,* Jocelyn mentions that our manner of meeting this aging time will depend on who we have been before. So in this light I share an important value for me, which began through grace a long time ago.

My first spiritual mentor, when I was 33 years old, said: "We are Peers." I said, "No, I am the one learning from you," putting her on a pedestal as the teacher. She replied, "We are each at the edge of our striving." She openly shared her own struggles as well as spiritual openings. This gift of peer-ship opened my heart to share my pain for the first time. Reciprocity has been a guiding light for almost 50 years, and transparency in relationships feels even more critical now in these elder years.

I recently visited with a friend with whom I have not spoken, beyond a friendly greeting, since before Kirsten's death. I asked how she was. There was a warm answer, yet I could sense something unsaid. The next day we shared our life journeys through the years, and she lightly mentioned that she looked forward to sharing more after dinner. When we sat down for tea, I asked if I could share something leaning on my heart. That conversation about a current dilemma led to questions about my grief and soul recovery after the accident. As she listened to my journey, I felt received, more able to face the dilemma I had shared. Then my friend said, surprising me, that she had decided not to share her current personal struggle with her adult daughter because it could not compare with the loss of a child. After listening to my story, however, she felt compelled to share her own current struggle. And her story tumbled out. We were in sacred space together, in peership. Instead of giving advice in my old age, I find elderhood is bringing me ever more to my knees in humility and transparency. It is increasing my compassion for the struggles and dreams of each person I meet.

WHILE I AM ALIVE

A child is born,
an elder passes,
buds spring forth,
old branches fall,
and yellow tulips bloom
in a pot inside my kitchen.

Can I make sense of life,
the cycles of birth and death,
of coming and going,
of growth and decay?

Perhaps only from my heart,
which can celebrate the comings,
and honor the leavings,
and stand cracked open
crying while I feel rain on my cheek.
While I am alive

Not only to celebrate and honor,
not only to notice and to note,
but to love this moment with joy:
this child's eyes,
this flower's screaming yellow petals,
this raindrop's soft touch.

And to hold just as dearly;
this person's pain,
this tree's broken limb,
this world's suffering.
While I am alive

June 13
2021
LB

All In

Jocelyn names Phase 12 as a challenging time. Here is a quotation from Corinthians 2: 4:16: "Though our outer nature is wasting away; our inner nature is being renewed every day." I wonder what capacities I will have, to meet a time of more limitations in regard to my body? What inner attitude of soul am I growing now that will allow forgiveness and gratefulness to come from the inside, no matter the circumstances?

So, here I am now, miraculously alive at 81. Through all the losses and challenges, I am here in joy, grateful to be alive each day. I am more aware of my aging physical body and work to support it daily. I swim to help my feet, as it's hard to walk from neuropathy and one shorter leg from an accident. I keep seeing what I can do now, aware of my physical limitations. Last year, in Costa Rica, I tried going in the surf, but my balance had changed, and I kept getting thrown into the sand. So, I went into the tide pools and floated in gentle waves of timelessness. I am having new thoughts about my future mental and physical capacity. While walking recently in the Red Rocks of Sedona, I realized that there may come a day when I will not be able to hike so vigorously, and I checked the asphalt paths good for wheelchairs. I have a new spiritual practice of asking for help when I need it, and allowing an arm when offered on a walk.

I feel closer to the threshold of death, especially in this last year. This brings an urgency, a heightened sense of less time ahead, and another awareness. Like a young child, my senses are more alert. I am more present in my body than ever before. I have a strange feeling that even though I have neuropathy in my feet, I feel alive all the way into my body, into the tips of my toes. I am more present on this good earth. This poem came recently:

I Am All In

I wash the dishes, feel the warm water and soap on my hands.
I stir the onions and mushrooms in the pan, feel the wooden
    spoon I know so well.
I feel soil under my fingernails, from my city garden or
    microgreen trays,
the smooth and gritty texture of soft earth on my palms.
As a part of everyday,
I make my own food, even for one.
Clean the cat box for my old cat.
Get down on my hands and knees.
Every day
I smell the rosemary and thyme sprigs I just picked.
I smell of squash baking in the oven.
I smell the roses in the winter bouquet.
I sing and feel vibration deep inside of me.

It is an awareness of a need
to be even more in my body than ever before,
as I prepare to leave this good earth;
to feel myself all the way into this vehicle, this body;
to keep healing what I can in the days I have left,
not just body but soul;
to love more and care more and be present more
to those in my life I am gifted to know.

It is really such a humbling,
that something so small as the soft hand of a child in mine
can send shivers of joy down to my toes;
a warm water foot bath can change my breath;
A conversation with a friend is a hug holding me close.
I am here; I am all in,
even now as my feet suffer from neuropathy;
And my short leg makes it harder to walk;
even as I carefully watch all I eat to work with heart health,
and make sure I exercise to keep osteoporosis at bay.

No, perhaps it is not "even now as I suffer"
No, it is because I lost one eye, but still can see;
Lost my face, but still can smile;
Lost my hip, but still can walk;
Lost my daughter, but find she is still here.
It is because I say now in this writing
with new tears that it is even more true what that voice
        said to me in ICU:
"Love is greater than loss."
Now at 81, 28 years later, I hear a new voice:
"May it be that Love is greater because of loss?"

Aging as a Blessing

I started this Chapter on aging with a poem about mustering
the courage to meet a dragon. While it was written about the small
dragon of disempowerment I faced in writing this piece, it could
also be about aging or death. Recently I dreamt the following:

I am climbing a vertical cliff of a steep mountain at a high altitude. I am worried about food, water and air. A guide is with me, helping me to release worries. She says we have enough to make it to the top. I realize that I must trust. I can still breathe at this altitude, and I am given food and water. I just need to keep finding handholds on the steep cliff. I did not know I could do this. I breathe. I am guided. I can do this.

The purpose of this journey up the rugged cliffs to the dragon's cave is about befriending the dragon and finding the jewels. The dragon, now a part of me, descends the mountain along with jewels of insight, helping me to love even more fiercely. I know I will meet more dragons, and hopefully gain more jewels. Jack met the dragon every day of his cancer, moving through fear to love, gifting us with his jewels of joy and connection.

A dear friend, age 88, named this journey in a recent conversation: "I am living with fear of dying. But larger than that is feeling loved by those around me, and curiosity about the mystery of what is ahead." As he named the interplay of fear, love, and curiosity, those of us sitting with him experienced his presence and striving as a blessing. In Beredene Jocelyn's words: "Even when older age becomes somewhat burdensome, the light filled soul aims to be not a burden but a blessing."

In a recent dream, I was under a huge enveloping tree that held my community in its shade. I awoke realizing this was the world tree, rooted in mother earth and reaching to the cosmos, nurturing and protecting all beings. It was the Tree of Love under which all might be healed. When Jack's sister Nancy called the evening he died, and asked how he was, he took a breath and said his last words on this earth: "LOVE, LOVE, LOVE." He was held by that tree as he crossed the threshold. Greater than all the topics discussed in this chapter is this power that we each name in a unique way, this invisible spirit that guides us, holds us, comforts us, and lifts us during the dark times and the joyous times. By whatever name we call it, God, Goddess, Divine, Sacred or Sophia, this power that lifts us is LOVE. During all the challenges of aging, it is the jewel, the mountain, the transfiguration of the dragon. During the rest of my life and through to my death, as the Stonehenge poem at the beginning of this chapter articulates, may the stones of our lives be raised by this guiding force—LOVE.

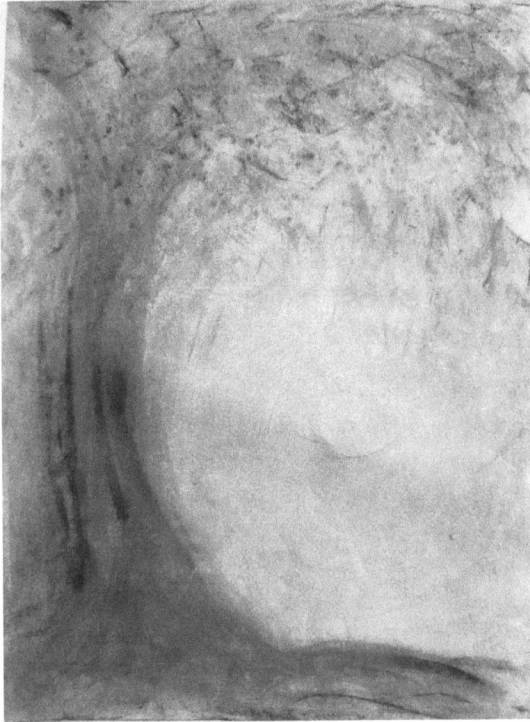

Linda Bergh is a striving human being exploring her elder years with curiosity, most recently as Biography and Social Art Facilitator and Natural Death Care Guide. Earlier careers include child psychologist, Waldorf teacher/teacher trainer, assistant professor of education, and public school teacher. She is fed by the beauty of all things large and small, by the joy of singing and dancing, and by the grace of the spiritual world.

All poems and paintings are original by the author

TRACING THE ARC OF LIFE: GIFTS OF AGING

Following a Thread

Karen Gierlach

The invitation to reflect on the last two decades of my life, now that I am over 80, has been a special gift. Since I am by nature more of a doer, I had not thought very much about the full sweep of these later years, even though my work as a biography workshop facilitator has been to encourage others to do just that! To assist me in researching my last 20 years, since I could not remember much in any particular order, I found a life chart I had made years ago. Alas, I had stopped filling in events and people at sixty-three. However, with the help of old emails, I have now reconstructed these more recent decades and discovered that on the one hand they have freed me from many of the constraints I experienced during my earlier years, and on the other provided a welcome long-range perspective from which to review my entire life.

One particular thread caught my attention. It is visible around my birth, childhood, and in my twenties. Then it mostly disappears and does not resurface until my sixties. Following the thread in the last twenty years, I can understand even more deeply how connected to my spiritual origins and to one intention my most recent activities are.

All my life I have been interested in "otherness" in people, cultures, languages, climates, vegetation, orientations. Up until my sixties that interest took me to many places and experiences. I will now follow that thread.

I was born in wartime London after the Blitz and before the first unmanned ballistic missiles began raining down on the city. When I was four, my parents and I moved to bomb-damaged northern Germany for my father's work, and we remained there for eight years. I have vivid memories of seeing piles of rubble everywhere, whenever we drove beyond our immediate neighborhood. (Current images of bombings in Syria, Ukraine and Gaza evoke those memories for me.) Even though I knew these sights were the result of actions in The War, my wise parents never me told that The War had been between us, the English, and the Germans, our former enemy, amongst whom we were now living. Thus, otherness did not provoke fear in me, nor did I learn what an enemy is. (A few years ago, I was attracted to the phrase: "An enemy is someone whose story I haven't heard." It is quoted at the bottom of every email I write.)

I learned German within a very short time, as is typical of young children, which provided a wonderful bridge to connect with the neighbor children and eventually my classmates and teachers at the Waldorf School. It was unusual for an English child to attend a German school in those immediate postwar years, but my father had attended Waldorf school himself, so sending me there was a natural decision for him. Lucky me!

Back in England, when I was 12, I encountered for the first time anti-German sentiments from some classmates and in the general atmosphere around me, though certainly not in the Waldorf school that I attended. The most dramatic expression of these sentiments occurred one day when my younger sister and I were walking our dog in the park. As we had done for most of our lives together, we were speaking German. All of a sudden, a passing stranger shouted at us to stop speaking "that terrible language." We were stunned into silence and from that day on, never spoke German to each other again. I soon realized that most Germans were considered to be Nazis by the English at that time, so I found myself defending the people I had lived among and attended school with and now sorely missed. I tried to explain that the people I knew were kind and good to me. But it became clear that I could not convince these critics, so eventually I stopped trying. Otherness had now appeared to me in a negative guise for the first time, and war clearly had much to do with that.

Once I began to hear and read about the Holocaust, I was better able to understand the strong negative feelings that the English harbored toward Germany. As a teenager I greatly admired those who resisted the Nazis. People like Bonhoeffer, the White Rose and the brave English and French women who worked as Resistance workers in Nazi-occupied France. Later in life I read with wonder and admiration the journals of Etty Hillesum, who approached her unavoidable fate in occupied Holland with intensified love and equanimity.

As I read more about the chronology of World War II, I noticed that many tragic and evil events occurred around 1942, the year I was born. These included the beginning of systemic mass killings in the gas chambers, of Jews and other prisoners in concentration camps. When I later learned from reading Rudolf Steiner about the preview we have of our lives before we are born, I imagined I must have been aware and distressed by the huge numbers of human beings who were wrenched out of life on earth, just as I was on my way into life on earth. Did I carry this concern with me unconsciously, as possibly a wish to help those suffering from the effects of war in the future?

Following the thread of my interest in otherness further, at age sixteen, I had the good fortune to spend a summer in Thailand where my parents and younger siblings were living for two years. In those days the long flight from London to Bangkok made several stops in order to refuel: in Beirut, I was both mystified and distressed by a large group of weeping and wailing women, veiled and dressed in black and speaking Arabic, close to where we disembarked. Bahrain was a nighttime vision of endless sand, men in flowing robes and their heads covered with white head cloths. In Karachi, we drove through the streets at sundown as the muezzin was calling from the minaret and everyone was kneeling to pray, wherever they'd been standing. I could hardly believe I was witnessing such an exotic sight with my own eyes.

Once in Thailand, the powerful tropical climate and lush vegetation, the incomprehensible language, the grace of the Thai people and the many colorfully decorated temples made every day rich and exciting. The aromatic and to me totally new food—this was long before Thai restaurants migrated to other countries—could not have been more different from German and English food. The entire visit was a feast of otherness for me.

Spending a year in Spain after attending high school in England, I was able to learn a new foreign language, make important karmic connections, enjoy wonderful art as well as new landscapes. At the same time, I could still see signs and hear grim stories about the Civil War that had so deeply divided the country. Franco was still running Spain with an iron fist, and the artist anarchist friends I met there complained bitterly about the lack of freedom and hope, as well as the widespread poverty at that time.

After returning from Spain and while attending university in London, I continued to travel all over Europe whenever I could. Once, when I had a job as an assistant tour guide, we visited Prague, which was very dark and sad at the time. As soon as the sun set, there were barely any street lights and none of the store fronts were lit up. One evening we were approached cautiously in an outdoor beer garden by two students who had recently been imprisoned for political reasons and wanted people from other countries to hear how unbearable life was for them under Communist rule. This meeting gave me another glimpse into divisions, enmity, the dark shadow of war and conflict.

Later I travelled further afield, to Israel, and joined many young people on the deck of a Greek ship that carried us cheaply and in a few days from Venice to Haifa. In Israel I worked on a kibbutz, quite near the Gaza strip. Beginning before sunrise to avoid the worst of the heat, large groups of us wearing little white cotton caps (not much protection from the sun!) climbed into trucks that took us to work in the orange groves. I remember being told with great enthusiasm by the young kibbutzniks how this new land (only seventeen years old at the time) was now the home of young Jews like them who would never again go like "lambs to the slaughter" as had happened in World War II. Even though they knew that the Palestinians would drive them "into the sea" if they could, this would never happen on their watch. I was inspired by their optimism and glad that now, after the devastating Holocaust, they would be safe in their own country. I loved living in community, eating together in the dining room, dancing the *hora* and sharing in the enthusiasm that permeated the kibbutz. The only Palestinians I met at that time were the armed Druze guards of the kibbutz. Little did I know then that much later in life the difficult relationship between Israelis and Palestinians would play quite a large role in my life.

At the end of my twenties, I arrived in the ideologically conflict-torn United States. JFK, Martin Luther King, and Bobby Kennedy had all been tragically assassinated by then. I found that I now had to find my place among the hippies or the anti-war camp or the straight people. I have never liked taking sides, and since I found commonality with aspects of all three groups, I found it a difficult fit. Eventually though, I, too, found my place in the United States. I married, raised two children, divorced, and worked for many years in Waldorf schools, in both administration and as a language teacher. During those adult years my focus became of necessity much narrower and focused on my family and my immediate environment rather than on far distant places or communities. My surroundings did eventually become more multi-cultural and tropical when, before retirement, we moved to Hawaii for a few years.

My sixties opened up many new experiences for me. With my second husband, we moved to the Bay Area for his teaching job, and I there discovered many volunteer opportunities that I could explore. My health was now much better than before my retirement, so I was able to be quite active during my sixties.

As a volunteer, I appreciated the opportunity to spend time with people outside of Waldorf communities, an impulse I had already followed when I graduated from Waldorf high school. Having been a "lifer" through the grades, I enjoyed leaving the Waldorf cocoon and in typical teenage fashion, even secretly hoped I would never return to it. That, of course, did not happen because I worked in several Waldorf schools for 25 years!

My first experience as a volunteer was to take a hospice training. I loved learning that our task was to take to the patients an attitude of being available to them and/or their caregiver in whichever way they needed. We were urged not to take any agenda with us, but rather to sense and listen to the needs of our client. This was a welcome change from the very agenda-heavy existence I had lived until that time, especially as an administrator. I met and learned many things about end-of-life experiences from a large variety of patients and their caregivers. It was a privilege to be at many different bedsides in multiple settings, offering what I could in companionship and taking an interest in their stories and concerns.

I also connected with plants and the beauty of the Sierra Nevada, by spending regular periods of time both in the Presidio National Park and in Yosemite during spring and summer. It was a special joy to camp in the mountains for a month at a time, together with my husband and a group of friendly volunteers. In Yosemite I was able to be of help to many overseas visitors by using the languages learned in my early years.

Around that same time, I reconnected with my interest in otherness when I chose to teach English to a delightfully international group of new immigrants in San Francisco's Mission District. Otherness, connected to war and divisions, surfaced even more strongly when I became a volunteer with the International Rescue Committee. My task was to visit and support a newly arrived refugee family or individual over a period of six months, as they found their footing in the United States. After those months they were deemed ready to become fully independent and embark on a new life.

Through the IRC I met a group of young, orphaned Burundians whose families had fled to the Congo during the Rwanda genocide. One day their village was attacked by armed gangs, so they had fled as children to a refugee camp in Tanzania and eventually were evacuated to the U.S. as teenagers. I was assigned to them because we could communicate in French until their English skills had improved. I was very moved by how much these young people had already endured and the courageous way in which they eventually travelled to other parts of the United States in order to find work and a new life closer to other Burundians they knew.

My second IRC assignment was with a young woman from Iraq who had to leave her country because she had been a translator for a British NGO after the U.S. invasion. As a result, she was marked as a collaborator and had to flee for her life to Jordan. After several years of trying unsuccessfully to make a new life in Jordan, she and one sister have now found a home in Europe after making the harrowing crossing from Turkey to Greece in a leaky rubber boat one cold December day.

At the same time as I was becoming a hospice volunteer, I was pointed to the work I really love by Lee Sturgeon Day, namely facilitating biography workshops. What particularly attracted me to this kind of group work was the social art aspect of it, through which we encourage the participants to take an interest in another person and to listen to them without judgment. In our naturally anti-social consciousness soul times, I found this practice of vital importance. Here my original interest in the other, which I have had naturally since my childhood, was an activity to consciously practice, not just on my own but now together with others. Surely such a practice can also help us resist the tendency to see others who are different, or think differently, as enemies.

Initially I facilitated workshops for Waldorf teachers and parents, in Waldorf teacher trainings and with anthroposophical groups. Eventually I was invited onto the board of the Center for Biography and Social Art by Signe Schaefer, where I met wonderful new colleagues from whom I learned much and with whom I later collaborated to bring a series of three workshops to different Waldorf schools, called Awakening Connections: Creating Community (ACCC).

During Covid, biography exercises proved to be very helpful for people in a difficult time. To meet the need for human connection, which was so missing during the lockdown, the ACCC team of facilitators created two-hour online workshops for Waldorf communities. Because we could use breakout rooms for small group sharings, a suitable intimacy was achieved, even though it cannot fully replace this activity done in person. The very positive responses we received from the participants thankfully allayed our doubts about working online, so we continued to offer the workshops until we all were able to reemerge and meet in person once again. We learned that biography work is extremely flexible, important, and possible to be offered in many different forms.

My seventies began as my husband retired from full-time work. As a result, we left San Francisco and spent three years traveling and working in different locations across the U.S. as well as in China. These years also included several major losses in my life: the passing of my very elderly father, and the subsequent dissolving and sale of our family home in England where my father had lived for sixty years. Too soon thereafter, my younger sister became seriously ill, and within six months she too had made her transition. These two very different threshold experiences reawakened many memories from my hospice years, though now in a much deepened and personal way. Both events left their mark in unexpected ways and made me turn more actively to including the dead in my readings, and for help and guidance.

Seven years ago, we moved to Sacramento where we have found old and new friends and enjoy the spiritual nourishment that this community provides. I continue to stay connected with "others" in the area, through teaching older adults at the local university and offering biography exercises to my neighbors, as well as at the local library.

Biography explorations have given me a valuable tool with which to now examine my own life more closely, with the understanding that we come to earth carrying interests and impulses that guide us unconsciously for many years. Through the many necessary human encounters and life experiences we have, we are given the opportunity to bring more consciousness and understanding to our actions and to fulfil pre-earthly intentions.

Beginning quite recently, in my late seventies, and even up until the present, I have picked up the "otherness" thread in a different way. I began creating international biography sessions, bringing together friends from Europe, the Middle East and from the Americas to meet and share in small groups how they live, how they feel about various topics, and what their hopes for the future are. This resulted in some lively and heartfelt exchanges, which revealed that all the people I invited were of similar orientations despite outer differences and living in widely separated areas and cultures. The wish they all shared was to bring more love and understanding into the world.

My most recent projects have included friends from Israel and Palestine. I had returned to Israel in my sixties, forty years after my first visit. Unlike the time when I had spent most of my time on a kibbutz in the south, during this visit I was also able to travel to the neighboring Palestinian territories. That experience opened my eyes in a new way to two very different realities existing side by side in the region and to the great tensions underlying so much of life there. Through Shepha Vainstein of reGeneration and her friends, I met many people involved in building bridges between the Arab and Jewish populations in Israel, as well as people in Palestine who have created bonds with peace-oriented Israelis.

A few years ago, I became connected to a family in Gaza who needed emotional and financial help. The periodic bombings of Gaza had brought me strong memories of war and conflict from my childhood days. There they were again! But now, rather than living among the so-called enemy and merely observing the damage that war creates, I have become proactive and able to come from a neutral, yet engaged, position.

Using a biographical lens, I recently created an opportunity for two women I know from the region, one from Gaza and the other from Israel, to share online their story and process of becoming peace-activists and now also friends. I invited a large group of interested and concerned individuals from this and from other countries to listen to the two women and, if they wished, to make a financial contribution to support the Gazan's family, who were enduring the war on the ground and had lost their house and home. My friends were moved by how these women, despite the ongoing war, had resolved not to automatically follow the common narrative of hostility and fear toward their neighbors. They maintain that to give in to those feelings could never lead to a peaceful coexistence in the future. Instead, human encounter, entered into with an interest to learn more about the other, is the key. These two are the embodiment of this approach and have upheld the resolve to keep talking, despite the events that began horrifically on October 7, and as the bombing of civilians in Gaza continues. Many of my friends who listened to their stories gave generously to help the family on the ground in Gaza.

A month later, as the Israel/Gaza war intensified and circumstances in Gaza became ever more desperate and dangerous, I returned to the same friends and added others whom I knew less well, in case they could help me raise additional money to enable one young woman I know there to leave and start a new life outside of Gaza. Many people generously donated a second time and others responded with new contributions, even people I did not know directly, until we had received what we needed and even a little more. This large and concerned community, with whom I've become connected over the span of almost my entire life, includes friends from my elementary school years in Europe, from the U.S. and overseas in my adult years, and friends and colleagues from my years in Waldorf communities. Also, newer friends that I have made, inside and outside of Waldorf circles. I feel deep gratitude for all these widely different human beings who have influenced, helped and taught me so very much, long before they were invited to contribute to my fundraiser.

The other day, I received a short text from my Iraqi refugee friend. A few years ago, I had made a contribution to rescue her second sister from an impossible life as a refugee on her own in Jordan. When I told my friend about this new Gaza rescue venture, she wrote: "Thank you for helping people be safe." When I read that simple sentence, I felt that maybe now, after living for so many years, I have been able, with the help of so many others of goodwill, to put into action something I had wished to do as I was on my way to earth during those war-torn times in 1942. I have journeyed from carrying an interest in others, to working with others through biography and social art, and now, with others, working for those who are suffering the effects of war. I wonder what will come next on my journey?

Karen Gierlach was born in England, grew up in Germany and has lived for over 50 years in the U.S. She raised two children, attended and worked in Waldorf schools for many years, and since retiring has enjoyed facilitating biography workshops within and beyond anthroposophical circles.

CRONEOLOGY

DAVINA MUSE

ON WRITING AN AUTOBIOGRAPHY
AT THE BEGINNING OF QUEENDOM

What themes she sees: the strands
That weave
Between the destined morning and the eve!
The power of silence to conceal, contain, reveal.
Pain's gifts lift in the dark places: the wheel
Turns, more thread is spun from Heaven's Light.
Babe, child, maiden, mother, Queen—
She grows, surprised; the soul Increasing
In the space between what will be and what's been.
(As one hand offers, the other is receiving)—
And in the fabric of becoming
Flash—in and out—
The precious marks of Angel's Might.

In what tongue shall I write of the decline, the death-processes, this last phase of excarnation from my body? In what tongue articulate the utter grace?

Father tongue: The science of aging, its biology, neurology, horology...

Mother tongue: Aging's intimacies of grief and love...

Elder tongue: That might be muffled by duct tape, or silenced by fear...or awe...

Perhaps I will speak in all three tongues, and in the sound and the silences you, dear reader, will find resonating your own experience...

And, I hope, some inspiration.

Certainly I write as a woman, and my woman's tongue, being a little older than my teeth, is age 74.

No getting out of this body in this lifetime; and being a woman has conditioned and grown me in body and soul, and therefore in spirit.

I was born in rural southern England, the first in my generation after World War II. There was still food rationing till I was 4. I remember my mother picking nettles for soup by the henhouse.

I think there was a special shine around us, those first post-war children, after so much death and destruction. I acquired a different special shine when my mother died tragically when I was 5, my brother and I having been sent to some kind of children's home during her illness. It was dark and smelled of disinfectant. My mother's death was a betrayal. Perhaps of the fundamental expectation of children to be loved and nurtured by mother. Like all betrayals it offered the opportunity for initiation into new levels of understanding, forgiveness, ways of being: new soul terrain. It has been a long journey, stopping at the inns of depression, grandiosity, escape, victimhood, acceptance, resilience: to heal the narcissistic scars of wounding. A long journey to learn that I am in fact good enough, that I can trust myself and the world, trust life, and receive the gifts of that painful initiation through loss.

Among those gifts are a desire to be of help to families in distress, and an almost unbearable empathy with the emotional lives of children. It seems there is a particular intelligence, of the heart, that is schooled by inevitable loss and betrayal when we can meet them with a quiet mind, accepting their offerings of possibility. All of this story informs my experience of aging, which is both unique to me, and shared with my generation.

A new moon teaches gradualness
and deliberation, and how one gives birth
to oneself slowly. Patience with small details
makes perfect a large work, like the universe.
What nine months of attention does for an embryo
forty early mornings alone will do
for your gradually growing wholeness.
     —Jalal-al Din Rumi, 1207–1273

There was a gradual awakening to the fact I was not only "special," but also very privileged. However, some privileges were denied because I was a girl. Visiting my brother for the first time at his elite boarding school, astonished by the beauty and antiquity of the buildings, the immaculate green of endless sports pitches, single rooms, servants, and particularly the art rooms. Plural. All this he had by virtue of his gender. It took a long time, and a launch into the feminism of the 1970s to come to terms with my frustration and anger at this personal and greater social inequity. What has been most helpful along with a long study of the Great Goddess, the Divine Feminine, and the Sophia, is the knowledge gained through anthroposophy that I have been a man in previous lifetimes; as an accomplice in both the evil and marvelous accomplishments of patriarchy I have a responsibility to help move humanity in the direction of Gylany, the Partnership Way.

Human beings have forgotten how really to become old,
 and we must learn again to become old.
We must learn in a new way how to become old,
 and we can only do so through spiritual deepening.

—Rudolf Steiner, *Ancient Myths and the New Isis Mystery* (p. 96)

1. *Aging Body...till age snow white hairs on thee*

Recently, in one of those transitional crises when the body announces its capacity to betray, I broke a femur and received, courtesy of the National Health Service, a replacement hip. Soon after, on a crowded Oxford bus, with those accoutrements of the elderly in hand—crutch and shopping trolley on wheels—I stood, maintained upright by the crush of other passengers. A 17 year old and a 20 year old were sitting in the seats reserved for elders and the disabled. Several older people were seated nearby. After clinging wildly to the pole for three stops, I mentioned in a humble way to the young people that I had recently had hip surgery and would appreciate a seat. Oh, they were about to give up their seats, etc. The elders around tutted disapprovingly. After a good deal of squashed maneuvering, I sat down.

Reflecting on this incident‛s many layers—my feeling of extreme vulnerability, my apparent invisibility, my own unwillingness to speak up for myself, the feeble solidarity from other elders—I came to an epiphany: this was my official induction into Cronedom. I have joined the cohort of the aged, the physically vulnerable.

The Celtic folklore of the phases of a woman's life, gender-specific to women, has survived 2,000-plus years of patriarchy, largely as an oral folk tradition. More nuanced than the Puer/Senex male archetypes of Roman times, it corresponds roughly with some of the 7-year cycles identified by Rudolf Steiner and others as markers for inner development in a biography. This Celtic perspective of the collective archetype of the feminine adds to the Greek triple goddess—Maiden, Mother, Crone—the Queen phase, between menopause and Cronedom. Thus, we women move through Maidenhood, Motherhood (a time when we may be giving birth to ourselves as much as to children), to Queendom, and then to Cronedom. So now in our time, the archetypal feminine is quadruple, and given how much longer many of us are living, there is more time to achieve these four-fold inner accomplishments. Each phase of development has special tasks; when achieved, these make a strong foundation for the work of the next phase. Identifying and inhabiting the Queen phase was so liberating for me, especially from the cultural smog of fear of aging that I had unwittingly inhaled, that I forgot—or denied—what would inevitably be coming next: Cronedom.

> Crone: an ugly, evil-looking old woman.
> Synonyms: beldam, beldame, hag, witch.
> Type of: old woman.

What?!! Who says THAT?! This is a terrible insult to the millennia's-long courage and fortitude of medicine women, white witches, curanderas, eldresses, anchorites, bag ladies with their supermarket trolleys full of hard-acquired wisdom.

(My inner feminist notes that there are no equivalents for male elders.)

OK, time for us baby-bloomers to do some more redefining—through living our own lives—of contemporary youth-worshiping, death-fearing narratives.

So now I am considering Cronedom, and my own Cronedom in particular. Have I achieved the tasks of my Queen phase? I am not entirely sure what exactly those are; and I have a sense of achieving, sometimes, the kind of compassionate empathy that comes through the experiences of adversity, through listening deeply with the ears of my heart to the suffering of others. Is this the "spiritual deepening" that enables us to learn how to grow old in a new way?

Now, in this time, what are the developmental tasks of the Crone? What sort of Crone can I become? What are my purpose and values as a Crone? Is my intention more important than values? How to maintain a balance between increasing gravitas and levitas—that lightness of being that can laugh at, and find dignity in, the innumerable indignities of droop, flab, fall, dither, hobble, etc. inflicted by gravity on the declining body?

A friend said to me recently that if all she does as an elder is to set an example to youngers of SLOWING DOWN, she will have achieved something worthwhile. It seems to me that slowing down is a radical act of kindness in the rush and overwhelm of everyday life. And it is something our bodies oblige us to do as we age.

I hold these questions with an open mind as I begin my slow pilgrimage-quest on the Crone path alongside my sister Crones and brother Elders, holding each other up when our knees give way, listening patiently to each other's organ recitals...

In addition to the cultural fear of aging, the Crone, as an individual and as an archetype, it seems to me, must face as consciously as possible, another fear: the fear of dying, and of death. It can be helpful to make that distinction. This may be part of the "great work" of the Crone and the Elder; work performed in the inner temple-theater of the soul. It is part of the spiritual deepening that Rudolf Steiner says is necessary if we are to find, or remember, new ways of growing old that include the experience of inwardly—in our spiritual life—growing younger, flourishing, becoming more fully a whole human being. This inner activity requires me to experience myself as more than body; that my body is the garment in this lifetime for my soul and for the spirit. This effort, to make the opacity of matter translucent by seeing through it to what is spiritual, can be a powerful disruption to the materialism that experiences death as an ending, a portal to darkness.

> ### Time (excerpt):
> *Where thou onely wert before*
> *An executioner at best;*
> *Thou art a gard'ner now, and more,*
> *An usher to convey our souls*
> *Beyond the utmost starres and poles.*
>
> —George Herbert, 1593–1633

I have now had the good fortune to accompany three elders right up to that mysterious gateway, and have come to experience time, not as an executioner, but as a gardener whose life-garden grows seeds for future lives and worlds. Each journey to the threshold was very different. From my own experience and study of transitions, I can see death as a transition process into a world both new and familiar, where as much or more will take place, as in life on earth.

If I were making a trip to Africa, I would study its geography, history, denizens, and so on, so that I would have some idea what to expect, and how to be respectful of different laws and customs when I arrived. In the same way I can research the record we have of the next world. In this regard, ancient Egypt, Buddhist texts, Steiner's clairvoyant pictures, and recent accounts from those who have had near death experiences, are all helpful in building a kind of growing trust that we are more than our carbon-based earthly bodies, that vivid experiences await us on the journey between lives. This transformation (rather than overcoming) of fear of death, of the unknown, may be the alchemical labor of the Crone; work performed not in the outer world, but in the inner laboratory of the individual soul, which in turn transforms the collective soul of humanity on our evolutionary journey, as one drop transforms an ocean.

> *The laboratory must once again become an altar.*
> —Rudolf Steiner, *Life of the Human Soul*, lecture 5

I apologize to gentlemen readers here, for writing mostly from a gender-specific Crone perspective. It's the only one I know as I look out from this body, and review a lifetime living in its shelter. However, there are many developmental tasks in our biographies that we face together, hand in hand.

2. *Maturing Soul*

> *There are things the old woman can do, say and think that the woman cannot do say or think. Before she can do say or think them, she has got to change her life...become pregnant with herself.... Only one pregnancy is harder: the final one which men also must suffer and perform.*
> —Ursula Le Guin, *The Space Crone*, 2013

So aging happens very apparently in the body.

And yet, as Steiner points out, when we look from the perspective of the entire human being, "only our physical body grows older. For from the spiritual aspect it is not true that we grow older. It is a *maya,* an external deception. It is certainly a reality in respect of physical life, but it is not true in respect of the full nature of human life. Yet, we only have the right to say it is not true, if we know that this human being who lives here in the physical world between birth and death is something else than merely the physical body" (*Ancient Myths and the New Isis Mystery*, p. 99).

So everything that follows in this essay is predicated on the reality of the intimate connection, the constant interweaving and metamorphosing, that is occurring every moment among body, soul, and spirit.

Steiner, and other scientists of wisdom, tell us that the disintegration processes in the body bring consciousness, a form of spiritual life. So perhaps in looking at the soul of aging we are looking at the processes of maturing: the driving work of the I, the inmost eternal realm of the self, to achieve sovereignty and development in thinking, feeling, and willing in its sojourn in an earthly body, in its connection with a soul, in a human biography.

"This confusion is the ruin in which the treasure will be found," says Rumi. The confusions of childhood and early adulthood led me on a search: through Divine Feminism, the Sufi path, and then by a circuitous route via my children's Waldorf school, to anthroposophy.

I realized I had no idea what "soul" means. For more than 20 years I have endeavored to find out, to experience more fully my inner world of thinking, feeling, and willing, and to have some jurisdiction over it. Steiner has been the best teacher, and doing the 6 basic exercises he gave for soul-development, the best soul-gym. In this process of immense learning, my inner world has gradually opened out of its narcissistic hovel, re-orienting to enter the palaces of the living sacred that is beyond the limitations of relativism and industrialized scientific materialism. By miracles of grace, I am beginning a more conscious and active co-creative relationship with the spiritual world, the earth and all her creatures and beings, my community, and all of humanity. The exciting part is how much there is to know, do, learn and become! I think the largest—and continuing—gesture on this journey has been the shift from knowing about what soul is, or might be, to actually beginning to experience my inner life, to be able to distinguish and separate my thoughts, my feelings, and my actions: to feel my Self within myself.

After this age (63) wisdom is gained and we disregard the critical world and may perform some of our greatest work!
—Rudolf Steiner (quoted in F. W. Zeylmans Van Emmichoven, *The Anthroposophical Understanding of the Soul*)

In his lengthy poem *Intimations of Immortality*, Wordsworth allows himself one line for "a thought of grief." He lived in simpler times.

As I have gradually woken up to the thoughtless desecrations, the greedy exploitation, the murderous destruction of earth and her creatures that have metastasized in my lifetime, how can I not be filled with shame? Grief? Remorse? Guilt? How do I face my grandchildren with that behind me? As I offer radical hospitality to the lamentations of grief, shame, remorse, each of these bitter inner experiences has a healthy side, so long as they do not paralyze me into the "Nothing I can do about it now" space. Sometimes it seems the best I can do in the face of the 21st century is pray, "Bless this mess. May the good prevail."

Is my remorse enough to wake the angels who can astonishingly help us heal each other and the earth, get up and walk our talk? Will my shame recruit mighty beings who can help us learn to love fully at the eleventh hour before the earth dies too young, thanks to our selfish prioritizing of convenience over connection? Can I in my crone-seed-like way, help to restore the spiritual bond that we have lost, or mislaid: the invisibly perceptible and experienceable bond between each other, the earth, and heaven? Can my healthy grief strengthen my resolve to differently live in this last phase of my life, to perform "some of my greatest work"?

I am finding out.

This job "ain't for sissies." It's a job for the wizened, the weathered, the ones who can care, who finally have time, who have learned how to persist, who have forgotten and remembered much, who don't care anymore about what others think; and who are willing to keep on humbly changing and growing, together. In that humility we step out of our safety zone, we lose full control and *power-over*, leaving room for the unpredictable personal *power-with* that is predicated on each one rediscovering the other in truthful vulnerability. It seems old age offers us this opportunity more than other phases of life.

> *We must sit frequently in the face of the truth.*
> —Pat McCabe, Native American elder

This, too, may be part of the work of the Crone, and Senex.

It may be a waste of energy to argue with what is. We can still protest, still do our best, however apparently small that best may be. We can still picture change for good, new futures, using the most powerful tools we have: love and imagination. At our age there is no point starting small, there isn't time. Better start big and bold! I invite you dear reader to join me in speaking to the manager of the hardware store and handing out leaflets of complaint, whenever you see Round Up (the death-dealing Glyphosate) still—still!—on the shelves. I believe this sort of activism with Earth and her creatures in mind, which seems small, when enough of us do it with conviction and hope, is big and bold...

At about age 56, after the sad and amicable ending of my marriage, and re-training as a family therapist, I realized that I didn't really know what love is; nor was I clear about my own experience of love, as an activity or as a feeling. As a boarding school survivor of situations that often force the feeling life into dumb numbness, it has been a long task for me to learn my feelings' sign language, to name, befriend, include my feelings. I am slowly learning to attend to what lives in me, and in the space between me and the Other and the world, that space where the Sophia dwells, her veil lifting...

So, I added to the task of learning about soul, that of understanding and experiencing more deeply, love, using my feelings as a perceptual learning tool. It has helped to have as a guide the Greek schema for four kinds of love—Eros, Philia, Caritas and Agape (divine love operating transformatively in the human heart)—as a sort of tracking device to help nuance and build this understanding of myself and in the world. One thing I have learned is that love is messy. Very messy. Creatively messy if my tidy self can stand it. I have to renounce the safety of detachment, distance and invulnerability, be willing to face challenges: How to love someone for whom I feel antipathy? A stranger? An enemy? How to love stupidity and ignorance? How to love evil? I am finding out.

Travels of a Magpie Soul, Snapper Up of Unrequited Trifles, Who Got Caught by Love

From the old stone walls
Of the many mansions of my father's house
I scraped off crumbling pieces of the Church of England
They are under my fingernails still.

On the path between Stonehenge and Avebury
I found the glimmer in a dewdrop
Of an ancient star
It was something about heaven and earth
That I stuffed in my pocket.

A tourist in the great halls of the Zohar
I filched a spoon from a table
And used it to sip the complex juices of
The psalms of David.

There is an unfinished caravanserai
On the Way of All Women.
From a drawer in a room under construction
I snatched a handkerchief
For when there is a need to weep.

Wandering in the glittering temple of Rumi
When I thought no one was looking
I borrowed a tile from the wall
One of the bluest
And put it in my bag.

I found myself on a scaffold
High up in the dome of the Agia Sophia mosque
I was given three stolen tesserae from the mosaic
    of St John.
Nothing was stolen by me, I am innocent
In this case.
I lost them, then found them again later in the
    laundry basket.

From the Cairo Museum
I delicately liberated memories
Of initiations
And managed to get them through customs
Undetected in the hem of my coat.

At Ephesus I stood
Before the statue of Diana
Counting her many breasts;
Climbing the Buddha-bedecked stone
Mountain of Borobudur
I grabbed a blessing for the embryonic girl-child
    within me.

Now I see that these were gifts not stolen treasure.
Why did I make myself guilty and ashamed for needing,
    for searching?

At last I came to a wooden temple on a
    snow-covered hill,
In flames it was. The ruins emerging like a crucifix.
    A sacrifice.
Apprehended at last, what I take from its resurrection
Is love and wisdom.

3. *Eternal Spirit:*
The "Years that Bring the Philosophic Mind"

The Inner child grows up—in the care of beloved community.

> *The soul has two eyes:*
> *One looks at time passing,*
> *The other sends forth its gaze*
> *Into eternity.*
>
> —Angelus Silesius, German
> priest and physician, 1624–1677

Native American wisdom science invites us to consider 7 generations.

This is good advice; but which way should I look? Behind me? Ahead? Very often faced with a choice of 2, I practice inclusivity and invite both options, knowing that often a middle way, or third movement, can arise. In this case it can be both moving and expansive to consider 3.5 generations of our ancestors, and 3.5 generations of our descendants. As elders we may have known and know some of them, and experience ourselves centered and present in the stream where time and eternity flow together. In this exercise, the eye that is gazing at eternity may catch a glimpse of karmic strands, themes that weave through a bloodline.... And the eye of the soul that is looking at time passing may learn to look to the future, and listen.

In the soul realm, I am still, to a lesser extent than in my body, gendered. According to wisdom science (never mind common sense derived from observation) the male physical body is stronger than the woman's; her subtle life-energy, or etheric body is stronger than his. She can host, nurture and birth life; in famine she endures longer. When we consider the subtle energetic body that connects us with the stars—the astral or soul-body—we are in a realm beyond gender, in the realm of the soul's invisible and still perceptible capacity for thinking, feeling, and willing, for connecting with the spiritual reality that dwells in all of life. The "I," too, sheathed in the soul, is beyond gender. In that realm of consciousness, I can, with guidance and grace, access pure spirit.

In my work as a therapist, I have come to see—and know—that there dwells in each of us the unwounded, unwoundable eternal self that is continuously becoming, over lifetimes. This perspective can be very comforting when we are lost or stuck, alone in the immediate and embodied pains of woundedness and victimhood. It also serves to disrupt materialism, a radical gesture I am taking on more consciously in my old age.

The path of the individual leads through great loneliness, but it is in this very loneliness that people seek each other...the world can become a temple to us which we can enter with new spiritual forces in deep connection with our fellow human beings...

Zeylmans van Emmichoven points to something that is profound for me: that now is the time to open to community, not only to become a temple, with its altar the laboratory of my inner alchemist; also, to co-create temples of community to welcome the lonely, the dispossessed, the excluded, those who are, in the words of the Hopi Prophesy, in the river with us now. To be honest, that is a terrifying prospect! Do I have the courage and the inner resources to take this on, this preparation for entering the great beloved community of heaven? Am I willing to leave the relatively safe space of my private individuality, what Steiner calls the Consciousness Soul? Can I develop in myself in old age the kind of love that loves a stranger, an enemy? The kind of love that transforms my isolated selfishness?

When I look with one eye of my soul at time passing, I am mystified by a paradox: that I am both entirely different from how I was 10, 30, 50 years ago; and I am still the same in some core acorn-like way—the acorn that wondrously contains and announces and births the oak tree of me in this lifetime.

My earth sign is Aries: beginnings are my forte. It has been a life-long task to learn how to complete, to stay on the path without leaving too much undone littered behind me. So, looking at the ending of life, the other eye on eternity, feels like new territory. How to do this bit well, with sincerity and wonder?

Recently a beloved Crone-friend advised me to "Look for the footsteps of the Christ" in my everyday life. If you, gentle reader, have trouble with the C-word, as I have (appalled by the iniquities committed over centuries in the name of Christianity), you can try substituting "mightiest perfect being of Love." Look for the footprints of that One.

We can find these footprints in Thinking as Consolation; in Feeling as Radiance; and in Willing as Sacrifice. So, when I hear or offer consolation, or see and feel the radiant shining of warmth and light from another person, plant or creature; when I see or make a sacrifice, great or small, I am experiencing the mighty being of love in thinking, feeling, and willing—I am learning spirit-beholding, spirit-sensing, and spirit-recalling.

Perhaps this Way of recalling, sensing and beholding is our Going Homework. As Elders we can dip into the untapped deep pool of our collective love and wisdom and keep offering...

Even if I am invisible, inaudible, even if I have to stand in the bus all the way home, as an elder, a Crone, I can still bless.

And be a blessing.

The vulnerability and humility we are obliged to experience in old age are not weaknesses. They can be openings to inner strength and connection with our divine humanity. In vulnerability and humility, we no longer have anything to defend, and in that place we are powerful, and finding our way to a new way of growing old.

Writing this essay has helped me set my intention-sails for the next stretch of the journey. Even so I have no idea what I will do and become between age 74, and whenever; or what inns I will stop at, what help, solace and challenges I will be given, who I will encounter on the way. I am finding out.

> *I turned the pages of my life*
> *And found that there was waiting there*
> *A page filled with such utter grief*
> *It bowed my back and greyed my hair.*
>
> *I turned the pages of my life*
> *And found at last a page of gold*
> *A page whose utter grace will stand*
> *When I am withered and grown old.*
>
> —Roger Wagner, 1948
> (with publisher's permission)

Davina Muse is a citizen of Britain, where she was born, and of the U.S., where she lived for 35 years before returning recently to England. She is the devoted mother of 2 astonishing young adults, and grandmother of 2, so far. Having also been a high school English teacher, a textile conservator, an advocate for Waldorf Education, a family therapist and parenting coach, an avaricious reader, and a mystical gardener, she is currently in training for her perhaps final career, which may include and transcend all the previous ones, as a myrrophore. Look it up. She is probably a heretic.

Somebodies and Nobodies: The Search for Meaning among Older Men

Christopher Schaefer

"As we grow older we begin more and more
to love the wisdom revealed by life."[1]

I am part of two groups of elderly men, one an in-person meeting in the town where I live and the other an international zoom group. Both meet about once a month, and both consist of mostly retired individuals with diverse professional backgrounds as well as different philosophical and spiritual interests. We work with a wide variety of themes, from what is happening in the world to more personal questions about our lives and how we relate to aging and retirement. When discussing the latter questions, it became clear that we tended to share a similar set of attitudes about what it meant to be a man coming to adulthood in the 1950s and '60s and the struggle and search for meaning and purpose as we retired.

Despite widely different career choices and countries of origin, we all felt that a primary obligation as a man coming to maturity was to provide financial and physical security for our family and loved ones and to be successful within our chosen career fields. Of course, I know other individuals for whom this is not the case. However, within these two groups we recognized something deeply ingrained within us, leading each of us to find meaning and self-worth within our work, within the external and public domain of

---

1 Rudolf Steiner, *Love and Its Meaning in the World*, p. 179.

society. The corollary of this was that we tended to expect our wives or partners to take most of the responsibility for children, family life and relationships, what I would call the more qualitative life world.

I am not saying that these attitudes were fully conscious nor, of course, that they were enlightened; but I would say that amongst ourselves we were able to acknowledge them as being fundamentally true, leading to the recognition that once we were retired, as I have been for some time at 81, we faced the question of who and what are we now? This dilemma is expressed by the title of this essay, *Somebodies and Nobodies*, the title of a book by Robert Fuller, which examines how society engages in rankism, judging people based on their position, age, rank and job.[2] It was also poignantly expressed in both groups at different times, for example when a retired academic, who had then become a hospital chaplain said to us, "now that I have given up the chaplaincy who am I, and how will people see me?" In the other group, a former high-level executive told us that in recently planning his 85th birthday party, his wife questioned his wish to include a manager who had given him a prestigious industry award twenty-five years earlier. "Is that really relevant today for you or our family?" she asked, illustrating the dilemma of older men seeking meaning by turning to past accomplishments.

From my reflections, and also based on conversations in these two groups, it is clear that in order to find new meaning, purpose and self-worth, older retired men who lived with fairly traditional views of what it meant to be a successful man in society, need to shift their focus more to what I previously called the life world. This more qualitative world of friends, family, relationships, feelings, art, nature, and inner or spiritual work is, of course, part of the life of all adults. But in my experience, it is not really seen or valued by many older men, witness how puzzled we are by how much women have to say to each other in conversations, in person or on the phone. Or the admission we make quite readily that we leave it to our wives

---

2   Robert Fuller, *Somebodies and Nobodies: Overcoming the Abuse of Rank.*

or partners to maintain the relationships with our children, grand-children and even often with the members of our own birth family.

So retirement, as well as our life-partners, our children and grandchildren, and our friends, can be the gateway to experiencing, valuing and being creative within this—for us—newer but always present life world. It is one of the gifts of modern society that, at least if we have reasonable health and a middle-class income, we can move from the world of doing toward this life world of being, of observing, of being present and of loving. When a person in one of the groups asked what we can give, pass on or teach our grandchildren, others answered that we can love them and be there for them.

In referring to the Steiner quote at the beginning of this essay, I would say we can learn to love the wisdom revealed by life for us as older men if we can more consciously participate in the qualitative social life world; this sustained us in the past and now can encourage us to honor friendships, family relationships, the beauty of conversation, and the blessings of human encounter. Part of this blessing is moving from being the authority, the expert, to learning from and being dependent on younger generations. On the way home recently with our sixteen-year-old granddaughter, my wife asked her what music she loved and played. She began to explain the different kinds of music she enjoyed for different activities and different parts of the day, playing them for us on her iPhone. Perhaps this sharing brought her contentment, for she then turned toward me and began rubbing my earlobe between her thumb and forefinger, a favorite activity and comfort to her when she was a young child.

The movement from expert to learner is quite naturally also accompanied by moving from helper and supporter to needing help and support. I am no longer so steady on my feet, and increasingly my children and grandchildren will help me on a steep incline or stepping off a curb. Recently, going for a swim with my son in quite high surf, it was touching to see him assess the waves, telling me when to enter and then holding my arm carefully as we scrambled out so that I wouldn't fall. After thanking him, I also had to acknowledge to myself that I was weaker than I used to be and needed the help he provided with such care and generosity.

Coping with illness, weakness, and the loss of hearing and sight are of course also increasingly with us as we age and spend ever more time at medical and dental facilities. In my friendship circle we refer to the tales of our ailments as the organ recital, as many people do, and try to limit this time spent on sharing our minor ailments. Yet as we grow older and lose evermore friends to serious illness, to cognitive impairment or death, the limitations of body and mind are a very real worry and companion of the aging process.

For many elderly people, appreciating nature and travel to foreign cultures can be other important ways of entering the more qualitative life world, giving pleasure and meaning to life. I try to spend time in my garden every day to observe plants, trees, birds and animals, as well as to tend to my flower beds. Since I have created three small ponds on the property, this includes checking on the frogs and fish and occasionally observing the blue heron who visits at least twice each summer, or watching the deer who often drink from the ponds in the evening.

This observing and appreciating of nature is an ever-stronger experience as I grow older; and each sunset, autumn leaf or hummingbird becomes an occasion for unique delight, if I let it. Perhaps this is due to the realization that my time is running out, that an ending is visible, and that the marvelous beauty of the natural world will not be available to me forever. Perhaps I now also have the inner space to fully appreciate it. Indeed, it seems to me that as we age, there is an ever-greater possibility of experiencing the joy of just being, of listening to and seeing the human and natural world around us. Perhaps it is a natural gift of aging, this appreciation of small things, of the beauty and love expressed in nature and human relationships. As a very old writer noted a few years ago: *"Here is the paradox simply told: even as I am moving into very old age, recognizing and recording my own diminishment as time passes, my truth is that this last decade has been the happiest of my life.*"[3]

Rudolf Steiner gives a reflective exercise often used in Biography Work that can be most helpful in entering the qualitative life world, in particular the community of life that has made our life possible. He suggests looking back at our life and bringing to consciousness the individuals who have helped us on our journey, opening doors for us, encouraging us and supporting us—parents, teachers, children, friends, and colleagues. When you do this earnestly, it evokes gratitude and humility because you realize that most decisions and indeed many of the accomplishments of your life have been made possible through the interest, encouragement and support of others.

For me a conversation with George O'Neil, a friend of my parents, was critical in my finding a relationship to Anthroposophy and to Steiner's work. I was a history and philosophy major in college and came home one day reading a thick tome by the German philosopher Martin Heidegger. George asked me what I was reading and how I found it, and then he said, here, read this book on philosophy by Steiner and I will read Heidegger and then we can talk, which we did.

Another important aid in our process of becoming, for both my wife and me, was going to an International Anthroposophical Youth Conference in Spring Valley, New York, in 1970 and through a conversation with Alan Howard, a British Waldorf Teacher living in Canada at the time, and Diana Hughes, a Waldorf teacher from Toronto, deciding to help start a Waldorf school in the Boston area with friends. Attending the Conference and helping to start a Waldorf school were central in determining our life path, for we met people who helped us to find our way to Europe and to our respective life works.

And on and on it goes for each of us. A teacher in junior high school who sees us and encourages us. The person who gives us

---

3   Sam Toperoff, "In the Land of the Very Old" (SundayLongRead.com).

our first job, or someone who asks us to help with a project. I am, for example, very grateful to a deceased colleague, Coenraad van Houten, for asking me to help him start the Centre for Social Development at Emerson College in England many years ago, certainly because of the things I learned from him and the many international students I met, but particularly because of the deep connection to Steiner's social insights this allowed me to develop.

Of course, such biographical reflections can be made in the middle of life, but as we enter our 70s and 80s, we naturally feel a deeper connection to certain people and to specific biographical themes and challenges that have made our life what it is. It is as if the years of our life have become a sieve allowing some things to fall away and others to become more visible and important. Two examples come to my mind.

Because I came to the United States as a child and then lived for some years in Europe as an adult, I have always felt a bit of an outsider, a visitor, with no real home except for the specific houses or apartments where we lived. This sense of being an observer has played into my work as a consultant and advisor, as well as to always having at least two jobs at any one time. This made my work life interesting but has also led to a lack of full commitment to any one thing. The older I get, especially now in my eighties, the more I see this as an important challenge to work with.

The other example is that I have been married for almost sixty years. Over two thirds of my life have been spent with Signe, and much of what we have become and what we have achieved is as a result of our life partnership. In getting older a deep appreciation and love for the other can grow, adding a sweetness and gratitude to our life.

We may think, particularly as young people, that we are the author of our lives, but the reality is that, all along the way, we are helped by the conversations and meetings with others, and with what I would call the spark of destiny and love woven into our life path. This reality is beautifully expressed in a poem by Rosemerry Wahtola Trommer:

THOUGH I RESPOND TO MY NAME, I AM AWARE

how completely the love of others
has made me who I am. How the work
of their hands is more me
than the swirls of my own fingerprints.
I am the project of love,
the product of compassion,
the sum total of kindness
and sympathy. Of course,
the cruelty, too. Of course,
the ugliness, the shame.
But it is love that rises in me,
like yeast in the living bread.
It is love I've received
that stands when I stand,
love that responds
when you say my name.[4]

Part of the wisdom revealed by life as we grow older is seeing the themes and patterns of our life's journey ever more clearly, often starting in childhood. I remember reading about a man who as a child was deeply affected by seeing a caged tiger in a New York Zoo and saying to his father how sad the animal looked. Alan Rabinowitz went on to become a world-renowned expert on large cats, in particular, tigers and leopards, and he played a central role in establishing sanctuaries for these threatened species in Central America and Southeast Asia. Many people know the story of Jane Goodall whose favorite toy as a young child was Jubilee, a chimpanzee doll,

---

4   Rosemerry Wahtola Trommer, "Though I Respond to My Name, I am
     Aware" (https://ahundredfallingveils.com/2023/02/14/though-i-respond-to
     -my-name-i-am-aware/). Used by permission of the author. I am grateful to
     Signe Schaefer for sharing this and many other wonderful poems with me.

many years before her work with chimpanzees in Gombe, Tanzania, made her famous.

In looking back at my own life, I can see that my first memory of a daylight air-raid on Frankfurt at the end of World War II affected me deeply, leading me later to wonder how war was possible, how could human beings destroy each other so wantonly, and often with so little remorse? Later as a university student I arrived in Berlin in August of 1961, and witnessed the building of the Wall and the massing of American, Russian, British and French troops. This then led me to study international politics and economics, thinking I could work for world peace at the United Nations or some other international agency. In the course of my studies and later teaching, my goals became more modest as I realized that conflicts and war did not only exist between nations but also in organizations, between groups and individuals, and also of course within me.

So my working with organizations and communities on relationships, including conflicts, was a natural extension of a question and concern based on a childhood experience. This life or biographical thread was of course not clear to me at the time that I made decisions about education and professional direction, but it became ever more visible to me as I grew older. Recently this life interest, and I would say karmic theme, has led me to a growing interest in nonviolence and to the imagination of the Beloved Community, a foundation of the Civil Rights movement led by Martin Luther King Jr.

Another gift, although more perturbing, as I grow older, is that at odd times I have memory pictures of where I have acted in ways contrary to my beliefs and values. This is painful as I recall a situation in which I acted in a dominating or bullying way at a conference, or said unkind or hurtful things to a colleague, or through lack of preparation or arrogance did not serve a client well. Then there are also the memory pictures of when I have acted out of anger, or have lied to loved ones. This process of taking stock, of seeing my limitations and moral failings, seems to be triggered by an involuntary memory picture and can then become the occasion for a more conscious reflection about my life and some effort to acknowledge and atone as I enter old age.

The distance, objectivity, and insight into one's own life and that of others that becoming an elder can give to us if we learn to ponder, reflect and learn, is also, I think, part of this love of wisdom revealed by life that Steiner describes. In the same talk Steiner then made the following statements:

> The truth, however, is that the wisdom one acquires in life is merely the means to unfold the seed of the next life. When a plant has completed its growth through the year, the seed remains, and this is also true of the wisdom acquired from life. A human being passes through the gate of death, and the ripening process of the spiritual core of its being is the seed of the next life.[5]

For Steiner, life is really the great school in which we can learn to become wiser, more loving beings through repeated incarnations in a human form. The wiser we become, the more gratitude and reverence we develop toward the natural, human, and spiritual worlds, which have given us this life, and the more we seek to love this world. For me, individuals such as Thich Nhat Hanh, the Dalai Lama, and Rudolf Steiner demonstrate this truth, as do other truly wise individuals whom I have met and known.

After death, Steiner suggests we digest the wisdom we have received in this life, reviewing our life as others and the world have experienced us; and then with our friends, colleagues and human community we create the next lesson plan for our future incarnation. This plan is then embedded in our organism as our destiny; we are born and develop as individuals, with our family, friends, teachers, partners and colleagues as our destiny companions. The more we are able to bring to consciousness and to develop gratitude toward our life path, toward our destiny and the people that have made our journey possible—with all of its challenges and opportunities—the

---

5   Rudolf Steiner, *Love and Its Meaning in the World*, p. 179.

more, I think, we can learn to love this world, which so desperately needs it at this time of struggle and chaos.

In my efforts to understand and work with the opportunities that becoming an elder offers, I am learning to value and cultivate my relation to friends and family, to the human, more feminine life world, and to see and experience the wisdom built into this world through karma and reincarnation. I hope this can be true for many other men as they become elders.

Christopher Schaefer, PhD, is a retired adult educator who for many years taught at both Emerson College in England and at Sunbridge College in New York. He has also been an organization and community development advisor for most of his life, working both with Waldorf Schools and Camphill Communities as well as with many more. He is the coauthor of *Vision in Action: Working with Soul and Spirit in Small Organizations* and the author of *Partnerships of Hope: Building Waldorf School Communities* and *Re-imagining America: Finding Hope in Difficult Times*. He lives with his wife Signe in the Berkshires of Massachusetts.

COMING OF SAGE

MARY BOWEN

Writing about my life is painful as well as enriching. The first 21 years were challenging, yet forming and giving strength for the following 61 years. Now, at age 82, I am officially an elder —although each day I feel younger and younger.

I envision my life as a tapestry with many textures, colors and patterns. In this writing I hope to reflect on the early years of marriage, parenting, education, spiritual research, death and dying, travels, community work, becoming an elder, and family that served to inspire my life.

I often think of the newborn baby coming to Earth as a pure spiritual being filled with wisdom and potential. The presence of a new baby can bring a sense of stepping over a threshold into a different world. A sacred world. The baby is held for nine months in the vessel of the mother near to her heartbeat and pulsing with the breath of the mother. The new baby needs rest, peace, warmth, food and protection. It is a slow process waking up to the world, rolling over, crawling, learning to walk and speak, a process of incarnating. Breathing in life and growing.

As we age, this process is reversed. We begin to excarnate, taking leave of the Earth. I now begin to feel myself less and less of the Earth—letting go more and more. (Although feeling younger and younger in spirit.) Our physical body often declines, we move slower, and experience aches and pains. We reflect on past experiences and sometimes forget being in the now. For example, going into a room and wondering why you are there! We make lists so as not to forget something important.

However, the young child and the older person often go hand in hand. This slowing down can be a comfort, especially to young children and babies. Rudolf Steiner, the founder of Waldorf education, spoke about the young child thriving with care from an older person. The newborn coming so recently from the spiritual world and the elder moving back to the spiritual world, in a sense they are in a similar space.

Given all the limitations physically of the elderly, I find this phase of my life to bring new insights. The slowing down is a blessing. I now have time for and interest in meditation, in reading Anthroposophy, time for naps; and I feel less stress. My quality of life has changed. What is important to me now has changed. My motto is now—"well, why not?" (And sometimes there are clear answers to why not!)

I am thankful for the life I have been given. There were many gifts. Life has been both arduous and abundant.

In my early 20s I met and married an adventurous soul, my husband Bruce, which led to us living in Hawaii. I thought he was so cool and original…a surfer! On reflection, I feel this is when my life really began. I now had a new freedom and could choose how I wanted to live life. In the course of fourteen years, we gave birth to our two children, Jennifer and David, both very great teachers for us. We both chose to become teachers and applied for our first teaching positions at public schools in Hawaii. The 1960s in Hawaii was a lovely place to raise children, and we both established our careers while making many important connections with other kindred souls.

We enjoyed our summers and evenings being in nature as much as possible. We decided to try to live off the grid, and built a wooden recycled A-frame house on 4 acres, thinking we could live a sustainable life style. Bruce thrived on creating a farmstead, but I was not as adventurous as I thought. No running water, or electricity, and the house half built while traveling many miles from the country to town to teach, so that we had funds to live on, was not easy. In 1977 we came to a crossroads and discovered a little homestead/Waldorf School right down the road. The initiators there led us to meet René Querido, an enthusiastic Waldorf master teacher who encouraged us to enroll in the teacher training program at Rudolf Steiner College. After a few years we found our way to Sacramento and began the two-year, full-time program training to be Waldorf teachers.

After teacher training, we accepted positions at Mountain Meadow Waldorf School. Bruce took a first grade, and I enthusiastically dove into the work of a Waldorf kindergarten teacher.

In January while Bruce was teaching sixth grade, a great sorrow fell on our family with his sudden passing, at the age of 47. Our whole community was in grief. We held a three-day home threshold ritual with hundreds of community members and family support. That karmic event and connection to his soul brought the spiritual world close to our whole family and community.

In the years that followed, I helped many other families when a loved one was crossing the threshold, often creating a sacred ritual after death or by supporting families while their loved one was dying. A very blessed work.

Life grew more arduous; life grew more abundant.

Working with and knowing about the spiritual world began when I was a very young child. I nearly died at age 5 and then again at age 33 when my son was born. I was in labor for two days and was transported in a cargo airplane to a larger hospital. There was a moment when I saw myself from above and felt I would leave the earth; however, a being met me and compelled me back, and I knew it was not my time to leave.

Then 15 years later with the death of my husband, our son David was grieving the great loss of his father, I was grieving, our daughter

Jennifer was grieving. It was all a bit much. I prayed, I cried, I went to work. It was a very hard time; however, I did feel his spirit was always near. Bruce was a pillar, he never left me in our 25 years together on earth, and his great spirit has continued to carry, counsel and inspire me to this day.

When we were in our Waldorf teacher training years we studied in the arts. One teacher told us about these wonderful paint brushes that she could get for only $40. Bruce was very excited about them and told me he ordered 2 for us. I was somewhat angry because we were struggling financially with no income for 2 years. The day the brushes arrived Bruce gave me one and I said, "oh no, you ordered these...we can't afford these!" He shook that brush close to me and said, "Mary Bowen, one day you will be glad to have this brush!" I tell this story because it leads to the next crossroads that I met a few years later. Bruce was often prophetic.

In 1986 while guiding young children at the Waldorf School in Ukiah I saw a flyer in the school office announcing an anthroposophical art therapist, Maria de Zwaan from Holland, coming to lead art workshops in Berkeley. The moment I saw her name I knew we had a connection. Here I stood at another crossroads, and I began intensive training with Maria. A group of 12 met for five years and culminated our course at Chartres Cathedral in France. I continued to study and work with Maria; and when folks in Sonoma County asked me to hold a training course, I decided, if Maria would help, perhaps we could continue a training in Nurturing Arts as Social Arts. Maria suggested she could be a Godmother and would help from Holland as well as coming to assist. The initiative to train began in 1995 as a 5-year program. The work became very full and there were many folks attending. I write this history as it very much relates to my life now in the phase beyond 63.

I grew up in a family where the elderly and needy folks in our community were a concern of my parents. In many ways they were social workers. Those down and out were welcome in our home. No one ever left without a good meal and leftovers wrapped for them. Many times, I helped my mother make meals for families who were suffering. Now as I age, I am thankful for the model my parents gave us to consider others before yourself.

Both my grandmother on my mother's side and Grandpa on my dad's side lived with us when they could no longer care for themselves.

My grandmother was a tiny Irish woman who sat by the bay window in a rocking chair near the flowering pots of purple African violets. She spoke softly and usually had a rosary moving through her fingers. I was named after her. She was a teacher in a one room school house and, in those years, teachers were not allowed to marry. She was courted for over 20 years by my grandpa. They married at age 40 and had 4 children by age 47!

My grandfather on my father's side lived with us from the time I was born as his wife died young. I was very curious about the grandmother, his wife whom I never met. He would not talk about her. My parents told me it was because she followed a Christian Science path, and grandpa felt she might have lived if she would only see a doctor. There was a great sadness in his soul around the death of his wife. This was the first time I entertained the idea that there were alternatives to the current medical model. As a teenager grandpa taught me to drive in his old green Studebaker. I learned to drive on a racetrack with a clutch. Grandpa was a Renaissance man—he carved, farmed, sheared sheep, cared for our horses, and wrote music. At age 77, he became our band teacher in a small private school in Iowa. He volunteered and provided all the students who wanted to play in the band with instruments. He was very much loved, and all the students called him "Grandpa." He lived to be nearly 100 and died when I was 33. The day he died, I knew about it before I got the phone call telling of his death.

One of my favorite authors, Selma Lagerlöf, recalls her grandmother in the story *The Holy Night*...

> When I was five years old, I had such great sorrow! I hardly know if I have had a greater since.
>
> It was then my grandmother died. Up to that time she used to sit every day on the corner sofa in her room and tell stories.
>
> I remember that Grandma told story after story from morning 'til night, and that we children sat beside her quite still and listened....
>
> It isn't much that I recollect about my grandmother. I remember that she had very beautiful snow-white hair. And stooped when she walked, and that she always sat and knitted a stocking.
>
> And I even remember that when she had finished a story, she used to lay her hand on my heard and say: "All this is as true, as true that I see you and you see me."...
>
> The thing I remember best, and that is the great loneliness when she was gone.
>
> I remember the morning when the corner sofa stood empty and when it was impossible to understand how the days would ever come to an end...that I shall never forget!...
>
> I remember something was gone from our lives. It seemed as if the door to a whole beautiful, enchanted world—where before we had been free to go in and out—had been closed. And now there was no one to open that door.[1]

In writing a chapter for this book we were asked to write about age 63 and beyond. In the book *Fulfillment of Old Age*, Dr. Norbert Glas writes we are finally born at age 63. We have come to the end of our partially unfree development and have now entered the era of inner freedom. Yes, coming to the age of 63, there I found a new freedom. This was a phase where my children were married, and my six grandchildren came to earth. I moved several times and made spaces in my home for community arts. Many elders passed into the spiritual world. My mother, father, aunts, uncles and my sister all crossed the threshold. Discernment became more important in my life.

---

1   Selma Lagerlöf, *Christ Legends*, Floris Books, 1977.

Turning 70 was another turning point. I moved for what I hoped would be the last time and thought now I stay here until I die. I gutted the house, created new lazured walls, and opened up a big room for arts. I felt, now I am really home! Adults came for classes and there was a rhythm in my life. Life was good. My hips started to hurt, and I had two hip replacements.

In the first week of March 2020, we started a biography course with 12 women. We modeled life-sized baby heads and carefully wrapped the sculptures with wet cloths and looked forward to our next session. The next session did not happen. The phone rang, and one by one each woman called to say due to COVID they feared leaving their homes.

We all faced the pandemic. Everything closed. How would my family navigate this? We had Christmas outside on the patio because…why? I still wonder. I decided to help my 9-year-old twin grandchildren with school on zoom. I was not welcomed to do that. I struggled through a karmic knot and had a big letting go. I was shocked.

Working with groups and now basically being shut in, I decided to get a puppy. Gracie was adorable and incorrigible. I thought…now I'm old and old folks love their dogs. I had thought I'll either get a puppy or a banjo…(I should have gotten the banjo!) But a miracle appeared. I met a man who was willing to build a fence so Gracie could not escape. A very beautiful quiet man who became a good friend and helped me to see that I was not really a puppy person. Gracie went back to the family from which she came and became a mother of 10 puppies.

Things change!

Little did I know that at age 80 there were still more changes. I sold the home I had planned to live in for the rest of my life and moved with my good friend (the fence builder) to a new home. We live now in a large home that provides room for both of our needs. The Orchard is a community for elders where we have a running creek, redwood trees, a warm salt water pool, walking paths, yoga and exercise classes.

Now my focus is on keeping my body healthy, movement, and my inner life. I often wonder when and how I will die, and then I remember it's up to God.

I am thankful for the life I have been given, that I can still live independently in my home, that my grown children and grandchildren live close by, and that the karma COVID brought to my life has healed.

My work continues, but at a much slower pace and many friends help me. I have been asked to continue in the practice of Nurturing Arts and Biographical counseling. When asked I am usually able to meet others. If I'm not taking a nap!

And now this chapter ends, and it is as true, as true as I see you and you see me.

...and I got a banjo!

Mary Bowen, MEd, lives in Sonoma County, California. She has taught Kindergarten, the grades and adults. For more than 40 years she has facilitated "Nurturing Arts," an Anthroposophical initiative that brings consciousness through painting, drawing, and sculpture. She also works privately in biographical counseling.

The Gift of Aging—
the Beauty in Getting Older

Joseph Rubano

I have a friend (Robert Johnson, now across the Threshold) who, in his becoming-suddenly-old phase, when asked how he was, would say: "Better than ever." We young ones in our 40s or 50s would sometimes laugh and almost make fun of him, saying to each other that we, too, were "better than ever." Even when we weren't. We enjoyed the light in his eyes and the hint of a smile, but we really didn't get it.

He would also often say, "I am learning so much"; but he wouldn't really try to explain or fill in the picture, even if he were asked. Perhaps he was referring to insights or understandings about how life or consciousness plays out. Maybe it was about seeing himself more clearly, or how he is or has been in relationship more clearly. I am not sure why he wouldn't say much; but I do know that some of the "so much" I am learning can be pretty embarrassing or humbling that it has taken so long to get so little—pretty obvious and seemingly unimportant, but actually very important—insight about how I am in relationship. Maybe we are all slow learners, or the most important understandings can only open in us in time.

Many times I would visit Robert and in the course of our conversation he would ask me "What is this world coming to?" He was deeply concerned, and he was genuinely asking. I think that he was hoping that one of his friends might have some insight, or a way of looking that would help to make sense and offer hope. The world outside had become very different for him from the world inside—or is it the other way around—the world inside had grown very different from the world outside?

This piece will have two foci. The first relates to "Better than ever" and "I am learning so much." The second will not attempt to answer the question "What is the world coming to?" but will speak a little about the experience of physical and soul pain and the capacity to bear "what the world is coming to."

I have to acknowledge an important thing right off. My life partner, of 47 years, and I are in good health. We have a comfortable home, food when hungry, drink when thirsty. We live simply. My relationships are for the most part good and healthy. I have family around me, I have lots of friends, I feel loved and valued, I still do the work I love, and I don't worry much about money these days. I have a friend who says that an important question to ask yourself in your old age is "Do I have enough?" I have enough. I realize that not every old person does. Life has been good to me. I am grateful.

I am also writing from the perspective of one who has been walking a spiritual path for over 50 years. Also, in writing this, I have asked a number of my friends (who have no or, at most, very little connection to our beloved Anthroposophy) what they would say the gifts or beauty of aging are for them. You will hear their voices, too. Of course, there are physical challenges—like my Italian grandfather, who was a machinist, used to say: "The machine-ah donna worka like-ah it used to! The parts they-a weara out." But I won't be talking about that.

I am 75 now and it is true for me that my experience of life is "better than ever." There are some outer circumstances and some inner developments that contribute to this. I have not lived what might be called a culturally determined "normal" or "successful" life in the world, so I could never hang my sense of self on some kind of external criterion for success (like money or prestige) in the way many men have or do. I struggled a lot because of this but, in the end, it has turned out to be a gift—in that I have invested a lot of time and attention, my sense of self, on my inner state of being and on my relationships. It has been a steady focus for over 50 years.

I encountered meditation when I was 22 or so after graduating from college. While, in growing up, I did love sports and the Catholic Church, yet meditation was really my first love. I loved the ritual of the mass and something about being in a Church and Christ and the saints—there was a mystery and a sense of the Holy there that I was unconsciously drawn toward. However, prayer was mostly rote. But meditation—sitting still and focusing feelingly inward—opened a whole new world to me. A world that touched the mystery I sensed in the Church and one that I felt immediately at home in. That inner world became my primary focus and interest and striving. My center; my love.

I worked as needed, met a woman, got married, became a father, and continued to work as needed. I owned a small herb company, did handyman work and trained as a counselor. I was lucky, life gave me teachers, friends and a wife on the same inner path. And finally, a work, counseling and facilitating groups, that enabled me to make intimate contact with others. So, the inner striving and the life of relationship has been my focus. In this I have been successful.

And part of the benefit of this, and one of the reasons I can say my life is better than ever, is that I seem to be able to help more people; more people are coming to me for help. I am so grateful to be 75 and have passed through the years of trying to find my place in the world and be "good enough" or "successful" enough. I have a client who is a marketing guy and two years ago (not for the first time) he was saying that I need to market myself, people need to know about me, and he would help. He said that I could offer this and that which would create a funnel for clients to come to me. He opened his arms wide and high and brought them down like a funnel in front of him. For years this idea that I had to find a way to market myself so that I could be successful was a source of not a little anxiety. But now, I was happy to say, "I am 73 years old, I am not interested in creating a business, if someone feels that I have something to offer them, I am happy to offer it." I could not have said that so clearly even 5 years previous. The truth is, I am probably busier now than I have been most of my life. I am a late bloomer. And, for now, this is a good thing.

One of the realities of aging is time. For many, life has slowed down, and they have more time for doing the things that have more meaning for them. Time for friends and family, for artistic expression, for a simpler life. That is a very real gift of aging, but there is another way that time is important. The older you get the more time you have invested in something. We can say that, in that time, we are practicing whatever it is we are attending to. The gift of aging is having had many years of practice. You get better at whatever you practice over time. Some habits of being, practiced over a long time, do not yield wonderful results. But some do. If we practice many years of aiming upstream, as a friend of mine likes to say—turning our attention toward an inner light, or loving, or waking up to the truth of our being and the truth of relationship—then after a while, we are graced with some sweetness from the fruit of our practice. My friend Joe M. is living what his parents taught him: that a person's golden years are dependent on the way they live their lives. Live a respectful, compassionate, and empathetic life and aging can be beautiful. It is so for him. If we have spent years studying spiritual texts, we will find that deeper layers of understanding are available to us. It is as if our soul has been changed, developed over time, so that insights can now quietly blossom there. It is a beautiful thing when that happens; it is like a soft diffuse light lights up in the soul. It nourishes. I am a lover of reading spiritual texts and this is happening for me more and more these days. Reading *about* is changing into *experiencing with*.

Murray (age 75) speaks of the blessing of time and practice:

I have spent over 45 years with spiritual practice being a foremost concern of my life, and 41 years giving enlightenment intensives—3 or 4 or 7 or 8 a year. I have become more and more free of the limitations and thought formations that held me back when I was younger. The last few years of my life have been very rich. This richness has been a function of my years of practice and experience. Since my late 60s and increasingly in my 70s I have more confidence and trust in myself than I ever did. I cannot say how it happened, it's been gradual and cumulative. Now I find myself in a space that is clearer and freer than anything I've known.... I simply know that I can trust myself.... I'm just hitting my stride and I couldn't be happier. It's taken a long time for this ship to come in, but it has come in.... At this juncture, my main concern is to pass it on; to pass on the wisdom of the teachers and the teachings, the wisdom of the truth that blossoms out of presence, out of contact, out of authentic expression, out of love and self-giving.... I have been a gardener these past 40 years and in that time many things have grown and blossomed, and it has been very good, but now it feels like a general harvest.

Spiritual ideas and truths sometimes open to us early on our path—we have beautiful experiences of openness and love. But then they are not so easy to access; they fade with the rough and tumble of life, with the speed at which life moves, and then other deep-seated habits of being come into play. The early openings are not lost, but the doorway narrows. And we have to learn how to not get caught for too long in the narrow doorway, how to open out and open in. In old age the doorway can softly open again and we can have access to the deeper truths. Our years of practice at aiming upstream, or years of experience from being knocked about by life and realizing what really matters, have created a fertile soil in our soul that we can tap into. The challenges of life continue but we are more able to integrate them. My long-time friend Richard (now 75) tells how, with age, his perspective has widened and, with the larger picture that he now holds, the stuff of life becomes less triggering, even irrelevant. He is affected but doesn't take it so personally. Slowing down helps. Actually, it is essential. Age brings a natural slowing down; a natural looking back and looking in. Whether and how we take advantage of it, is another story.

I remember when I was around 60 and hiking in the Anza-Borrego Desert, that in climbing rocks I moved more slowly. I noticed this and thought, to my surprise, that I was finally moving at the speed that felt right for me. When I was younger, I could never relax enough to slow down; I had to get somewhere. I had to achieve, accomplish, prove something, be successful. Those thoughts were lodged in me. Whatever I did achieve or accomplish was not quite enough. I was not quite enough. Anxiety was my constant companion. After 60, something started to change, and after 66, when the financial pressure I have always felt began to ease with an unexpected gift and my starting to receive social security, a new level of relaxing was experienced. This too is part of the "better than ever." Several of my friends, those who are also blessed with a certain level of financial comfort, have said the same thing.

Also, when I was 60, I gifted myself a month retreat in a friend's meditation cabin at Tara Mandala, a Tibetan Buddhist retreat center in Colorado. I decided not to bring any reading material. I figured, I have read so much spiritual stuff for over 37 years that if I couldn't handle 28 days without reading, I was in big trouble. I brought a journal to write in and following the suggestion of my friend's wife, Tsultrim, the resident teacher there, I made a schedule of four, two-hour meditation periods a day; and I stuck to it. It was really good. I had just started leading retreats, doing the work I felt most inwardly and directly connected to, and was hoping this personal retreat would strengthen or deepen something in me that would be important in the next phase of my life.

During my sitting periods I began to notice how the thoughts in the mind create my reality in the moment, but that they are not necessarily real. I noticed how worry thoughts would rise and how I would be carried into them as real; feelings of anxiety and fear would begin to course through my body. But when I placed my attention on the sky and the true nature of the mind as open and spacious, empty, the thoughts and accompanying uncomfortable feelings would dissolve. They had no reality aside from my feeding them. I got pretty good at dissolving thoughts that did not serve. We have control over where we place our attention. Of course, you have to do this over and over again, but once you have seen it happen and you know there is a pathway back into the open, it is forever possible. Once you know the feeling, you might even find that the open calls to you. Now it is not necessarily easy because some thoughts have a strong gripping power, but it is possible, and you know it.

It is sort of like this: it used to be that you often were walking as if wading in 4 inches of mud without really noticing. But once you have found the feeling of firm ground you can notice when you are stepping onto a sink hole and then you can decide not to shift your weight fully onto that foot.

Now after many years of watching and practicing, I have come to the point of being able to observe the mind, and see old familiar thoughts appear. These are thoughts that give rise to feelings that do not serve life, do not serve love or relationship or joy or beauty, and certainly not truth. When I place my attention on this, I can almost see a Being taking form; a shadowy, ghost-like Being that, somehow, I used to identify with as me. As soon as I notice the untruth, the unreality, of the thought/feeling creation, something in me sparks awake, causing me to pause, and in the pausing, it begins to dissolve; and then the letting go. This letting go gesture is one of the fruits of years of watching and remembering to not identify with what appears. And, for me, this fruit has ripened in my late 60s and continues ripening. The sweet taste and resulting smile is part of my daily diet. It's having a certain sense of acceptance of, humor about, and appreciation for being who I am.

One night, recently, I was rolling around on the floor, as I do before getting into bed, and one of those shadowy thought beings appeared and I started laughing as I saw the untruth—I remember saying something like—"it's not real, it's not like that at all," and laughter arose in me. Patricia heard me laughing and asked what about—I simply said, "it's not real; this that arises in my mind, is not real," and the laughing came again.

I don't remember what shadowy being appeared that night, but it could have been one connected to a fear of not being enough, or comparing myself to someone, or a sense of being a failure. Sure, it is true that I have failed, that someone is better than I am at this or that, and that in some sense I am not enough. But that is not the full truth. Enough/not enough; failure/success; better than/less than— that kind of judgement misses the point, and we suffer because of it. But in my advanced age I am no longer held captive by these judgments for long. Sister paradox has helped me with this — being willing and able to see that there is truth in both ways of seeing. (Enough and not enough, failure and success, better than and less than, can live in the same room together without being a problem!) Yes, and.

My friend, Christine (74), writes of the capacity to stand between two feelings/thoughts; that holding the balance is more possible as she gets older. To hold the balance between fear and trust, anger and acceptance, sadness and joy, troubled and grateful, despair and consolation, giving up and being interested—"to hold the balance and to feel—even if only for a short precious moment—right to the core of me the stillness, comfort and beauty of being whole and in full agreement with what is."

You know how much you love that old raggedy sweater, that old shovel, that totally out of date bike. I have come to love this raggedy old, nicked up, rusty old me; and while holding the opposites, an inner light can shine, and a quiet smile lights up in me; sometimes even laughter.

You are the one seeing, noticing. You are not what you see or notice. This one (the "I") who is seeing, I sense more and more— that is the gift. It also has no substance, like the ghost Being has no real substance—in fact, it has even less substance, but more Reality.

Two years ago, after being grabbed by and grabbing hold of a particular belief and feeling state and then allowing it to dissolve, I wrote this:

MAKE BELIEVE

It is all make believe
My unhappiness I mean
Probably yours too
The one making me unhappy
does not exist
—not the way I think
There is no body who doesn't want to help
No one taking pieces of dried bread
or stealing oranges from small trees
No one feeling the pain of loss
or the upset of not having
That inner gripping, clutching
That soul disturbance—
Self-inflicted
There is no Other doing anything to you.
Just sit there
Feel it all
Do not move
Do not move
In that unmoving, listen, breathe, feel
You will want to move—don't
You will start to move—stop
Breathe, listen, feel
A gripping
A letting go
Gripping
Letting go
A hint of a tear
A hint of a smile
Notice
the revealing True
In the gaps
The split seconds
of falling away.

The rest
is make-believe.

I was one time sitting with a Ute elder, Grandma Bertha, who was 80, and she was saying how she accepts her children and grandchildren just as they are, without judgement, with appreciation. I was impressed and asked her how long it has been like that for her. She said, since last year, and laughed. The gift of old age.

Then when I was 63, I did a 3-day solo time, where I sat for 3 days and 3 nights on the land of Madre Grande Monastery outside San Diego. The rules of the Solo are that you are open to the world, no tent; you fast, taking only water; and you stay in one place. There is nothing you have to do. I opened to the quiet that comes with being still. During that time, I experienced the warmest love and deep appreciation for this person that I am. I opened to images of me going through life in my own quirky or graceful way, seeing my "failures," not enoughnesses and "successes," and accepting it all as me with nothing to change or judge. I saw that loving oneself is a doorway to loving wider and wider. Then spontaneously came the appreciation for people in my life—one by one they appeared in consciousness, and I spoke each name and gave thanks. Widening love. I saw clearly that we have the capacity and indeed the choice to either love oneself or disapprove of oneself—to either love others or disapprove of others. We have the capacity to choose love.

We can choose to open to quiet. I was helped in this "opening to quiet" with an old favorite verse by Steiner that I meditated with many times during those 3 days:

> Quiet I bear within me
> I bear within myself
> Forces to make me strong
> Now will I be imbued
> With their glowing warmth
> Now will I fill myself
> With my own will's resolve
> And I will feel the quiet
> Pouring through all my being
> When by my steadfast striving
> I become strong

To find within myself
The source of strength
The strength of inner quiet.

I think this slowing down and being with Quiet is a gift and a need as we get older.

Christine wrote this: "My skin is getting thinner. Not just in a physical sense. More than before I feel the need for quiet moments, to let my eyes rest on small things like the rose hips on an otherwise bare branch in winter, the first snowdrop..."

I remember visiting a friend in her 90s; she would tell me about how interesting it was and how much she enjoyed watching the squirrels running up trees and the birds taking from the feeders in the yard. And my mother-in-law was always commenting on the beauty of flowers, or the many shades of green in the trees, and the colors in the sunset sky. I didn't appreciate this at the time. I wasn't old enough yet! The gift of old age is noticing the beauty, having the inner quiet and inner simplicity to perceive and be deeply nourished by the beauty. Doug (76) puts it simply: "The essence of being has become more important than doing in my old age." I have heard that when we humans really meet, perceive and take in the life of nature around us, we are serving the elemental worlds, the elemental beings. The old ones are doing a great and important deed here.

I just learned of a recently published book by Gabriele von Arnim, a German writer and journalist, called "The Comfort of Beauty." She is 78 years old and says that she needs beauty, the comfort of beauty. She goes on to say: "Comfort does not mean that everything will be fine. Consolation means building banks on the river of pain, moorings where you can tie up the boat, get out and rest."

We can ask ourselves, where do I find rest? What can I relax into? Here I find another gift of aging — resting in the unknowing. I have many friends who will admit that the older they are the less they know. But this is not experienced as a bad thing; it is not that they are needing to know more and more like in the past, though there is a continual openness to learning and discovery. It is more that we can rest in the unknowing. Be amazed by how much there is. Wonder. Something in us relaxes more deeply, opens more softly to or from an inner depth, where an insight might come, from which a feeling like knowing arises and touches us. But it is a "knowing" that cannot be held on to; it can be experienced, felt as a soft breath of warmth that nourishes us beyond knowing. Maybe these insights can rise because we are open to not knowing, and the passageway is less obstructed by what we think we know. A gift of aging is the wisdom to release the grasping—being content with a momentary glimpse, seeing the momentary glimpse as both little and not little at all. Just as we need to rest our eyes on small things in nature, we need to notice, open to and enter into these flashes of inner light with awe and gratitude. In our slowing down years, we are more able to do this. It just takes noticing and a subtle attentiveness that allows the world to enter, that allows spirit to enter.

I say "it just takes noticing," which is true, but it is true only after years of creating an inner soul soil from which to see. When we have practiced a long time, we can become aware of the "most precious fruit" of the practice, as my friend Edrid (now 79), a long-time walker on the spiritual path, calls it. And this most precious fruit that he has discovered is being authentic and at ease in himself, at peace in his relationships, a sense of belonging, a stable equanimity, and being established in what he calls the ground of being. "There is no longer a grasping for this or that, or a pushing away. Whatever comes, comes, and it is not that big a deal.... Used to be, I had to work at seeing, now my eyes have changed, the seeing is more integrated in a natural view of things." Love and appreciation more naturally flow from his core, and he is more in touch with a wisdom that knows what works to make life better for himself and for others.

Edrid and I also talked about the gift of a long marriage (50 and 47 years respectively). We have come to accept our partners and the dynamics between us as part of the dance—old irritations have not disappeared, but they are not a big deal. The love and friendship, the gratitude and humor of it all are the embrace that we live in. The small stuff dissolves in that magic potion.

Seeing more clearly and wisdom. My friend, Tsultrim (now 76), a long-time Buddhist practitioner and teacher, said something similar in that she is finding that she is doing less formal meditation practices, but the natural luminosity of the world has become more of a steady state of living and seeing for her. Richard (75) speaks of how after years of meditating he is seeing that spirituality is life itself as he identifies more and more with Self. And Nama (76) writes:

> With over 45 years "on the path" and decades of experience and study, particularly natural health and spiritual realms, I feel I've genuinely moved into my "wisdom years." I have a fair amount of knowledge and wisdom about life to share, which seems to flow quite naturally and with confidence when called for (and sometimes even when not! Haha).

We are learning to let go, release the grasping. We become less attached to preferences. The older we get the more we open to the reality of death and dying. We know it is closer. Death is a great teacher. In my twenties I read the Carlos Castaneda books. In one of them, Don Juan says to live your life being aware of Death on your left shoulder. Allow it to wake you up.

My friend, Squidge (80 years old), accepted my request to look at what gifts of aging she has found in her life. She wrote:

> Aging. At first it seemed like a betrayal; like driving around in a vehicle which is designed to drop a fender, then lose suspension, then the steering wheel....
>
> Then, off in the distance, or in a dream, or during meditation...appeared the fierce Goddess Death looking me right in the eye with the stern instruction to PAY ATTENTION; that each moment is equal to every other. and what I NEED to do is be present with whatever that moment is. Seriously. Not conceptually but through every sense of perception.

From this assignment, arose a sense of theatre and humor about the character I played; one so certain about her self-owning separate self. With some perspective and tenderness, that is funny; not tragic.

She goes on to say:

> I made a vow 5 years ago at the first of the 4-year Wabanaki Healing Turtle Island Ceremonies, not to protect my heart from being broken (which it is every day for the suffering of the innocents) and not to take refuge in negativity, I keep that vow but adding the yeast of humor at self makes it possible for me to see bigger.

We know death is closer. We contemplate death. One day we will no longer be here in a body. I noticed that I did not like the feeling that comes in me when I think of death, so I decided to contemplate death as part of my daily meditation practice. Sitting on a pile of rocks facing the ocean one afternoon, I contemplated death and when I opened my eyes the ocean appeared more alive and beautiful than usual. An inner warmth and gratitude filled me, for the ocean, for my life, for my family, for my wife sitting next to me. I remember when I was preparing to move from a home I had lived in for 15 years, how precious the last months were. I was able to take in the beauty of that place more fully and regularly and to feel the love and gratitude I had for that place and those people. Edrid said that in accepting the reality of death, in addition to being in awe and wondering what it will be like, and his hope to be able to meet it with the same interest and focus he brings to meditation practices, he is finding that instead of working to improve his situation, he is more interested in working to improve the situation of others.

When I spoke with my friend Gary, who is almost 83, and asked him about the gifts he is finding in his aging, the first thing he said was "letting go." He noted a number of letting-go's—when he was around 60, he noticed that a lot of old guys he encountered weren't happy. They were very opinionated and told the same stories over and over again. He noticed they were attached to their beliefs. He said to himself, "My beliefs will not serve me in the rest of my life." He made a vow that, moving forward, he would not be a prisoner to his beliefs. Letting go. He committed to live his life moving in the direction of love, and he noticed that one can't be attached to being right and at the same time choose love. He has made it a practice to let go of having to be right. It is a daily practice because "the silly stuff keeps coming up and then you have to start over again."

He also mentioned the loss of physical vitality with age—a loss, yet also a great opportunity. It depends on what you are aiming toward. If you are aiming toward letting go and choosing love, then getting old is the perfect opportunity to practice. He is noticing that choosing love has become a more conscious choice since turning 80. One helpful thing here is the natural diminishing of sexual energy—the focus is more on giving, less on getting. It comes down to what are you choosing to practice, what are you investing your time and attention in? The fruits and gifts come with years of practice.

Five of my men friends, who have given me input for this writing, have mentioned this diminishing or the extinguishing of sexual energy and desires as a gift in that it is no longer a distraction or a driving force; no longer a burr under the saddle! One said he is freer to appreciate the beauty of women without trying to get anything. The grasping gesture is released and the openness to beauty and giving increased. However, this is not just a male thing. A woman friend of mine, Osha (80), said:

> It took until age 65 to realize that what I most want in a mate is kindness. Before that, it was hotness. Hotness and kindness are an unlikely mix. There's something to be said for waning hormones!

Richard, speaking from a different perspective, remembers turning 60 and noticing he was finally old enough to playfully interact with a young woman without them feeling he was coming on to them. He was freer to touch strangers with a loving playful heart.

Another friend, Yoah, a long-time meditant and spiritual practitioner now 76, finds he is no longer seeking, nor is he practicing any formal meditations like before. He is opening more and
more to the Quiet—peering into the unknown—spending more
time in what he calls "depth contemplation," being witness to the
play of consciousness. And in that interior space, or arising out of
that interior space, is the making of art, computer drawing, which
he engages in with the full attentiveness of contemplation. With
less being demanded from the world and free from self-imposed
"shoulds," two friends (Nama, 76 and Robin, 71) spoke of the
freedom to simply do what arises,

> to be content to live each day as it is given to live—as a gift....
> And because we are less restricted by social norms or wor-
> ries about what others think, we feel freer to be our eccentric
> selves.... Gratitude abounds.

I have another friend, Susan, who is 73 and has had to deal
with many health issues in the last 10 years. Pain is a daily companion. She was always a doer, a choleric force. If she was angry,
she would go out to the garden and work hard and long. She had
not an ounce of the phlegmatic in her. Being older and being physically compromised has asked her to see the world with the eyes of
a phlegmatic, more inwardly quiet, slower moving, mellow, peaceful. She is grateful to be connecting with others from a different
place in herself. She is even grateful for the pain. It is transforming
her. She has had to learn to ask for help and rely on others. The
constant pain has been an invitation to turn to prayer and the
spirit regularly. She invests more time and attention on study and
spiritual meditative practices.

Several of my friends mentioned that now with more time, less
doing, they find that they are looking back and reviewing their life
more. In addition to being able to accept themselves more fully
(Osha has a needlepoint pillow in her kitchen that says, "Every
day I live I get more like myself"), they are finding that they are

increasingly able to see the destiny connections through their life. They are more inclined to find the gratitude and the gifts from the difficulties in their life than they were when they were younger. We are accepting how life has been and seeing the good—putting the attention on the learnings, the development, the gratitude. Sure, there are the disappointments, the unlived life, what we did not accomplish; but now we are more attentive to what psychic food we place into our soul, what thoughts and feelings we choose to live with and feed. The mind continues to be the mind; unasked for and unwanted thoughts and feelings continue to appear. But they are no longer held onto like they used to be. There is no longer a home for them in our soul purified by many years of practice and the closeness of death.

Friend Paul (77) wrote this:

As we age—if we can keep the ferment going, not let it solidify—there is a live inner culture better able to digest all experience, not entranced with the superficial dualities, and thus naturally able to embody and give voice to a gentleness, a reconciliation of realities, and in that way be of unknowing service to the world.

Now, "What is this world coming to?" And how do we bear the pain of the world? Squidge touched on this earlier in her vow—"not to protect my heart from being broken (which it is every day for the suffering of the innocents) and not to take refuge in negativity." Being willing to feel. The older we get the more vulnerable we become—we are less strong, we can do less, our balance is not as good, our senses not as alert. We are aware how fragile life is. How tentative our life is. We have experienced loss.

This all opens the heart of compassion. Our willingness and capacity to feel deeply is a gift. It opens us to others. I find that I am more easily moved to tears. This is true for many of my men friends as well. Tears are a gift; they wash me open. I become softer. In this soft opening I can make a more direct, intimate contact with the world of nature and with the people in my life. And this is one way of bearing the pain of the world—be open to relationship. Give more attention to the spirit light inside. And do whatever you can do to help others in small ways.

A friend of mine, deeply moved by the war and suffering in Israel and Palestine, took an honest look at his life and saw that he had to change something in himself to bring healing to the relations in his family. "How can I say I want peace in the world, when I haven't worked for peace in my family." He took new steps in being willing to be vulnerable and making honest contact with the people in his household. He lowered his barriers and initiated the opening of channels of communication.

Years ago when I was studying with Martin Prechtel, a very special man, trained as a Shaman in a Guatemalan village, he taught us a Maya blessing: *Long life, honey in the heart, no evil, thirteen thank-yous.*

I can now see how this blessing captures the gifts that are possible with old age. With a long life we can develop the capacity to love with a sweetness of heart created from a whole lot of work and years of gathering; we have come to the point of a developed and cultivated soul whereby we are able to bless and not inflict harm; and we are filled with gratitude for life thirteenfold. When my mom was dying, lying in bed holding my hand and looking up at me, the last thing she said to us was "I don't know what to say except I love you, thank you." Maybe there really is nothing else to say.

Here's a poem I wrote when I turned 70:

TURNING SEVENTY

7 is a line
sweeping along the horizon
suddenly falling
on a sharp angle
down.

Let it be a long fall;
The flames of color
long hang on the trees;
Sun glow,
even when the day is grey,
Beyond bright
when with sunlight.

To be this 70-year-old man
is like that
Years of stored sunlight.

There are caves
where fish live
that have lost their eyes
to darkness.
In the sunlit cave of my heart
new eyes are growing.

Seventy,
and all my friends are getting older
The great river of time
is washing over us,
altering favorite features
depositing others along the banks.
There is another river of sky
where in the changing shapes
old friends begin to recognize each other,
see past the dark outlines,
the shadows
that hold the light in place;

See deeper
to the precious center.

Oh, wonder of wonders
It is an amazing thing to be a person;
To withstand the shock of meeting another;
to return to an emptiness
you know but do not remember,

where the familiar ghost of "I am"
appears as outer form
lingers and falls away
like a breath,
like the last leaf of autumn,
revealing a clear sky
of awe
at the creation of each moment
and you as part of the creation.

Seventy years
And every friend
becomes more real
As I see
how they carve me
into being.

Joseph Rubano has been living in an old-world style multi-generational household with his wife, daughter, son-in-law, and three grandsons since 2005. They live in Oceanside, California, where he has a Biographical Counseling practice and offers Enlightenment Intensives, Desert Solo Vision Quests, tends a backyard garden, and watches over a beehive. His third book of poetry, *This Crazy Love Life,* will be available soon. Visit his website JosephRubano.com.

"There Is So Much to Admire, to Weep Over."

Alex Reid

I know, you never intended to be in this world
But you're in it all the same.

So why not get started immediately.

I mean, belonging to it.
There is so much to admire, to weep over.

—Mary Oliver, "The Fourth Sign of the Zodiac," part 3

I t is evening where I live, mid-February. The air is mild, the sun is low in a pale, clear sky. Bats wheel overhead, scraps of black emerging from the Botanic Gardens where they have hung all day upside down in shady trees. The city is humming with Saturday night summer. I've been to a movie, alone. I am content and a little lonely.

Did I choose this? Was this aloneness in one of the boxes I packed before birth, or something that has come to meet me along this life-way?

Boxes: There is so much to admire, to weep over...

In the 1950s, before television "arrived" in Queensland in 1959, we listened to the radio. On Monday night there was Pick a Box. Most of the details of this show elude me, but I know there were contestants, and now, as I think about it, I suppose they answered questions. Bob Dyer (from Tennessee, so exotic) and his "lovely wife" Dolly hosted this show. He called her Doll. I can see the faces and clothes I made up for them, still. Every evening it came to the time when Doll helped successful contestants to choose a box…in it might be a fridge, a diamond necklace, a new car, or a dream holiday, or…or nothing. Before they got to open the box, Bob would offer money: "the money or the box!" We held our breath, waiting for it to turn out well, or poorly. Sometimes they lost everything in their bid to win more. We groaned.

None of this matters except for this: over time, "Pick a Box" became a metaphor for an imaginary parallel life in which a locker room of boxes contained all my imagined best life-choices: a life as a wife on a remote cattle station, where I was a fearless horsewoman, gardener, and cook, with a family of five or so girl children and a two way radio. In this box, I was a closet poet, another Judith Wright. Or, an alternative reality: a box in which a religious and devoted doctor and anthropologist became a missionary in Aboriginal Communities far from boring Brisbane. And so on. Remember, Dear Reader, I was nine or ten.

Of course, in time, I got to open my boxes, none of which held possibilities that I imagined, though many of the opportunities and challenges in them were predictable, if you remember I was a female, a first child, born in 1948, into a family of decent, unambitious people.

Most of the men in my young childhood had been to war and were recently discharged from the Army or Air Force. Many of the women I knew (my aunts, my mother's few friends), had been seconded from offices into factories during the war. In the late 1940s and early '50s, having married, they were attempting to become good wives and mothers, in the new houses being built in new suburbs of sub-tropical Brisbane.

[Did] you need a little darkness to get you going?
—Mary Oliver, "The Fourth Sign of the Zodiac," part 3

For example, a profoundly anxious and at times paranoid mother, a people pleaser father who increasingly self-medicated his anxiety and work related overwhelm with alcohol.

Did I choose **this** family? (Not in pick a box of life, that's for sure!) And yet, I did.

In the box I chose in this life, there was a young woman from far North Queensland, from "the country." She had been sent to "the south," to Brisbane, to begin work, in order to avoid the imminently invading Japanese. There she met a young man who would have loved to be a country boy, as his cousins were, but this was not in his box. When the war ended and he was discharged from the Air Force, they bought a block of land near where he had grown up. They married and settled into the little house he built for them to live in, while he built the big house where my sister and I would live out the years until we could (escape and) move into our adult lives. For me, this meant as far away from Brisbane as possible.

Now, at 75, I look at the other boxes that awaited me in the light of my fantasy boxes. A mixed bag of five children, three of whom are male. A life in country towns and cities in Australia and in other countries, no horses or religious vocation. I am yet to find and open a box that says poet. A box that said "teacher" (one of only two possible boxes for girls from families like mine, who matriculated in Brisbane in 1965; the other box said nurse). A box labeled "Anthroposophy," which I would look into at 21, in New Zealand, close the lid on, and open again two years later, in England. There was a box labeled "farmer/gardener," funnily enough, but it contained dairy cows and a biodynamic farm in England. Eventually I discovered there were two boxes labeled "husband." Or perhaps it was one box that contained two husbands?

Vocations, intentions, intimation, choices, boxes? Who knows?

But here is a question, one that I live with patiently, and, despite my love of Rilke, incredulously: Why on earth would I have chosen twice to live with husbands whose boxes said "serious illness" and for whom and with whom I have made, each time, a reluctant transition from partner to carer?

The first time, I was 40, my husband, X, was 45. He developed an autoimmune disease, which was treated with, among a litany of other drugs, very large doses of corticosteroids over too long a time. He could not work. His appearance changed, moon face, buffalo hump. His confidence in himself waned. His bones became thin, and cracked. The pain and other effects of his illness remained intense. He injected blood thinning medication daily. After five years, it was impossible to tell which awful changes were symptoms of disease and which were side effects of medication.

I am more creative fixer than nurse. Mostly, up to that point in my life, I had been able to make things work, or workable enough. But in this, I could do so little, despite initially doing a lot: research, mining knowledgeable contacts for ideas, asking questions of medical professionals, involvement in appointments and decisions and making my best efforts at kindness and care. Eventually, after too many years, I faced a truth. I could not make him better.

We left the community where we had lived for ten years. I cared for him as best I could. I accompanied him on visits to doctors and visited him in hospitals, and looked after him when he needed it at home. I learned to be effectively, a single parent and shouldered the care and maintenance of family and home. I learned that there was not much space for me to have needs or wants. As X's life became smaller, more circumscribed by incapacity, pain and uncertainty, the gaps between his possibilities and mine grew unbridgeable. I yo-yoed between compassion, and compassion fatigue. Real fatigue was constant. Here was a man, who through no fault of his own, was in a situation that no one could envy and whose plight made others who enjoyed good health and were well and able to live, feel almost indecent. I did what I could, I returned to teaching to earn an income for the family; he stayed in the home and when he could, played the piano. He suffered. We all suffered. We separated. I lived with the image of a rat (me) deserting a sinking ship.

≈

I'd been to the river before, a few times.
Don't blame the river that nothing happened quickly.
You don't hear such voices in an hour or a day.
You don't hear them at all if selfhood has stuffed your ears.
And it's difficult to hear anything anyway, through
    all the traffic, the ambition.
                    —Mary Oliver, "At the River Clarion"

The second time I realized I had opened the seriously sick husband box, I was 65, and my second husband (Z) and I had been together for a little over two decades. You would imagine I may have learned stuff having opened this box once already. But sadly, I approached this completely different and all too familiar situation as if it were my first time, and with almost exactly the same skill set and orientation toward making him well again, as I'd had in the past. Slow learner? Needed another round to learn what I could not learn before? Dear Reader, draw your own conclusions.

...it's difficult to hear anything anyway, through
    all the traffic, the ambition.
                    —Mary Oliver, "At the River Clarion"

Of course, it was once again my job to save one dear to me. (I realize now that this was a box I opened in my childhood with my mother but that I did not recognize, yet.) At first, I was active in searching for a medical doctor who could work with complementary medicines to treat Z's acute anxiety. This failed majestically, despite the doctor's good intent and experience. Z was daily more delusional. He paced and shouted "Father, Father, Father," he was terrified of something he could not name. He hit his head against the unforgiving stone wall of our house, he was unable to sleep, unable to eat. An itchy rash covered his body. Acupuncture put him to sleep for an hour or so, a small respite for all.

I searched for a psychiatrist. When (finally) I found one who could see him, Z was immediately admitted to a psychiatric hospital.

Neither of us had slept properly for 2 months. Memorably, the psychiatrist said, "This is the sickest man I have seen walk in off the street in my career." Z was from the first moment deeply suspicious of this man, his ability and his motivation. By the end of their relationship, Z loathed him with an unreasonable hatred.

This time in the psychiatric hospital began 4 years of periods of various drug therapies, and Electric Shock Therapy. Periods in hospital were interspersed with temporary "betterness" and return to home, which never lasted long. Mostly because this suffering man, even when "better than he had been," was paranoid, delusional and locked in an internal hell in which he was being poisoned, stretched on a rack, fed feces. As well, he was deeply contemptuous and mistrustful of the medical system, and of the doctors who worked in it, seeing them as ignorant but willing participants in a medical system that supported Big Pharma.

I alternated between relief that he was once again in hospital and feelings of despair at his intense suffering and the feeling that nothing was helping and that these times in hospital were going nowhere. I felt powerless to help him or myself, and there was a terrible familiarity to the feeling of being, yet again, inside a bubble of paralyzed hopelessness. That box.

After four years, two things happened almost simultaneously. One was another series of Shock Therapy treatments. The first cycle of ECT had not helped him at all and in fact had rendered him catatonic. I was understandably reluctant to agree to another cycle. But at this time, he spent his days searching the hospital for the bodies of the people he had murdered. He could not have a shower because he knew he would be gassed. Nights terrified him, because he knew that he would be tortured by being stretched on a rack. He was so thin, so tortured, so unable to live that I was told this treatment would be mandated by a Guardianship Board if I did not give permission. I caved.

Around the same time a buyer appeared for the farm that Z had owned for 30 years, and that I characterized as "his dream, my nightmare." But in truth, it was always a cross between a dream and a nightmare for Z…because so much always needed to be done. After 30 years of weed-indecision, inability to repair fences and do general maintenance, because it would cost too much money, because he was exhausted, because the problems were too big, the land and buildings were in a sorry state. Acres of blackberries covered hills and gullies, completely out of control. It was a striking metaphor for what was happening in his mind and body: so much potential, so much chaos.

Then, something happened. Was it the ECT? Was it the relief of the farm and all the failure it represented, being taken off his hands? Both? Neither? Who knows. All I know is this: mysteriously, with no help from me, really (aka the fixer), his mental health gradually began to change in a positive direction. The way I thought of it, was that he became more user-friendly. He came home to the new house I had bought in July 2016—all in all he had been in hospital for the better part of four years.

> I'd been to the river before, a few times.
> Don't blame the river that nothing happened quickly.
> —Mary Oliver, "At the River Clarion"

BUT.

Neither of us was the same person we were, to ourselves or to each other, that we had been when this began, in 2012. My husband was recovering from acute mental illness, the after-effects of ECT (particularly short-term memory loss), and four years of being a bystander in his own life as he had known it. I had lost all trust in his capacity to be rational, or even in the possibility of him returning to himself, the benign eccentric I had known him to be. I was often confused about whether what he was saying was reasonable, especially in areas where he had previously been an expert. As months went on, I had to make many decisions about things that affected us both, always wondering not only if this was a good decision, but also if I had the right to make it. This began, I think with the decision to sell the farm, which felt at once like a pragmatic necessity and a deep betrayal. There were many more decisions to come, all of them tricky. I was plagued by the question of when it was reasonable to make a decision for another adult.

It is 2024, and Z has been living at home, unmedicated, for seven years. Last Friday, the postman delivered a letter that looked official. As we sat down to eat that night, I asked Z if I could open it. He agreed, where formerly he has refused. His way of managing mail is to put the unopened letter into a large box with years of unopened mail. It is too frightening to open a letter, as it might contain bad news. The bad news this one contained was a fine for $900, for a speeding ticket that had been issued four months ago, and that had remained unpaid, despite regular notices and warnings. (These of course were in the large cardboard box in his study with all the other unopened letters.) He had a panic attack; I paid the fine. Later we agreed that from now on, it was probably a good idea for me to open mail that came for him, and to let him know whether he needed to attend to it. I am no longer so confused about what I need to do; his adult right to open his own mail is not working. I will from now on open all his mail. This is an important marker. Over the years since 2016, incident by incident, this is how I have moved inexorably from partner to carer. This is visible, necessary and pragmatic, here is another thing to do, to protect us both—another bridge to cross. But there are other much more nuanced, more subtle shifts, which are painful for both of us and hard for each of us to bear, for different reasons.

I rely on him for nothing, to avoid inevitable disappointment, and/or complication.

Sometimes he asks me, with great grief, why his beloved only daughter does not make contact with him. The reasons I give him are true: she is a young mother of three young children, she works in a demanding profession (medicine) that gives her a particular view of your mental state and an opinion about what you could do, which you do not agree with. These responses do not comfort him, so they don't go in. He asks me the same question again. I tell him my truth as I understand it, again. We go on.

He tells me, yet again, about someone he must have offended because said person is cold to him, or is avoiding him. It is true, they are avoiding him, but not because he has offended them. I would feel cruel if I were to tell him a possible reason, which would be that he lives on Planet Z and everyone else lives on Earth and his missionary zeal to tell people about what he sees from Planet Z is of no use to them, on Earth. We can no longer have guests to stay, as sooner or later he feels they are ignoring him, or he believes that they have done something to hurt him, or they have broken one of his invisible, unarticulated but vital rules. He retires to his room and does not appear for the rest of their visit, which is noticeable and disconcerting for everyone except him.

We cannot go to dinner with friends as he is offended that no one wants to talk about his interests, or to listen to him. We cannot go to the movies together or share podcasts as he is only interested in Conspiracy Theories and the work of a couple of doctors who inevitably disappoint him. He cannot leave home for more than a few days without becoming anxious that he is becoming unwell, which means we have to return home:

> *There was someone I loved who grew old and ill*
> *One by one I watched the fires go out.*
> *There was nothing I could do*
> —Mary Oliver, "At the River Clarion"

This is true. I am sad and sorry as I gradually come to accept this. It is a slow process, but an important one in learning. I can watch this; I cannot, nor should I try, to change him. The fixer is redundant.

However, more complex and outweighing the dilemmas of decision making, the taking on of daily practicalities, the attempts to explain others' or his own behavior, are other changes between us.

Recently I read a description of Ivan Ilyich by Leo Tolstoy. It put into words two aspects of our situation very clearly.

> The main torment for Ivan Ilyich was the lie, that lie for some reason acknowledged by everyone, that he was merely ill and not dying, and that he needed only to keep calm and be treated, and then something very good would come of it. While he knew that whatever they did, nothing would come of it except still more tormenting suffering and death.
>
> —Leo Tolstoy, *The Death of Ivan Ilyich*

The first part highlights the impossibility of having a truthful relationship: if I do not collude with the delusion that Z has cancer and is dying, I am repeating the behavior of all of the ultimately frustrated health professionals Z has consulted over the years, trying to find an acceptable reason for his suffering, or a cure. A more dreadful outcome is that I become a threat, a cold-hearted person who does not take his suffering seriously. Doctor shopping becomes a preoccupation. To suggest that this is a fruitless search for recognition of his suffering is not helpful. He wants a cure for his suffering. I can give him an explanation, (unprocessed complex trauma), but I cannot help him find the magic key that will relieve his suffering. I now know this. This is another touch-star in my wayfinding.

Intimacy, cornerstones of which are truth and trust, in the sense of an adult speaking to an adult, is gone. But when I try to find a way to articulate this to a person without insight, I fail, again and again.

> Apart from this lie, or owing to it, the most tormenting thing for Ivan Ilyich was that no one pitied him as he wanted to be pitied: there were moments, after prolonged suffering, when Ivan Ilyich wanted most of all...to be caressed, kissed, wept over, as children are caressed and comforted. He knew that it was impossible; but he wanted it all the same.
>
> —Leo Tolstoy, *The Death of Ivan Ilyich*

A craving "to be kissed and caressed and comforted" is easy enough to meet if it is, in fact, to comfort a beloved child. But what if it is an adult who needs to be caressed and comforted constantly, who wants sexual intimacy and who cannot understand why this might not be a mutual desire. Gradually he accepts "that it is impossible, but he wants it all the same."

This is a very uneasy place for both of us. I would like to say, "I can be your friend, I can be your carer, and I can be your companion, but I can no longer be your lover." But the words stop in my throat, and it becomes a statement by action or inaction. To say it directly, feels like kicking a man when he is down. To not say it, feels dishonest and uncourageous. I am stuck. I know the truth of Mary Oliver's words:

> *As for the body...it wants to polish itself; it*
> *wants to love another body; it is the only vessel in*
> *the world that can hold, in a mix of power and*
> *sweetness: words, song, gesture, passion, ideas,*
> *ingenuity, devotion, merriment, vanity, and virtue.*

I wrestle with my shame and sadness and resentment and our mutual losses. But I remember her injunction to *"Keep some room in your heart for the unimaginable,"* and gradually I find I can say the unimaginable: "I cannot"...do this, or fix this, and I do not have to.

≈

> *There was someone I loved who grew old and ill*
> *One by one I watched the fires go out.*
> *There was nothing I could do*
> *except to remember*
> *that we receive*
> *then we give back.*
>
> —Mary Oliver, "At the River Clarion"

We receive, then we give back.

Z continually asserts that he loves me. That he is lucky to have me in his life. That he is grateful for all I do to support him and to manage our life together. He is stalwart (or deluded, take your pick, but in the end, does it matter?) in this commitment to his view of me and our relationship, even if his view of me is, in my opinion, delusional and his view of our relationship is one I do not share. This steadiness of commitment feels paradoxically mad, and a grace, because "Grace is both mysterious and hard to define. It can be found when we create ways to find meaning and dignity in connection with each other, building on our shared humanity, being kinder, bigger, better with each other" (Julia Baird, *Bright Shining*). In spite of ourselves and in our own ways, we try to be kinder, bigger, and better with each other every new day.

Mary Oliver understood this:

> *Of course, for each of us, there is the daily life.*
> *Let us live it, gesture by gesture.*
> *When we cut the ripe melon, should we not give it thanks?*
> *And should we not thank the knife also?*
> *We do not live in a simple world.*
>
> —Mary Oliver, "At the River Clarion"

I thank the melon and the knife for all I have learned, for all I might never have been able to learn without all that has come from Z's mental illness. I thank X for the prelude. I thank my mother for situations that taught me to rely on myself, and to affirm to myself "this is not rational."

I have come to see how trauma comes home to roost; how unprocessed, unacknowledged trauma can only be suppressed for so long. I thank family and friends who have listened to me rant frantically, be resentful, complain about my lot and through their listening and compassion help me to find ways to keep loving the *melon and the knife,* and moreover continue to be able to be grateful for both. There is grace in this.

When Covid happened to the world, many of the people around me struggled to live with the immediate and multiple uncertainties it brought into their daily lives. I began to realize that thanks to eight years (then) of living alongside mental illness, I had a post graduate diploma in uncertainty. The daily practice years of living without having any sense of control over what may come toward me has not only brought acceptance but a love of, and deep appreciation of mystery.

> *Said the river: imagine everything you can imagine,*
> *then keep on going.*
>> —Mary Oliver, "At the River Clarion"

I have and I do. What if, through you, I am able to become more wonderingly aware of my own madnesses, more conscious of the pitfalls of not grieving, not processing, not being vulnerable and open about my struggles? What if this is part of our life contract, made before birth? What if you are my teacher just as much as I am your carer? What if you are bearing your struggles—obsession, anxiety, inability to know trust in life, addiction, depression, for all of us—for they are certainly illnesses of this country at this time.

And it is true, in spite of all the grief and the obsession at its root, that I admire your tenacity, your courage, your relentless search for help, even while I despair of its fruitlessness.

> *Said the river I am part of holiness.*
> *And I too, said the stone. And I too, whispered*
> *the moss beneath the water.*
>> —Mary Oliver, "At the River Clarion"

Through Z, I have come to understand this. I began saying, early on, even when Z was floridly psychotic, "this too is just another way of being human." I can now say, truly, "You are still holy, even in your madness. You are still part of the whole fabric of things, even the unseen things we can know only after death." Moreover, he helps me remember that

> *He's every one of us, potentially.*
> *The leaf of grass, the genius, the politician, the poet.*
> *And if this is true, isn't it something very important?*
>> —Mary Oliver, "At the River Clarion"

≈

There is so much to admire, to weep over. (Mary Oliver)

So, the big question: how to love what is, to be grateful for the grace that "occurs in the space between people" (Julia Baird). Learning to, trying to (on good and bad days) practice acceptance as a way of loving what is, has brought me to new comprehension of forgiveness, kindness and an openness to the sheer wonder of all that it is to be human and to receive the gift of life.

I could not learn this in my forties. It has taken me another thirty years of living, softening, preparation, to approach the mystery of choice, and the boxes of Acceptance and Grace. I remind myself that every day is a choice, and:

> *What I want to say is*
> *the past is the past,*
> *and the present is what your life is,*
> *and you are capable*
> *of choosing what that will be,*
> *darling citizen.*

> —Mary Oliver, "Mornings at Blackwater"

I remind myself that in spite of whatever is happening in Z's head or life, I must practice choosing in freedom, in order to love and accept what is or what needs to be, without rage, resentment or despair. It brings me again and again to the practice of forgiveness of us both, kindness to ourselves and to each other. And to know the grace of a kind of honesty that was not open to me before this.

As a child with an unreasonably anxious, paranoid and fearful mother and a largely emotionally absent father, I learned to get what I wanted/needed through willful determination, secrecy and deception. Of course, the price was high—eternal guilt and for the latter constant fear of being caught out and the shame and punishment that ensued. But I wanted so much that was out of the reach of my mother's imagination and the only way I could see to out-maneuver her fears for me and of me was to go for what I wanted and to lie about what I was doing. And I did. At 13, I lied about the fact that there would be boys on a church camp, so that I could go away for a delicious week with other kids. At 14, I changed my clothes behind a tombstone in the cemetery that bordered the tram stop, so I could go into town looking like my girlfriends. At 16 I lied about being picked up for a school dance by my 17-year-old boyfriend; I said his father would be driving. And so on. The belief that I could do what I wanted to do only if I kept it undercover began around three, and persisted far beyond its use-by date and created habits of secrecy that were hurtful to others. Finally, through the possibility and necessity of living with Z, I can choose to...

> *come to the pond*
> *or the river of your [my] imagination*
> *or the harbor of your [my] longing,*
>
> *and put your [my] lips to the world.*

—Mary Oliver, "Mornings at Blackwater"

I can "put my lips to the world" and allow myself to try for what I want. Also, I can say "I can't." This is an amazing freedom and one for which I am immensely grateful.

> ...I have known a wine,
> a drunkenness that can't be spoken or sung
> without betraying it. Far past Yours or Mine,
> even past Ours, it has nothing at all to say;
> it slants a sudden laser through common day.
> ....
>
> Maybe there was once a word for it. Call it grace.

—Judith Wright, "Grace"

Alex Reid—at almost 76, I am more than anything, grateful for the gifts of long years. I have lived a fortunate life and remain interested and alive to what's next.

Mary Oliver's poems are from *Evidence: Poems by Mary Oliver*, and *Red Bird: Poems by Mary Oliver*. (both published by Beacon Press).

HEALTH QUESTIONS

New Perspectives on Health, Aging, and Biography Work

Douglas Garrett and Renee Meyer, MD

*"Health and illness do not need to be seen as simply a conse-
quence of the correct or incorrect interactions of molecules,
but occur as a harmonious or disharmonious interaction of
forces of the physical, living, emotional and spiritual organization of the human being in an organ, organ system, or in the
whole organism."*[1]

Introduction

When we are young, let's say between our birth and age 21, our
health is usually good. Our maturing physical body is generally
healthy and working well; it's just the way it is. Yes, we experience
childhood infections and fevers, and yes, there are many children
and young people who face more serious health conditions. But it's
observably true that for most of us, our health, our physical well-
being, is just there, without much thought other than the annoyance
of occasional interruptions.

In middle life we may experience our first encounter with a
chronic illness, one that persists and requires attention. Chronic disease conditions such as high blood pressure, high cholesterol, arthritis, diabetes risk, and vision changes may develop.

As we age further in life these chronic conditions may continue
to need our attention, and/or progress to more serious manifesta-
tions, including heart and circulatory diseases, chronic lung disease,
and kidney disease. Mental and emotional health concerns rise

---

1   Peter Heusser. *Anthroposophy and Science, An Introduction*, p. 316.
     By the author: "This book is an attempt to create the foundation for a
     complete scientific and empirical integration of the different medical
     approaches in the biological and psychological sciences."

along with these increases, including depression and anxiety about the physical conditions themselves.

> ...there is really no possibility of speaking about the healthy and the diseased human being in a way that accords with the facts, unless we go beyond the physical body and include also in our consideration the higher members of the human being (e.g., soul and spirit),...for the nature of illness is simply not demonstrable from the physical body alone.[2]

Health of our physical body is foundational in supporting our work and play throughout life. But what about the health of the human soul and spirit? Rudolf Steiner (1861–1925) updated age-old concepts of Body, Soul and Spirit for modern times, enabling us to consider health from these vantage points, as well as the physical.[3]

Steiner's research identified how the soul and spiritual forces within us create our living physical physiology within three systems: Nerve/Sense system (brain and nerves), the Rhythmic system (heart and lung and blood/air circulation), and the Metabolic/Limb system (digestion, hormone regulation, energy production and movement).

Health

> ...the human being can better maintain his psychophysical health in the face of external stressors if he can develop an inner sense of coherence based upon the comprehensibility of the world and on the manageability which results from this, but especially on the meaningfulness or significance of the person's own life and biography. This can only be achieved by the intelligent spiritual core of the human being.[4]

One early example of work in human health, of developing an "inner sense of coherence...comprehensibility of the world...and

2   Rudolf Steiner, *World History and the Mysteries*, p. 111.

3   See his *Theosophy: An Introduction to the Spiritual Processes in Human Life and in the Cosmos* (pp. 21–41) for descriptions of the physical body, the soul and the spirit.

4   Peter Heusser, *Anthroposophy and Science*, p. 199.

manageability" is that of Machteld Huber, M.D., PhD, a former anthroposophical medical practitioner and now medical researcher in the Netherlands. Dr. Huber has made a significant contribution to an expanded understanding of health and well-being through developing a concept called "Positive Health." She had experienced an illness early in her career, and through this experience realized that her perspective as a patient extended far beyond what she had learned as a doctor. This experience sparked her curiosity about health and well-being beyond the traditional medical boundaries.

> Health care should focus far more on what patients want to change, on their personal preferences rather than on standard outcome measures, and on opportunities instead of limitations. This provides a fruitful basis for shared decision-making in health care.[5]

Dr. Huber's work presented a dynamic concept of health focused on resilience, functioning, and self-governance—terms that arise out of knowledge of the human being as threefold. Six interrelated dimensions of wellbeing were identified (the authors here note them in their relationship to the human Body, Soul, and Spirit):

> *Body*: *Physical Wellbeing*: bodily health, fitness, and vitality. Daily Functioning: an individual's ability to perform daily tasks and activities.
> *Soul*: *Mental Wellbeing*: emotional balance, coping skills, and psychological resilience. Social Wellbeing: relationships, social connections, and community engagement.
> *Spirit*: *Quality of Life*: overall life satisfaction, purpose, and fulfillment. Spiritual Wellbeing: inner values, purpose, and connection to something greater.

As we age, the Soul and Spirit aspects of life become even more important for us; and we could say that these aspects "open up to

---

5   From "Handbook: Positive Health in Primary Care—the Dutch Example" available from the Institute for Positive Health (https://www.iph.nl/).

us more." When older we are at a life-stage where we can look back and reflect, and come to perhaps wiser judgments about our lives than we were able to when we were younger.

Illness Processes

> Becoming ill is a process of unbalance in which the qualitative patterns of each one of these systems (threefold physiology) interfere with one another so as to generate disharmony.[6]

We might say that for minor or fleeting illnesses we use the word "sick," while for more chronic and disabling conditions, we would probably use the word *ill*. The word *ill* itself comes into Middle English (1150–1500) from the Old Norse *illr*, which meant "evil, difficult." In Middle English it became the word we know, *ill* with the meaning of "wicked," "malevolent," "harmful." We can relate to these meanings when we are ill. When we are younger illness is experienced mostly as acute, short-lasting physical conditions that are bothersome interruptions in our lives and activities. When we are older, and burdened by chronic illnesses that are more long-lasting and not easily made better, managing illness can be physically and mentally debilitating and rapidly can become a part or full-time job.

Through the interactive weaving of the spiritually endowed forces in the human being—the Etheric, Astral and Ego/I activities—our threefold physiologic systems (Nerve/Sense, Rhythmic, and Metabolic/Limb) strive to achieve a balanced working together in the physical body. These three systems are like two opposite poles (cool and warm), with a middle system that works to balance the two extremes.

The Nerve/Sense system we could describe as the cool pole, originating centrally in the head as brain and sensing organs (eyes, ears, taste, balance) and radiating as peripheral nerves through the body. This pole plays a crucial role in perception, cognition, consciousness and self-awareness—activities of the astral and I-forces. We

---

6   Paul Heusser, *Anthroposophy and Science*, p. 289.

can recognize its role as a forming and directing influence in the body. Nerve tissue has low vitality and low regenerative capacity. Healing in the nerve-sense domain may occur as scar, rather than renewal. The gift of being able to sense and experience the world, to have awareness, to sense and reflect upon our own nature, and to form concepts, also carries a catabolic tendency toward scarring, rigidity and death.

The Metabolic/Limb system might be seen as the warm pole. Its center is the abdomen and the organs of metabolism and growth, the stomach, liver, pancreas, intestines. Etheric forces are dominant here; heat is generated through the activity derived from digestion/hormone production, energy production/movement, and upbuilding human tissue. The Metabolic/Limb system plays its life-filled role in breaking down foods and rebuilding human cells from them, with concomitant heat and energy transformation, and supplying overall vitality. The Nerve/Sense system is symmetrical, cool, forming, with low life forces. In contrast, the Metabolic/Limb system is asymmetric, brimming with heat, energy, reproductive capacity and growth. We can recognize in its role an "inflammatory, dissolving" influence in the physical body.

The forming and scar-forming forces in the human Nerve/Sense system and the inflammatory, dissolving forces in the Metabolic/Limb system are mediated through the actions and forces of the Rhythmic system: the heart, lungs and the circulatory system that carries blood and air to all human cells. The Rhythmic system can help regulate fluctuations back toward balance throughout the physical body by increasing and decreasing pulse rate and breathing rates (the ventilatory rate), and by signaling secretion of myriad biologic factors and hormones to maintain balance, harmony and life rhythms in the body. We can recognize the beating heart and the regular ventilatory rhythm of the lungs as "sense organs" for the whole body. These organs observe and respond to the circulatory volume and flow of blood cells, blood content, and oxygen to every part of the body.

When more profound imbalances occur in these systems and bodies, we experience "becoming ill." In fleeting sickness, the balance is restored as the immune system, a protective activity of the I/Ego, overcomes the foreign protein substance, the "not me" of the disease. However, chronic illnesses are evidence of a "detente" of sorts. There may be partial healing, but an imbalance often persists.

Growing Older

Many people begin to feel the breath of mortality sometime in their 70s. As seniors, we may think enthusiastically about some new long-term goal or project, and then that breath whispers: "but wait...think about the time you have." We find ourselves looking at the future more cautiously.

What we will begin to experience is the slow loosening of our spiritual forces. The physical body will suffer decline as the higher beings—the life force (etheric body), the senses and soul forces (astral body), and our spiritual inner flame (our I/ego) begin to shift in their moorings.

These spiritual forces had found anchors in the physical body. The astral forces have worked through nerve tissue and the senses. In time the eye dims, hearing is impaired, balance may be compromised in the inner ear, in the cervical spine mechanoreceptors, and in the cerebellum. Fear of falling may appear as balance becomes uncertain and eyesight is less acute. Social isolation can develop as hearing becomes more difficult. We can fail to hear or misconstrue conversation. However, we can readily sense the impatience of others and that we are being passed over in a group discussion. These sensory changes increase potential for withdrawal and injury.

Our sense of life, the inner feeling that there is balance and harmony within the body, may be lost. Small disturbances like toothaches, joint pain, indigestion may take on exaggerated importance and will require our inner discipline to quell the fear they can produce. These distressed reactions might be viewed as flare-ups of astral body activity on the soul level, as its penetration into sense tissue encounters more obstacles. The I/ego-organization, previously able to apply the reins to astral excesses, may also be pulling away.

Our human forebrain is an important anchor from which the "captain of the ship"—the I/ego and its organizational principles— influences all aspects of our fourfold being by governing and harmonizing activities of the nerve/sense (astral) and life (etheric) forces. More rigid and "stuck" thinking, irritation and anxiety suggest that unbridled astral dynamics are at play without the calm reasoning influence of the I/Ego. Digestion is also an example of the I/ego organization's harmonizing effect. The I/ego organization guides full breakdown of the ingested food, so that all traces of the food's identity—its foreign "not-me" qualities have been removed, and the substance is ready to be incorporated into "me." The flowing etheric forces dominate in the fluid content of the small intestine by absorbing nutrients and rhythmic movement. In the large intestine, astral forces achieve the right consistency through gradual drying by absorbing water, and irregular kneading contractions, leading to a mostly unconscious and regular process of nutrient absorption and effective excretion of unusable matter. For excretion, the elimination of "not me," which is a conscious activity to some degree, the I/ego organization moves from guide to participant.[7]

Diverticulosis and its complications and gall bladder dysfunction are very common as we age. They are associated with failures of the precise and finely distributed oversight of the I/ego organization, with resultant weakened tissue strength, sclerosis and loss of fluid movement (weakened etheric forces); cramping and contractions, scarring, imprecise amounts and consistency of secretions (unregulated astral forces).

The accumulation of multiple illnesses and injuries over a long life can change the brain. Its tissues may become scarred, sclerotic, more opaque, and unresponsive to the I/ego organization's calm

---

7   Art van der Stel's article "The Spastic Colon" further illuminates workings of the 3 spiritual principles in digestion. Available on the Anthromed library website Anthromed.org.

leadership influences. The elderly person can report feeling adrift, unable to be fully present, especially in the mornings. Ego forces may hover around the physical and etheric body instead of readily reconnecting with them after sleep.

Illness and debilitation may be inevitable and powerful in their ability to throw us off balance. But there can be miracles along the path. Even as the physical body is struggling with new injury or illness, our life force (etheric body) continues to attempt healing with great determination. Wounds heal, bruises clear up, muscle injuries resolve, broken bones sometimes reunite even in advanced debilitation and functional loss. And impaired heart, lung and kidney function may improve.

Wisdom, a spiritual treasure, can await the older person despite the losses and progressive weakness of old age. Wisdom can enrich the older person's own life and the lives and futures of others. Wisdom is mostly reserved for the elderly, as wisdom may require a long background of accumulating life experiences; it is the informed and detached distillation of knowledge that can be imparted to the benefit of others. Wisdom requires continued experiences and reflection, emotional growth and moral development over time. It is a particular attribute of some elders, and can promise purpose and the beauty of a long view to those who attain it.

Empathy and understanding toward those seeking advice are crucial components of being a wise, useful guide. The very process of aging can help equip us with the necessary selflessness to see the needs of the other. We must all part with our youth and vanity, must accept with some grace our own infirmities and those of our spouses and friends, must endure the suffering and loss of many we love and watch our own context and relevance diminish by their absence.

Aging, losses, and experience alone are insufficient preparation for the great gift of wisdom. By regularly meditating with reverence and reviewing our lives in the light of spirit, new insight can buoy us. We may find joy in the discovery and affirmation of purpose and direction in our lives. Our discoveries may help guide others who are searching for perspective, caught in the worries and unsettling pace of their lives. This biographic journey can offer inward healing—perhaps just the right kind of strength to move forward with courage, leading us

> To purpose in living...
> To peace in our feeling
> To light in our thinking
> And teaches us trust
> In the workings of God
> In all that there is
> In the widths of the world
> In the depths of the soul
>
> —Rudolf Steiner

Healing Processes

> We are so overwhelmed and impressed today by a clinical/medical/psychological impulse that sees human problems and illnesses all as pathologies, that we are missing the developmental perspective. How can we loosen the prevalent view to bring movement into healing?[8]

In the quote above, a biographical counselor who has worked with medical patients asks, "How can we loosen the prevalent view to bring movement into healing?" This "loosening" can begin through expanding our self-knowledge and recognizing that we are much more than our physical bodies. In health, illness and healing possibilities, this picture provides us more to explore and work with than physical symptomatology alone—a "whole picture" of ourselves as human beings.

---

8   From an interview with Leah Walker, MEd, LPC, CHom, Counseling, Biography Work, Homeopathy.

A truly rational therapy is founded on a knowledge of the supra-physical in human nature.[9]

Spirituality is also an essential element of a fully "human" medicine.[10]

When we are ill, we naturally want to be relieved of our pain and discomfort. But if symptoms are only lessened or not relieved at all, can we still experience healing? The word "heal" comes to us from the Old English *haelp,* which meant "wholeness, being whole." The sense of being "healed" is to be restored to wholeness. This restoration may not be a return to a previous physical state—which might not be possible—but a journey toward a new experience of wholeness—a new elder flowering...

In the Human Body, Soul and Spirit, the interrelationships and balancing of the inner spiritual forces—Etheric, Formative and maintaining life forces; Astral, Sense experience and conscious-ness; and "I," or Ego, the inner knowing and directing individual-ity—within the three bodily physiological systems of Nerve/Sense, Rhythmic, and Metabolic/Limb, "bring movement into healing." These interrelationships work together within all six of Positive Health's dimensions of health and wellbeing.

Each individual requires their own unique path toward healing and restoring the disrupted harmonies in their human fourfold and threefold natures. In itself the "I," the spirit, is never ill, but its guiding activity may be obstructed as the physical body becomes scarred, more opaque or stone-like through injury or illness. Astral forces may be unleashed or misdirected without the steady, guiding spirit flame of the "I." Etheric, reparative forces often need to be strengthened.

9 Rudolf Steiner, "An Introduction to Anthroposophical Medicine" (https://www.anthromed.org/library/2018/12/6/an-introduction-to-anthroposophical-medicine).

10 Peter Heusser, *Anthroposophy and Science,* p. 200.

This obstruction of the "I's" guiding activity can be a call to identify ourselves more with what is deeply inside us and what is coming toward us from the future—both long held values and newly arising values—finding what is meaningful to us beyond just our bodily existence. We can ask about an illness, for instance: "What is this illness teaching me about my life? These are explorations into our Spirit—*Quality of Life* and *Spiritual Wellbeing*, and the necessary adaptations to our *Daily Functioning*. "Healing"—wholeness in the present time and present situation, whatever it is—becomes, as we age, more and more a matter of adaptation to a new wholeness through our Soul and Spirit capacities.

In addition to medicines and remedies, lifestyle adjustments, art and movement (eurythmy) therapy, rhythmic massage, music therapy, biography and social art (in groups or one-to-one sessions), improving social interactions, and helping the world in some capacity, are ways to find new perspectives and purpose.

> We do not grow old in vain, for the spiritual manifests itself within us in ever new forms. What thus arises within us, manifesting itself from within, will continually appear to us under new aspects.... To live expectantly, to expect something from the aging process year by year is the result of consistently and earnestly adhering to the thought that everything around about us and within us is the creation of the Spirit.[11]

Biography work in aging and illness— the medicine of meaningfulness

Dr. Bernard Lievegoed, a Dutch medical doctor and psychiatrist, and considered the "Father" of biography work, wrote the following in the introduction to his book *Phases: The Spiritual Rhythms in Adult Life*:

> ...the human being is seen as a physical being [the biological image of the human being], as a psyche [the psychological image of the human being], and as a spirit being [the biographical

---

11 Rudolf Steiner, *The Spiritual Background to the First World War*, lect. 15.

image of the human being]. The path of an individual's life [his/her biography] can only be appreciated fully as a unique personal "work of art" if these three viewpoints are combined to form a single image.

In our "spirit being," which unlike our physical body never gets ill, lives the image or path of our biography, our life-story—the unique path of our life or "personal work of art" as Lievegoed calls it. In our biography lives medicine and meaning for our Body, Soul and Spirit.

Margli Matthews, a biography counselor, wrote the following in her introduction to Gudrun Burkhard's *Biographical Work: The Anthroposophical Basis*:

> By making concrete, detailed pictures of both the inner and outer phenomena of our life and looking at it all as a self-less witness, we can begin to discern the truth within. This, Gudrun Burkhard suggests, is **preventive medicine** [bold by authors]...when we take on our self-education together with others, we consciously work to transform conditions and tendencies that otherwise might lead to illness.... By consciously taking hold of the material of our lives we access and generate healing substances from our biography that are available for our further creative endeavors...

The "healing substances from our biography" arise both from the dissolving of old inner images and the forming of new ones in the Soul through the biography processes and experiences. Dennis Klocek, in his *"Esoteric Physiology: Consciousness and Disease"* writes that "Images are a primary way for potentials to become substance." With these dissolving and forming processes, levity (lightening) forces can be released that have anabolic potential (constructive, upbuilding metabolism) throughout the human organism.

Artistic and other meaning-discovery activities utilized in biography work (new approaches to biography work are constantly being developed) are self-connecting and also encourage a more artistic (flexible and dynamic) approach to living. This flexibility and dynamism is of particular help as we age and face hardening forces in the physical body and in the soul. Biography work, particularly in its artistic/play aspects, we could say helps our Body, Soul and Spirit "dance together!"

As elders we can investigate, through our own biographies, important questions such as: What do I still hope to achieve? What matters to me? What is essential? and What do I need to stop or cut back on? We can also investigate and come to better understand, accept and work with our own health challenges. Here are two personal examples and a case situation with a biography client in 2023:

Douglas—7 years ago, at age 67, I began experiencing left hip pain. It would hurt, then get better, then begin to hurt again. X-rays were taken that showed osteoarthritis in the hip joint, and a bone spur that had grown and was the source of the pain. Pain relieving medication could help, and if the pain worsened further, a cortisone shot was the next step. Sooner or later a hip replacement was on the horizon (and done in February 2023). I had arrived at the body-part replacement stage! This was the medical picture. But was there a "biographical picture" of the situation?

When I was 25, I had open-knee surgery on my right knee for torn cartilage, then several arthroscopic "clean up" surgeries in the following years. According to the orthopedist, this "weakness" in my right knee caused a skeletal imbalance that contributed to developing the bone spur in my left hip. Makes sense, right? The story that I always told about the torn cartilage was that it happened while playing basketball in college. I told this story because I was ashamed of the real story. The real story is that one night my girlfriend went out to dinner with her girlfriend, and I was jealous and suspicious. So, I lurked around her apartment waiting for her to get home...spying on her. When they arrived, in order to not be seen, I dashed around the building...and suddenly heard and felt a pop! I had torn the cartilage in my knee.

Upon "biographical reflection"—looking into my concrete experiences—the true cause of my hip pain and subsequent surgery was really jealousy and suspicion, emotional weaknesses in my soul. Coming to this admittance and realization, I could ask myself how I am doing today with jealousy and suspicion toward others. While I recognize that tendency still remains within me like an echo, I am able to not act upon it today and can receive people at face value. The "biography" of the situation has enabled me to find greater self-acceptance and meaning in the whole experience.

Douglas—another health situation. After years of suffering with BPH (enlarged prostate) that affected my sleep, in 2022 I had an in-office procedure and then finally a hospital surgery to correct it. Even the gold-standard surgery did not work, and what was discovered was the "problem behind the problem," an enlarged (hypertrophic) and irritated bladder. Again, here is the medical picture...what might a "biography picture" add to it?

Looking into my life experiences, I remembered that I had been "pee-shy" for most of my life—unable to urinate when other boys or men were around. In addition, I experienced sexual anxiety and was sexually avoidant. I did not know it at the time—and being younger and intensely self-conscious I did everything to hide these conditions and of course did not seek any help—but these behaviors were rooted in anxiety and fear and had their physical effects over time on the urogenital system in my body. From this I realized that I could not be upset with my bladder about this condition; it was something my fear and anxiety actually inflicted upon my bladder over many years. With this self-acceptance and sense of meaningfulness about the situation, I am currently managing it with anthroposophical remedies (including therapeutic movement work—eurythmy) and a low dose pharmaceutical medication.

Case situation: 63-year-old woman diagnosed with uterine cancer

SM, a 63-year-old woman, was diagnosed with uterine cancer in September 2022. When she heard about biography work, she agreed to 5 sessions that took place between February 24 and May 23, 2023. All the sessions took place via Zoom because of travel distance.

The biography process began with a conversation to identify a question she would like to investigate through her own life experiences. In the conversation a number of questions were on her mind. She settled on two to begin the biography work: "What is important?" and "What is fulfilling?"

The first session began with a quotation from Margli Matthews:

> Biography is a way to become active and awake to our own life story, entering into a dialogue with it, questioning and listening to it so that it begins to reveal to us its secrets and riches.

SM then worked with rice on a plate—a warming and grounding exercise—running her fingers through the rice and seeing if a form emerged. Then she spoke about the form.

In the first 4 sessions, different quotes were used, including one in sessions three and four that SM's friend had shared with her that she found particularly powerful:

> My life, and the lives of everyone around me/Are the means by which the universe continues to evolve/The nature of that evolution is changed by what we do and fail to do/We are the Eye ("I") and the Agent of Creation/And our lives matter beyond anything we can imagine/I am ready for the transformation. Are You?/It begins with us: with each one alone, with all together.

A postcard exercise was included in sessions 1 and 2. SM selected from four cards that were shown on screen: "Pick one…what does the card say to you about your question(s)?" Note: SM's question changed after the first session, from "What is important" and "What is fulfilling? to a more sharply focused, visceral question, "What matters to me?"

The central exercise for sessions 1 to 4 was a self-made drawing experience on a large sheet of paper folded into three separate panels or drawing spaces. (SM was asked to place herself in each drawing.) In session 1 the theme worked with, in left to right drawings, was "important changes" that came about in your life between birth and 21 years old, then between 21 and 42, and then between 42 and 63. The theme in session 2 was "memories of longing," beginning in the left panel with a memory from her adolescent/teenage years, on the right during her adult years before age 63, and in the center the "present time." SM titled each drawing and did a 5-minute writing exercise on the "threads or themes" she recognized in the three drawings. In session three we worked with the theme of "turning points" during 0 to 21, 21 to 42, and 42 to 63. When completed, looking at each drawing, SM was asked "What one word represents a strength in you in that life situation?"

In session 5, the final session, the central exercise was a clay exercise (will). After warming the clay and forming a sphere, SM was asked to let a vessel of some kind form in the clay, a vessel that will hold "possibilities you want to create over the next year." Then she told the facilitator first about the vessel itself, and then about the possibilities for herself that are contained within the vessel.

SM reported after the sessions that she felt more at peace and had begun a gratitude journal.

Final thoughts

> We elders become rich in soul-spiritual things if we do not let ourselves be put off by our corporeality.[12]

> A biography [life story] takes shape in time as it unfolds between birth and death. The resulting shape is not an object to be discerned with the senses. It develops over time and arises from the qualities of time—past, present and future. A biography can only be seen inwardly as the panorama of a life if we concentrate on crystallizing out the sequence of

---

12 Rudolf Steiner, *Getting Old: Excerpts from Rudolf Steiner's Complete Works.*

experiences and events…. Through a series of metamorphoses governed by specific laws, physical organs as well as mental and spiritual faculties are developed as these gifts interact with external circumstances and events. Capabilities can be used to shape one's sphere of life and to realize ideals and aims. Every human biography is unique since the variety of given and added inner and outer possibilities is so enormous that no life is the same. Yet every biography is founded on a generally valid human blueprint that is modified by personal and suprapersonal influences.[13]

Douglas Garrett is a certified Biography and Social Art Facilitator. He works with people around important personal questions through investigating their own life stories, events and memories utilizing artistic practices. He has a particular interest for what Biography and Social Art can contribute in the field of health and our well-being in body, soul and spirit.

Renee Page Meyer, MD, is licensed in Internal Medicine and Geriatrics and certified in Anthroposophic Medicine. Mostly retired from medical practice, she is currently Director of the Acorn School of Charleston, a Waldorf-inspired early childhood and elementary grades school. Anthroposophic thought and writings have enriched her life.

---

13 From "A Patient's Biography as an Aid to Diagnosis and Therapy," Research at Klinik Oeschelbronn, Germany. Hans Werner, MD, Hans Broder van Laue, MD, and Elke E. van Laue, curative eurythmist.

THE PARADOX OF AGING

ANN SAWYER

I like to humorously describe old age as having a light, bright, vital spirit that is stuck in an old jalopy, held together with duct tape and glue and more, needing a lot of upkeep and maintenance.

Rudolf Steiner said this more succinctly,

> Everyone knows as a fact of experience that our physical bodies age; we grow older and older physically. And everyone understands what is involved in aging. But where our etheric bodies (life bodies, chi, prana) are concerned the opposite is true, we grow younger, ever younger.[1]

This is the paradox I am experiencing at age 75 years. And, as we age, the spirit of wisdom, Sophia, adds to our knowledge and experience the ability to reflect both within and looking out, beyond the self, to enable deeper understanding full of compassion and benevolence.[2] This is the kind of wisdom I have garnered from 50 years of being a psychotherapist, from my spiritual studies, and from life itself. This wisdom inspires/pushes within me to be shared and used. How do I satisfy my body's need to slow down and attend to my decline when my life forces push me to engage, reach out, use my lively spirit, and my wisdom for the good?

What path should I take? I do not know. This dilemma is evidenced in my recent behavior. In May 2023 on my 75th birthday, I retired. Then in September, just 4 months later, I went back to work.

---

1   Rudolf Steiner, *Initiation, Eternity, and the Passing Moment.*

2   Rudolf Steiner, *Isis, Mary, Sophia: Her Mission and Ours.*

Both decisions were not made without considerable thought, there being strong arguments on both sides of the question.

On One Side of the Paradox: Illness and Decline of the Physical Body

It is jokingly said that when you get people over 65 together, it is unavoidable that the conversation will turn to health, and it is true more often than not. Understandably so, for individuals 65 and older, 85 percent have at least one chronic condition, with 33 percent having three or more. And 40 percent of people over 65 take 5 or more different prescribed medications per week. Note all these statistics are for the elderly still living in the community, not in a care facility.[3]

Lifespans, how long a person can expect to live, have increased to 77 years. But perhaps more important is the concept of health span, the number of years a person has relatively good health and full functioning, which is on average 65 years.[4] I see many of my older clients struggle to keep going with their multiple health issues. So much of their time and energy are taken up going to doctor appointments or medical tests, often three or more times a week. Taking care of their health becomes an all-consuming, full-time occupation.

Health problems can strike anyone at any time, there are so many factors that contribute: genetics, lifestyle, environment and exposure, past actions and damage to the body, and just plain luck. Some jobs and careers are so damaging and toxic to the body that health problems follow, some medical procedures to treat one problem sadly create another, unknown genetic vulnerabilities can be triggered at any time, or depression can paralyze a person from taking care of themselves.

In December 2021, when I was 73½, I passed out at work. With no prior symptoms or any indication, I had a total heart block,

---

3   Denise Orwig, Nicole Brandt, et al., "Medication Management for Older Adults in the Community." *The Gerontologist,* vol. 46, issue 5, 2006.

4   Institute of Health Metrics and Evaluation, University of Washington.

which means that the atrial neural node responsible for signaling my heart to beat malfunctioned. I was lucky in the circumstance and by 4:00 that afternoon I had a pacemaker, and the next morning I was discharged from the hospital. Not realizing the seriousness of my episode, nor honoring my aging body's need of time and rest to fully recover, understandably I shortly succumbed to COVID. After being confined to bed for almost 4 weeks, I was left so weak that I needed a cane to walk.

These two health events were the first time I had been sick in 21 years. Luckily for me, I had been gifted with illness in the 1990s and early 2000s, first with strange symptoms, followed by a full Multiple Sclerosis attack and constant debilitating symptoms. I declined rapidly physically, cognitively, energetically, and was put on full disability. I began to research in hopes of finding something to help me fight this disease. A coherent approach began to form in my mind. Though MS is both a neurodegenerative and an autoimmune disease, one intervention seemed to stop the cascading biological changes that led to symptoms, namely, a dietary regimen so as not to eat those foods that activate the immune system, which starts the chain reaction.

I can still recall feeling a deep knowing, that filled my being, that the dietary approach held truth, hope, and recovery. With self-discipline I didn't know I had, born out of sheer terror of the future looming all too real before me, I followed the strict food regimen, exercised and embraced low stress and good rest, resulting in a return to full health after three years. I did not cure my MS, just reversed, recovered, and now control the disease. I have had to keep this strict diet, as MS will reactivate with my laxity. A few years later, I was diagnosed with breast cancer, which was quickly and successfully resolved by conventional medicine.

I call my MS the gift of illness. It was a turning point in my life. Before MS, I had gotten chubby, was eating poorly, and was on my way to high blood pressure, high cholesterol and who knows what else. Instead, by eating a pristine diet, exercising, and getting sufficient rest, I had even more energy and vitality as I returned to my active life.

My total heart block followed by COVID, were a mirror of 21 years prior, again having two serious health diagnoses within a short time frame. Using what I had learned from my MS experience, I further tightened my eating to focus on building my strength and health, returned to swimming—this time covering a half mile three days a week—also to a yoga class, and began walking with a friend. The results were that I returned to better health and vitality than how I had been right before these two health events. Luckily, I experienced no negative consequences or loss of function because of these two illnesses.

Rudolf Steiner said this about illness: "When we understand spiritual development and its costs—namely, human illness—as polar aspects of our humanity, we begin to approach illness and the healing forces it requires in the right way, with both heart and mind." Following this, he said, "Where there is spiritual development, as there is in human beings, symptoms and illness must appear as its shadow." [5]

The heart block experience did serve to bring my aging and the decline of old age into focus. Disease and health problems are not necessarily part of the aging process, but being old makes us more vulnerable. With the one exception discussed below, all our body systems are weakening and slowing down, the speed and rate of decline unique to each individual. We can slow the process through lifestyle, but it doesn't change the end point.

There is meaning in illness and the older person's greater vulnerability. Note that spiritual development is also skewed more toward the aged population, as maturity gives a depth of understanding and a capability to see beyond the immediate. I still remember James Hillman, a well-known Jungian psychoanalyst, suggesting at a conference I attended years ago that the dementias allow an individual's

---

5   Rudolf Steiner, *The Healing Process*, pp. 145, 146.

soul to process and work on remaining life tasks without the constant outside distractions.[6] As we grow wiser in our elder years, it makes sense that the aged experience more illness and disease, as the shadow side of greater spiritual development.

I looked for meaning in these two recent health crises since I had found that my MS and cancer had served to lead me back to myself, to a spiritual path, and interestingly, to a better, richer, and healthier life. Were these two recent health events a wake-up call as well? Had I strayed from my life path again? My recovery from MS was all about living at that present time, returning to my busy life, and not being hindered by disability. I, like most people in their early 50s, did not put much thought into my older years, what my decline would look like, or how my lifestyle, activities and health habits might affect my later years. It is only since my latest health challenges that I realized MS was a gift that keeps on giving. Having to eat so carefully, exercise consistently, and get enough sleep since 1997, has probably prolonged my health span, allowing me to do just about anything I want at age 75. I take no prescribed medications. For this unintended consequence of MS, I am very grateful.

People often say, "Age is just a number," but that is not true. We older people can look great, have a lot of strength and vitality, be active and disease free, but to some extent, we are all declining, and in all body systems. Often an older person appears to be doing very well, but when one problem comes to the fore, other areas of decline manifest soon after. This often silent but ubiquitous decline is the hard truth.

After my total heart block and COVID, I began to notice and acknowledge the subtle signs of my aging. I got tired more easily and earlier in the day and no longer enjoyed going out in the evening as I had, my balance was shaky, and sometimes I had trouble

---

6   James Hillman said this at a Mental Health Conference where he was presenting in Las Vegas in the mid 1990s. See his book, *The Soul's Code: In Search of Character and Calling* for more on his views of soul and inner daimon, guide.

with word retrieval or people's names. These are all signs of normal aging, normal decline. I can still claim good health, full functioning, energy, and good cognitive ability—just slower, less efficient and with a greater need for rest.

The Other Side of the Paradox: Soul and Spirit, Spirituality

My deep knowing experience back when I was struggling to find a solution to my disabling Multiple Sclerosis, gifted me with a second insight, which was just as important as changes in diet to restore health. I just knew with deep conviction that in order to fully recover, I needed to find a spiritual path to develop my inner self and connect with the divine. Unknowingly, I was following Rudolf Steiner's next admonition when he added, "They [symptoms of illness] can be mastered only by individuals who also turn to the light in the right way."[7]

With the same strong conviction, I began to read all I could about spirituality: Edgar Cayce, New Age, and I even joined the modern Rosicrucians, receiving their monthly packet. It was by chance, on a weekend trip to Chicago having recovered quite a bit, that I read an article about Rudolf Steiner in the *Tribune*. For me, it held truth, and his work became my focus. I ordered and read a great many of his works; not understanding much of it, I read them again.

Prior to my Multiple Sclerosis manifesting, I had lost myself in the busy-ness of my life with three children and a husband, my job, my community, and my friends. My individual "I" was drowning in everyday life. With my increasing disability due to MS, I had to stop and get off the merry-go-round of activity that was my world. Unable to do much at all, with little mobility beyond hobbling, exhausted after any effort, and having various parts of my body numb, tingling or not functioning, I spent my days alone in my house.

Besides working hard to follow the diet, I got to know myself better, and with my spiritual reading I started to see the world through a different lens. This deeper and wider perspective helped me not

---

7   Rudolf Steiner, *The Healing Process*, p. 154.

to get lost in self-pity or despair in the face of Multiple Sclerosis. In fact, I began to see purpose and meaning in my illness.

By profession, education, and experience, I am a LCSW licensed psychotherapist. Helping people, I realized, is not only my vocation but also my avocation. Even my MS turned into a helping others project for me. As word of my recovery spread, friends and relatives put me into contact with others struggling with their MS. From telephone calls to share what I had learned, this mission grew into my sending to anyone seeking help a 72-page booklet I wrote. Eventually, Penguin, the large publisher, published "The MS Recovery Diet" I wrote, with another MS person doing the cookbook portion. Selling over 25,000 copies, this book is still in print. By age 60, having devoted so many years to illness and then to spreading the word that recovery from MS is possible, I was ready to return to work.

My hiatus from my profession had been fruitful in many ways as it gave me a deeper, sustaining perspective on my work. I better understood living with chronic illness, the feeling of being broken, flawed, as well as the guilt and shame one feels with such illnesses. On the positive side, I discovered the power of finding a healing path even if by unconventional means, and faith in the beauty and meaning of all life. I now carried joy and optimism about people that guarded against the cynicism so dangerous to my profession.

At age 68 I was invited to do biography work, a method of following the ancient dictate to "know thyself," with Patti Smith. We worked for a year and a half, discovering purpose and meaning in the sequence of events in our lives. I wrote at the time, "*The hurts, disappointments and sadness of the past have been transformed/transcended. The sting is gone. In part this was accomplished by seeing the purpose and meaning to what we suffered and how it served our evolution.*" Biography work also made clear to me that helping people was my mission in life. And, in helping others, my soul and spirit grow larger and deeper. This work, though helpful at any stage of life, had a greater impact and more growth resulted because I was in my elder years.

Religious institutions are shrinking, and the culture is becoming more secular. Yet interestingly, the Pew Research Center, in a 2023 study, found "overall 70 percent of U.S. adults can be considered 'spiritual' in some way, because they think of themselves as spiritual people or say spirituality is very important in their lives."[8] This is in contrast to 2007 findings that about 50 percent of adults were spiritual, noting this number was up from previous studies.[9] In my practice, where people will tell their therapist what they don't say to others, I have noted a hunger for connections to the spiritual.

My own understanding and growing spirituality have led me to not just study for my own benefit, but with an increased energy, to try to live my beliefs for the benefit of others as well. Again, turning to Rudolf Steiner,

> There is much truth in this recommendation. If in old age one has an interest that completely occupies one's soul and spirit, that fills one with enthusiasm, this will make one more youthful.[10]

The Dilemma of Wisdom

Throughout the ages, cultures have looked to the elderly for their wisdom, but that no longer seems to be the case in our modern society. With the increasing life span resulting in greater numbers of the elderly lost in dementia or very frail, the modern picture of aging has grown darker, clouding the image of the wise old sage. Youth is so valued that the culture is replete with advice on how to look young, stay young, even to the extent of erasing the signs of aging through surgery.

Science supports what older cultures knew. Dr. Sherwin B. Nuland writes in his book *How We Die*:

> Interestingly, recent research suggests that certain cortical neurons seem actually to become more abundant after maturity

---

8 Becka A. Alper, Michael Rotola, et al., "Spirituality Among Americans," Pew Research Center, Dec. 2023.

9 Russell Hemlich, "Mystical Experience," Pew Research Center, 2009.

10 Rudolf Steiner, *Health and Illness,* vol. 1.

has been reached, and these cells reside in precisely the areas in which the processes of higher thought take place. When these findings are added to the confirmed observation that the filamentous branchings (called dendrites) of many neurons continue to grow in healthy old people who don't have Alzheimer's disease, the possibilities become quite intriguing. Neuroscientists may actually have discovered the source of wisdom which we like to think we can accumulate in old age."[11]

He further notes that with this exception, all the rest of the brain shrinks with old age.

Sadly, there is no mechanism in our culture for the transfer of this wisdom to the younger generations, nor do they look for it. In theory, the process of cutting back and retiring is an ideal time for the older worker to pass on their wisdom. The reality is that only 37 percent of older workers experience a planned retirement and only 30 percent continue to work for pay part-time after they retire, both opportunities lost to pass on wisdom. Sadly 56 percent of people must retire (age 62) before they planned (age 67) due to failing health or the employer has restructured, gone out of business or eliminated their job. [12]

According to a New York Times article, only 6 percent of U.S. senior citizens live with extended family, as was the custom in the past, so the wisdom no longer naturally transfers to grandchildren.[13] Isolated from the work world, and not integrated into a multigenerational household, set off in some senior living community or in a facility offering some level of care, there is little opportunity for all the richness of wisdom accumulated over many years in the older populations to be shared and used by the younger generations.

I feel that I have been generously gifted with wisdom thanks to the thousands of clients I have seen in therapy, where I learned

---

11   Sherman Nuland, *How We Die*, p. 56.

12   *USA Today*, Jan. 24,2024 by Daniel deVise. Statistics taken from Employee Benefit Research Institute, Transamerica Center for Retirement Studies, Harris Poll 12.2022.

13   *New York Times*, Nov. 5, 2023.

something from each person's experiences and their return to better wellbeing. I have within me this multitude of life's lessons, which is inspiring/pushing me to share. I am not the exception, most of the aged have a similar storehouse of wisdom that could contribute to the health of our culture but instead lies unused within.

Cultural Expectations—Retirement

After my recovery from COVID, I returned to work, but began to think about retirement. After all, I was almost 74 and most of my peers had long since retired.

Retirement is held out to be the "golden years," the time when the elderly can enjoy life and do what they always dreamed of doing. Following this, the advice is to retire at an earlier age in order to have the physical health and stamina for overseas travel and the like.

But what if this prescription does not fit? I recall a former client of mine with a PhD in education and a 50-year tenure as a grade school principal, who retired at age 75 at the urging of his family and societal expectations. He hated retirement but tried to make the best of it. He volunteered several days a week at the information desk of the hospital. He was such a well-known figure in the community, many visitors or patients would stop and talk with him, especially other elderly people. He shared with me that most of them told him they were unhappy in retirement as well. Like him, they apparently felt like they had been put out to pasture with no purpose or meaning, and less connections to other people—all the factors generally needed for a satisfying life. He did not experience a degree of decline or compromise to his functioning until about 2 years before his death at 85. That is not to say that there are not a lot of retired people who love the freedom of not working, following their interests and hobbies, and thoroughly enjoy retirement. Retirement is not a one size fits all proposition.

Like my client, my family urged me to retire, worried that work was wearing me out and would shorten my longevity. The fact I was already 13 years past the usual retirement age, and my perception that we baby boomers are not graciously stepping aside for the younger generations to take leadership, gave me pause. I did not want to be one of the people holding on beyond my time. So, I decided to retire. I chose my 75th birthday as the date and had a party to celebrate this new transition.

I, too, did not like retirement, even though I was working only two days a week before I left. I kept busy, traveled a bit, kept up my exercise, spent time gardening and with my family. But I missed the intimacy and depth of thought and feeling of doing therapy, I missed the sense of purpose and meaning, even joy, I got from helping people. Frankly, my life has been such that I did not have a bucket list; I had mostly done what I wanted to do. My retirement lasted 3 months, before I asked to come back to the group practice.

Resolving The Paradox...or as much as I could

Luckily, I have the kind of profession and, in my case, the kind of employer who was willing to (1) take me back and (2) allow me to design when and what I wanted to do professionally. Instead of individual therapy, I chose to do group therapy, two groups, each based on a novel concept. The first integrates exercise, socialization, and therapy, all shown to be effective in treating depression, instead of relying on medications. The second group integrates spiritual work, specifically drawing on the wisdom of biography work, along with psychology, with the focus on self-discovery and building strength to "follow the laws of one's own being" in the words of Carl Jung.[14] The goal is to help people discover their inner authentic self, including their higher self and the beauty that lies within them. These two groups have shown that they meet the needs of many clients and have been very satisfying to facilitate, but they do not require too much of a time commitment for me.

Another venture, done with a friend from anthroposophy, Susan Kurz, is a larger undertaking, but we both feel inspired and share a commitment to it. We wrote a small book and designed a program

14 Anthony Storr, *The Essential Jung*, p. 197.

named after our book, *"Solving the Mystery of You."* Through biography work, psychological understandings, and spiritual wisdom, the goal is to bring more people to know and value their own inner being and relate to the divine within. Through this we hope to expand and reach more people beyond those already doing esoteric studies. We do not know the outcome but are energized to pursue this program wherever we can. Our goal is to have this program transcend us, since we are both now 75 years old. As a result, we are looking to find a younger partner who can join us in this "Solving the Mystery of You" program, and who will take ownership and continue this work after we are no longer able.

A solution in part for sharing my wisdom was offered to me after I started writing this chapter, which was to be the instructor for second-year graduate students in their field placements, helping them learn to be therapists. Again, I have limited hours, to honor my age, but this assignment draws on my many years of experience and learning.

This follows what Dr. Ehrenfried Pfeiffer said in his 1949 lecture in Spring Valley, New York,

> So while the body ages, something is preparing which leaves the body young, at death. Physically we grow older, as soul-spirit being, we grow younger. It is complicated because the two streams of ongoing and reversing time are always working against each other. The etheric dissolves with the physical as we age, the astral grows younger. Health means that these two processes are well-balanced, in harmony. Disease means that these two streams are not completely balanced.[15]

I have tried to adhere to that admonition.

Looking Ahead

Another challenge of aging is that though we know the end point, death, we don't know exactly when or how we will meet our end of

---

15 Enrenfried Pfeiffer, "Health and Disease," notes from his lecture of May 1, 1949, Spring Valley, NY.

life. Much as we don't want to admit it, we elderly are fragile and even previously inconsequential events like a fall, can snowball to cause our death. Or we can live to 100, as many more people do, and then worries focus on if we will still have the means to support ourselves. Being an older person means to live in a certain mystery.

So often, I see clients who are plagued with pain as their constant companion—be it from their backs, joints, migraines or from other conditions—which robs them of life. Or others with multiple autoimmune disorders, who never feel well and do their best with no real solution since these diseases stymie modern medicine. Or people who had hard physical jobs throughout their lives and now their bodies are worn out, or ones whose workplace involved toxic substances for which they are paying a price in their health. I admire their courage to live with these health challenges, determined to live the best they can.

It is true that lifestyle can do much to increase the health span for some conditions like diabetes, obesity, heart disease and some cancers. But lifestyle changes are limited in impact as well. Sadly, our culture is quick to judge the disabled and those in early decline. Add in depression, so common now, which is a powerful force that can prevent many people from doing what they need to do to improve their health. I am incredibly grateful and feel blessed that I can claim such good health, so that I can invest my energy in manifesting my younger spirit.

So, I intend to work as long as I am functioning at a level that I can be of real service to others, not so they can be a service to my ego— hanging on for my own needs rather than others' need. I have seen that as well, an older therapist who falls asleep in sessions or barely remembers their clients or their problems. People are generally kind and indulge these misguided elderly, I don't want to be one of them.

Old age is a time to withdraw: "The essential value and meaning of old age can be found in the disengagement from the demands of the external world. This stage of life deserves the kind of environment that fosters the activity of contemplation and reflections, a place where memory images can be brought up, relived, and revered. This is the way the psyche sustains its sense of continuity as preparation for death."[16] As previously reported, James Hillman, a Jungian analyst, suggested a spiritual purpose for dementias, saying that the soul has work to do without the outer world intruding.[17]

The need for time and space to do this end-of-life task is clear, but exactly how many years are needed? Again, it seems to be unique to each individual both in time and depth. If a person retires at 62 and dies at 102, that is forty years of life without obligations, yet it is obligations that often give us purpose, meaning, and the connections so needed in life. I'll never forget hearing the famous playwright Edward Albee, speaking at a conference on death, say, "It isn't death that bothers me, it is those who die before they are dead." I see this in my practice, people who quit life, never leaving their beds, watching TV 24/7, drinking to drunkenness, often for years from retirement to their death. On the other extreme are those who never acknowledge aging and death, living in the illusion of eternal youth. Or there are the people whose lives are ended suddenly, with no warning. Death is not something many people accept, but rather deny and avoid it, often to the extent that the elderly are left to face it alone.

Many never address these end-of-life reflections so profoundly needed by the soul and spirit. But then, when is the time to withdraw? Is it when our health span limits us, bringing mortality closer, or when we are given a terminal diagnosis? This is a challenging judgement to make. I hope that I can make a timely decision and face my mortality with grace.

Ann Sawyer is a student of life as seen in her 50-year career as an LCSW psychotherapist and in her 30 year spiritual quest through Rudolf Steiner's works and Anthroposophy. She is the author of *The MS Recovery Diet* (Penguin, 2007) and, with Susan Kurz, *Solving the Mystery of You* (Garnet Drake, 2023).

---

16 William Bryant, *The Veiled Pulse of Time*, p. 98.

17 See footnote 6.

DEATH IS PART OF THE STORY

Death as a Process of Grace and a Doorway into Light

Karen Nani Apana, PhD

I'm approaching my eighth decade of living and find myself attending more funerals and memorials than weddings. I look around at my aging community of family and friends and realize this is the path we are on: leaving this life is the last door we will walk through as we close this chapter of our biography.

How will we enter this last door? Will we remain unconscious and in denial, or can we prepare for our death in a meaningful way? Will we welcome this significant event with ease when our time comes? This article hopes to shed light on the process of transition from life to death for the living, the dying and those supporting them.

Personal Biography: The Death of My Father

My father, Herbert Lau Apana, died unexpectedly at the young age of 42, leaving behind a 36-year-old wife with three children ages 16, 7, and 3. As a family we were pushed into funeral arrangements that were very dissatisfying, because we were deprived of the opportunity to be involved in any meaningful way with the death of our father. From this biographical experience, I learned in hindsight that "participation is the golden key" that unlocks the door to grace and healing when dealing with death.

The funeral industry had taken control of the death process, in the same way that hospitals had taken control of the natural process of birth. It was a hands-off experience for our family with the assumption that the funeral institution was providing relief and support for our grieving process. My mother gratefully accepted these conditions as she was overwhelmed and had a life-long fear of death from her own earlier experience of her father's accidental death.

My encounter with death at the early age of 16 marked a pivotal spiritual experience for me, igniting my journey to seek the answer to the greatest mystery on earth. I had the immediate realization while viewing my father's corpse that what I was seeing was "not my father." The true essence of my father, his life-spirit, was no longer present. This startling realization started me on my path to search for the meaning of death and eventually led me to discover the writings of Rudolf Steiner, who has written more about death and life after death than any other Western philosopher and spiritual teacher. [1]

Seeking to understand death and life after death have become major themes in my own biography. My personal experience and dissatisfying closure with my father's death, along with the discovery of Anthroposophy, have guided me to an alternate and more healing path. Sharing this information with individuals and families has allowed me to provide much-needed support through the transition of death and beyond.

As is so often the case, our early biographical experiences can lay the foundation for our future karmic work. The focus of this article, in addition to sharing ways to support people who want to understand the process of death, includes discussion on how we can use biography work and other ideas to support the person who is preparing to cross the threshold. I've also included some ideas of how we can prepare for our deaths in a meaningful way, while we are still alive. My intention and hope are to help alleviate our fears around death and make it more approachable.

---

1   Rudolf Steiner, *Life between Death and Rebirth.*

How To Open and Continue
the Conversation about Death

When someone we love is in the process of dying, we can accompany them on their journey in a beautiful and loving way, by being present and accepting what is happening. If the person is unconscious or has cognitive issues such as dementia or Alzheimer's, it helps to remember that they can still hear our thoughts through their unconsciousness. We can continue to talk to them even if they look unresponsive. No matter the outer manifestation, we can be supportive of the dying person by giving them warmth and love. We can say inwardly or out loud, "I love you and thank you." These simple words have a power that can bring inner peace and calm to the speaker and the one who is spoken to.

A beginning step is to gently ask what someone believes will happen when they die. This will help us understand where the person is and how much else they might want to hear. It also informs us about the fears they might have about dying.

I asked this question of my 94-year-old grandmother, with whom I was very close, when I thought she was nearing death. She was born in the early 1900s and Grandma immediately responded that she believed she would go to Heaven if she had been a good person. At the time, I affirmed that yes, she had been a good person and would indeed be going to Heaven! That was the extent of our conversation. (My grandmother eventually had what I consider a "good death" as she died in her sleep.)

From the teachings of Anthroposophy and Rudolf Steiner we learn that when we go to sleep each night, we all have a mini-death experience, as our physical and energy bodies stay in bed while our astral/soul and higher-selves travel to the spiritual spheres and gather wisdom and understandings for our daily work and life. The difference between going to sleep and dying is that in death, our etheric cord is severed from our physical body, and the physical body stays behind while all the other bodies eventually disperse over time.[2] (The slow dispersal of the other energy bodies is why anthroposophy and other spiritual practitioners believe that it is supportive to have a three-day vigil prior to cremation or burial).

The course of dying is an excarnating process. Everyone's death takes a different amount of time, and there can be a notable waiting period. Sometimes those on the threshold of death are waiting for visits from friends or distant family members, or need an emotional issue to be resolved before they can let go. There can also be strong unconscious fear that arises, even when someone says they are ready to go. Sometimes the people who have the closest ties to the dying person must leave the room, as the dying person doesn't feel free to go, due to the strong attachments. I was told the story about a friend who demanded that her family leave the room so she could concentrate on leaving!

Each family must navigate this part of the journey for themselves, and it helps if those who will be left behind can meditate, pray, and communicate to the person in transition that they are free to release their spirit from their body. Family and friends can consciously work to not cling to the dying person and help them with their transition.

Bedside Biography Work

If the dying person seems resistant to letting go, this can be a good opportunity to do some bedside biography work. Doing this end-of-life biography work can be satisfying for both the dying person and the listener. It can be a simple process of asking the person to tell a story from another time in their life or share an early childhood memory. Once they begin to tell the first story, others usually follow. The listener can also ask questions or share photographs from the person's life to stimulate more stories. The listener can take notes of the stories as a way of tracking what has been important

---

2   See, for example, Rudolf Steiner, *An Outline of Esoteric Science*, chap. 3, "Sleep and Death."

for the person who is dying. You often hear stories that were never shared before, and these can be written down to be shared later with friends and family members.

Signs of Excarnation

When someone is coming close to the threshold of death, they start to turn away from the physical world of food and drink. These are signs of the excarnation process that demonstrate how the soul and spirit are letting go of the physical attachments of this worldly life. It is important to understand this phase and honor it, and best not to force people to take nourishment unless they request it. The person often begins to sleep more, as if they are entering a cocoon, preparing for their final step in transformation from an earthly being to a fully spiritual being.

Fairytales, Inspirational Reading, and Music

When we are turning away from the earthly world, we are more open to the world of imagination and pictures. This can be a time to read fairytales or tell stories to the person who is dying. In fairytales the archetypal images speak more directly to the person who is loosening from their intellectual capacities. The story themes can be about individuals taking an arduous journey but who eventually are able to reach their destination. This can also be a time to read inspirational books like poetry, anthroposophy, the bible, or any book that is significant for the dying person.

Singing and using the human voice also support the process. Soft music can be played, using instruments such as the harp, lyre, guitar, and flute, as well as single long vibrating tones. There are local community groups called threshold singers, who visit those who are dying and sing in a cappella voices to bring harmony and ease to the death process. Their songs are about going on a journey and can be composed according to each person's life.

Death the Reverse of Birth

The death process is simply the reverse of birth since the person who is dying is being reborn back into the spiritual world. As the person's incarnated spirit is seeking to be released from the physical body, there are similarities to the birth process, such as the laboring that takes place before the spirit goes. I was fortunate to be sitting with a friend who had been lying unconscious for a week; suddenly she sat up, opened her eyes wide, and looked at everyone present with consciousness, then closed her eyes and died. Any time we can be present at a death is a gift, just as it is a gift to be present at the birth of a child.

After Death

An important transition for both the living and those who have died comes after the threshold of death has been crossed. Depending on where the person has died, tremendous healing can take place when we are able to spend quality time with them. This can be arranged after a medical doctor or hospice nurse verifies the death, and the requirements of each state and the appropriate paperwork are filled out.

Once these verifications have taken place, family and friends are free to wash the body of the deceased person. I recommend mixing water in a bowl with the addition of an essential oil, such as lavender, rosemary, rose or lemon. A washcloth can be dipped in a bowl of water and used to gently wash the person's body. The body can be dried and then anointed with a scented oil such as myrrh, or again with lavender, rosemary or whatever you wish. The washing and anointing of the body have been performed in many cultures over the centuries and these actions serve as a way of blessing the body and thanking it for being the vessel of the spirit it has housed.

The Home Vigil

A home vigil allows the person who has died to separate with ease, as well as to help the living to accept the death process. There is often a tangible feeling of a spiritual substance present during a home vigil. There is also a strong sense of reverence, as the spiritual presence of the dead person and other spiritual beings can be felt. The length of time of the home vigil is up to each family. Even a few extra hours with the person's body in a hospital or nursing home has important value.

For many individuals, experiencing a home vigil is a life-changing event that reorients their lives. Tremendous grace and healing can be experienced when people are able to have home vigils. Opening one's home to the community brings another level of support to the family and the deceased person. I have personally witnessed the transformation of a dead body after a three-day vigil. The etheric forces appeared to re-enliven the body over the course of the three days and the person's face became rose- colored. I believe this transpired due to the tremendous love forces that were generated by the care of the family and the visitation of the members of the community. [3]

The Presence of Angels
and Other Spiritual Beings at the Vigil

If we are attuned, we can sense that there are other spiritual beings present during the dying process and at the vigils. We can sometimes feel the presence of other family and friends who have already crossed the threshold, who are related to the dying person.

I believe as does Iris Paxino, author of *Bridges Between Life and Death,* that it is important to keep speaking with those who have died, as they begin their journey after death. If a person has died unexpectedly through an accident, it can take longer for them to realize their new reality. I also suggest that if individuals feel they missed saying good-bye, they can have that conversation by writing a letter to the person who has died and express their thoughts and feelings. From my years of experience in biography counseling, I have discovered that our relationship to those who have died does not end with death. We can continue the relationship, seek repair

---

3 Medium Article by this author, "How to Have a Home Death," 2020

and healing (if it is needed), since those who have died are now able to recognize what needs to be reconciled. Candles can be lit, as we keep the ones who have transitioned in our thoughts, and like candles, keep them lit so we do not extinguish in our hearts and minds those who are no longer physically present. We can do a simple meditative practice of sending light and warmth to the person who has died with an accompanying verse, such as the one at the end of this essay.

Continuing to Work with Those on the Other Side of the Threshold

Iris Paxino's book can further our understanding of how to work with those who have died.[4] From Paxino's understanding, individuals who have died can sometimes become stuck in various states of consciousness and need the spiritual support of those of us on this side of the threshold. Steiner concurred in *The Presence of the Dead*,[5] when he emphasized that we (the living) need to have spiritual thoughts to take into our sleep to support the dead, as these thoughts are spiritual food for those on the other side. Paxino also quotes Steiner in her book:

> Those who have remained behind on earth have a far greater influence on the dead than the dead has on himself or others who have also died have upon him. It is really the individual who has remained on the physical plane, who had established some relationship with the dead, who through human will is able to bring about certain changes in the condition of souls between death and rebirth.[6]

Steiner recommends a practice of "reading to the dead," which means reading spiritual material to help them orient in their new world of the spirit, especially if they have been antagonistic toward

---

4   Iris Paxino, *Bridges between Life and Death.*

5   Rudolf Steiner, *The Presence of the Dead on the Spiritual Path,* chap. 3.

6   Rudolf Steiner, *Life between Death and Rebirth,* lect. 3, Dec. 3, 1912.

spiritual ideas. Now they will seek out these thoughts to help them navigate their new terrain.

Preparing for Death Consciously

How can we begin to prepare ourselves for our eventual death? We need to understand that we live in a culture that believes material reality is the only reality that exists, and this idea alone creates an unconscious fear of death. Can we move beyond this false idea, to reflect on what happens when our material corporeality ends? I believe one solution is to address the topic of death directly. We can reflect on what messages we have been given about death, directly or non-verbally. We can take an assessment of our feelings and knowledge about death. Write down our ideas of what we believe about death, so we can become conscious of them and begin to explore their validity.

If there is an inner resistance to looking at the topic of death, try to see how to soften it. Accept the fears and don't let them dominate; send fear of death inner warmth and love. For example, there's a movement called The Death Café, in which people come together in a café or home to discuss death when it isn't imminent. These meetings can help normalize the conversation around death and allow people to explore their beliefs or fears with others. Perhaps you can visit such a group or begin the discussion with family and friends who might be interested. Consider this activity an inquiry or research project into the topic of death.

The Continuity of Consciousness

I also believe reading biographies of individuals who have had a near-death experience (NDE) can give us a view into the world beyond death. While each story is different, there are themes and patterns in the NDEs—i.e., seeing others who have already died, experiencing a powerful light and spiritual presence, strong feelings of love and wellbeing, and a definite reluctance/resistance to return to their earthy life. An important and consistent theme is that all the individuals who have NDEs return to their earthly life, stating they are no longer afraid of death and dying. People who have had near death experiences have experienced a continuity of consciousness that continues after physical death.

I had the special opportunity to meet and talk with Dr. George Ritchie, who'd had a significant NDE. Ritchie gave a talk when I was at graduate school at the California Institute of Integral Studies in San Francisco in the early 90s. He told the story of his near-death experience, which he also wrote about in his book *Return from Tomorrow*.[7] He recounts the nine minutes he was technically "dead" and what he experienced during this time. In my personal meeting with Dr. Ritchie (we had breakfast together after attending a Christian Community Service in San Francisco), I experienced a definite light within him. George talked about how, for many different reasons, he had not known how to share this experience afterward. His friend Raymond A. Moody Jr., MD, had encouraged George to write his book. George Ritchie's story became the first documented NDE. Dr. Moody went on to write a book about his patients' NDEs, *Life after Life*.[8]

In the classic book on biography, *The Human Life,* by George O'Neil and Gisela O'Neil,[9] the editor acknowledges that during the three-year period between 1975 and 1978, the reality of near-death experiences entered the mainstream culture of consciousness, verifying the continuity of consciousness after death. At that point, NDE research had validated more than eight million NDEs, and I know at this time that there are many, many more documented cases.

Another significant NDE biography to explore is that of Anita Moorjani. She was born to Sindhi Indian parents, raised in Hong Kong, and had been diagnosed with Hodgkin's lymphoma. At one point, her organs shut down; she was in the hospital surrounded by her family, and doctors were telling them that Anita was on her way

---

7   George Ritchie, *Return from Tomorrow*, Revell Books, 1978.

8   Raymond A. Moody Jr. *Life after Life*.

9   George O'Neil and Gisela O'Neil, *The Human Life*.

out and to say good-bye to her. During this time, she had a major NDE, which she describes in detail in her memoir, *Dying to Be Me*.[10] Not only did Anita return from her near-death experience but within a week she was totally free of her lymphoma. The medical world has taken on studying her case to understand why her cancer went away.

Anita continues to give workshops around the world and can help people release their fears of death based on her own NDE.

I believe reading these biographies can help prepare us for death, because in all the NDE cases when people return from their near-death experience, they are no longer afraid of death; they have experienced continuity of consciousness beyond death, along with a loving light and feelings of goodness and well-being.

We can also work with our personal meditations to help us release our fears regarding death and to connect with our higher-self and our Angelic helpers. We can continue to do our own individual biography work, which will help us gain insights. The more we can come to realize that death is an important part of our life on earth, the more we can come to accept it and be prepared for it.

Conclusion

I hope that these ideas have brought inspiration and a new outlook on the process of death, the last door of our earthly biography. My wish is that these thoughts can help evoke healing and freedom from fear of death, as well as grace and ease when you are facing this mystery of transformation.

---

10   Anita Moorjani, *Dying to Be Me*.

VERSE FOR ONE WHO HAS CROSSED THE THRESHOLD

Upward to you strives the love of my soul.
Upward to you flows the stream of my love.
May they sustain you,
May they enfold you,
In heights of Hope
In spheres of Love
—R. Steiner[11]

Karen Elaine Nani Apana, PhD, is currently a practicing Biography Counselor in the San Francisco Bay Area and teaches Biography workshops throughout the United States and abroad. She also taught art and counseled high school students for more than 16 years at the San Francisco Waldorf High School. Podcast "That Good May Become," season 4 "Seven Year Cycles of Meaning," episode 25.

---

11   Rudolf Steiner, *Verses and Meditations.*

Memories of the Future

Christa Hornor

My earliest memories are of bombs falling on our home during a World War II attack in Germany when I was not yet 4 years old. My mother, my two sisters and I, were huddled in the cellar of our building, surrounded by neighbors who had also taken shelter, when the sound of more than 200 bombers approached our city. Then, for almost 30 minutes, the bombs fell.

It was April 4, 1945—World War II would end the following month, but our city had been targeted by the English. Nordhausen was targeted in part because the V2 Rocket, which destroyed much of London, was being manufactured within a few miles of our home.

Once the bombing stopped after destroying 80 percent of the city and our building now in flames, we evacuated our home through rubble and flames. We were surrounded by death, flames, and total destruction. As we evacuated, planes continued to target those of us, still alive and running, with rapid gun shots from above!

If it had not been for my mother's extraordinary courage, strength, and determination to protect us, and with an abundance of luck and guidance, I would not be writing about these memories today. That experience, all of it, serves as the backdrop to an extraordinary life that followed. The unexpected and major changes that came my way brought perspectives about life that may have been designed for or at least prepared me for what was to come.

Leaving Germany in 1949 and heading to Damascus, Syria, with my mother, sister, and my mother's new husband, a German scientist invited by the President of Syria was, to put it mildly, dramatic and unexpected. This was the second life phase, which shaped my attitudes and outlook on my life and the lives of my family.

Suddenly, my life became an adventure, privileged and extraordinary. In spite of my youth, I was aware and wondered why we had survived and why I had "cheated death" three times by the time that bombing took place. Even prior to my birth, my mother, due to illness related to her "condition," intended to terminate her pregnancy with me but changed her mind at the very last second while the procedure was taking place and managed to carry her pregnancy with me to full term.

Then, not long after my birth, we were to be taken to a concentration camp due to my Jewish heritage on my mother's side, but we were "overlooked." My mother and sisters and I were the only members of our large family that were not taken to Auschwitz.

These past realities were integrated into my fundamental sense of wonder and gratitude for life. I met most of my days with a "what's next" attitude. I was not often disappointed.

The future is veiled, as has often been said. That's a good thing if we wish to lead our life in freedom, for we might not want to go to sleep if we knew what awaited us tomorrow. Along my own "veiled" journey I have continued to live a life of remarkable opportunities, challenges, and encounters with events and personalities that are rare in an ordinary life.

I so often felt privileged and wondered why I had been given such strong life lessons and opportunities—many of which I had, I thought, created out of my sense of adventure and imagination. Something my mother had always pointed out, saying, "You are most like me, for you and I share and seek out the adventure in life." My mother was the true adventurer and I only a novice imitator of her style and abilities.

That I had survived and benefitted from so much, was often a wonder to me—so much so, that I began to think I could easily die without regret, having almost reached the finish line. My 75 years of life had been so unusual and fulfilling on so many levels. Socially, personally, professionally, and, most of all, as a mother of five. I felt truly blessed and privileged that our family not only lived within reach of each other, but there was also so much love, understanding, respect, humor, and support for all concerned within the families of three brothers, two sisters, and their twelve children.

Then, suddenly, life had another lesson to present before my ultimate departure. It is, and will always be, the ultimate. It was as though life had now distilled into a heavy, lifelong mantle of pain, from which I had been spared during my life's journey. But now, it was presented, and I was to wear it forever, and there was no way of laying aside this painful event.

The news came by telephone on July 16, 2016. I was to attend a dinner party when a call from my eldest daughter changed this last chapter of my life forever.

"Mom, where are you? Are you alone? Please sit down, I have some terrible news. We have lost two members of our family." My heart stopped, and I demanded she tell me who it was. At first, she was hesitant to say and, as the eldest of my five children, wanted to tell me in person. She was on her way, but it would take another five hours to reach my home. It became obvious to her, from my response, that there was absolutely no way she could leave me wondering who of my beloved family it would be that was "lost." Then, she told me, "Mark and Mina are gone"—Mark, my oldest son, and his little girl Mina had drowned in Hawaii. Mark had attempted to save his child who had been swept away by a "rogue wave" in a tide pool on the Eastern shore of Honolulu. Their drowning was witnessed by Mark's other two daughters.

How does one heal from such an overwhelmingly painful loss? The shock, denial, and excruciating process that followed are impossible to communicate to anyone who has not experienced the loss of a child.

Once I understood that healing is a process, I began to understand that this journey of loss and healing is part of the human experience on planet Earth. It is impossible to live our life without loss, pain and suffering. I wish it could be otherwise, but it just is not, as I so brutally learned with the loss of my son.

When losing a parent to death, or a friend in later years, there may be an ultimate acceptance in most instances; but when losing one's child at the prime of their life—my son was 46 years old, and so fully engaged, loved and respected by so many—it is different, as parents who grieve for their deceased children will say. Nothing will ever be the same, and it takes courage to live through the mourning process. It also takes courage and willingness to heal to the extent possible.

If one is to heal, distinct processes must occur. The first is the mourning process, grieving through the stages of loss, which include shock and denial, bargaining, withdrawal, depression, guilt, anger and finally acceptance. I wonder now if at a younger age I could have found the strength to support my family while they too were mourning the loss of their much-loved brother every minute of the day.

We live in a culture that for the most part does not honor these processes. I have experienced that people who I thought might understand and support our pain, suggested we go on with life as if one could actually just do so. This does not honor the healing process; and if we do not embrace and work through the healing process, our next loss will reopen the wounds of the loss that was not healed.

Grief has enveloped me now for almost 8 years. It has transformed me in ways that I had never thought possible. Now that I am in the last stage of my life, and after having lived a truly fascinating, and purpose-filled life, having seen almost the whole world, and most of all having brought my children into the world, I am at a loss with the "old" me.

The "loss" is due to seeing the world in a totally different light than I had ever seen it before. I now see it, and life, in a much more objective way. As I experience life now, I also, simultaneously, feel much more connected to other human beings. I feel a tremendous sense of compassion and love for others, especially when they too have lost a loved one.

My concern for world affairs has become stronger, and my disdain for materialism is profound. I have found myself becoming even stronger, and more determined, in the ways in which I set boundaries and priorities.

I am getting to know a different me. First let me say that I don't feel old, I'm not even certain how "old" is supposed to feel. I do now, however, experience a very profound change that has taken place, which is the result of "grief." The loss of my son, his father, and my granddaughter, all within a five-month period, led to an understanding of physical death. It did so beyond what I could have anticipated or expected, with a shattered heart. It did not instill a fear of death.

It led me to the accounts of NDEs, or near-death experiences, reported by mainstream scientists, universities, and countless individuals from around the globe, reporting their experiences during clinical, yet temporary physical deaths.

These insights coupled with my own biography, have brought me to a very different understanding and perspective of life. With the loss through death, the experience of life has changed every aspect of living. It has presented daily experiences in a more focused, deeper and often, also, more painful way. It has brought a newly awakened status to the experience of being alive.

I have lived my life focused on my world and the world of my children and grandchildren, and other family members. What I now sense is how we are all very much part of the entire universe, and do not just live in the world that we have created for ourselves. I now experience the oneness with all there is, especially when I am in Nature. I experience the realization that the "hand" that created the smallest little flower in the forest, is the same "hand" that has also created me. I am part of the forest as much as the forest is very much part of me. This is not just a "poetic" thought, but the deepest reality.

Living each moment in deeper, more aware, and often in more painful ways, means that life has brought me to a more awakened state in which I now encounter almost all experiences.

A well-known philosopher, Alan Watts, once told me many years ago: "Where there is a lot of pain, good things can grow." I wish I could tell him today how well I understand his statement now. He said it more graphically at the time. He said: "Where there is a lot of manure, good things can grow."

Memories, I have observed, serve as the threads that weave together the fabric of our lives. Every moment is etched within recollections that hold immense personal significance. Whether my memories have taken me to extraordinarily positive and exciting moments of life, or to the most painful moments imaginable, all are necessary for growth. Suffering, whether physical, emotional or mental, has led to personal development and progress. Life has demonstrated, at every step along the way, how challenges and difficulties are essential parts of life that need to be embraced in order to learn from them and grow.

Reviewing my life at my present age of 82 has given me the final opportunity of acceptance, strength, endless love, and a deeper understanding of life, which I wholeheartedly dedicate to my son for his supreme sacrifice given to us, his family.

Christa Hornor was born in Germany during Word War II and emigrated to the U.S. in 1953 with her parents. She studied Waldorf education, philosophy, and the arts. She raised five children, after which she became a professional fundraising consultant, primarily for the arts, education, and programs to develop and support the lives of women in third-world communities. She continues to enjoy photography, international travel, and her 17 grandchildren.

LOSS AND TRANSFORMATION

LORNA KOHLER

Our lives can be experienced as a series of seven-year cycles. Each cycle is ruled by a planet, and each year of each cycle is ruled by the same succession of planets. This is my understanding of the correlations given by Rudolf Steiner:

Cycle	Moon	Mercury	Venus	Sun	Mars	Jupiter	Saturn
Moon	0–1	1–2	2–3	3–4	4–5	5–6	6–7
Mercury	7–8	8–9	9–10	10–11	11–12	12–13	13–14
Venus	14–15	15–16	16–17	17–18	18–19	19–20	20–21
Sun	21–22	22–23	23–24	24–25	25–26	26–27	27–28
Sun	28–29	29–30	30–31	31–32	32–33	33–34	34–35
Sun	35–36	36–37	37–38	38–39	39–40	40–41	41–42
Mars	42–43	43–44	44–45	45–46	46–47	47–48	48–49
Jupiter	49–50	50–51	51–52	52–53	53–54	54–55	55–56
Saturn	56–57	57–58	58–59	59–60	60–61	61–62	62–63

Within each seven-year cycle, the Sun is at the center, flanked by Venus and Mars, Mercury and Jupiter, Moon and Saturn. The Moon, Mercury and Venus cycles enliven the physical, etheric and astral body of the child and adolescent. The Sun cycles focus on the development of the soul. The Mars, Jupiter and Saturn cycles enhance the connection to spirit.

This pattern uses the same sequence of planets for the cycles and the years within the cycles and is, therefore, complete and self-contained.

However, with the discovery of outer planets not visible to the naked eye, it is possible to extend this idea to include Uranus, Neptune and Pluto:

Cycle	Moon	Mercury	Venus	Sun	Mars	Jupiter	Saturn
Uranus	63–64	64–65	65–66	66–67	67–68	68–69	69–70
Neptune	70–71	71–72	72–73	73–74	74–75	75–76	76–77
Pluto	77–78	78–79	79–80	80–81	81–82	82–83	83–84

The outer planets, with their longer orbits, are present as the rulers of these seven year cycles, while the progression of planets visible to the naked eye still influences the individual years within each seven year cycle. Of course, many people live beyond 84, and new celestial bodies are being discovered, including Chiron, the Wounded Healer, Eris and Sedna.

In charting the Moon, Mercury and Venus cycles of my life, I became aware of a pattern of radical change in the Saturn year of each cycle. At age 6, my family moved from a colonial farmhouse in Rhode Island to a garden apartment in San Francisco, far away from three generations of extended family. At age 13, my family moved from the city of San Francisco to 250 acres of land near the town of Calistoga, where I rode the school bus to 8th grade at the elementary school and missed my three closest childhood friends, piano lessons and ballet classes. At age 20, I took a leave of absence after two years of college, working for five months to earn money to finance living in London and exploring Europe and the British Isles. I celebrated my 21st birthday with youth hostelers from all over Europe, singing together in a pub in Limerick, Ireland.

The Saturn year of my Saturn cycle ended with ten days of caring for my mother-in-law, Ellen, newly diagnosed with metastatic cancer of unknown origin. Her son and daughter-in-law moved Ellen and her beloved cat "T" from her home in Wenatchee, Washington to an assisted living apartment near their home across the lake from Seattle. I offered to sleep on the floor next to Ellen's bed. We awakened at dawn to birdsong, with Ellen in an expanded state transcending the limitations of cancer and the loss of her home. We enjoyed the most amazing, heart opening conversations in those precious early hours. During the day, I practiced my oboe and English horn parts for a production of Oklahoma. Ellen had played violin in pit orchestras for musical theater and knew the words to all the songs, which we sang together after I put my instruments in their cases. When we talked about death she said, "To me, it is all life." I was able to share this with family and friends at her memorial in Wenatchee later that summer.

Ellen died on the 63rd anniversary of my birth, the beginning of my Uranus cycle, at the very hour of our magical conversations. During the Venus year of my Uranus cycle, age 65, I completed my second recording of original songs for voice, guitar, oboe, English horn, with my daughter Thea providing a cello part for one of the songs. My daughter Zoe listened with me for the sequence of songs and provided a photo for the CD cover. I gave a CD release concert with Thea playing the oboe and English horn parts on her cello.

The Sun year of my Uranus cycle brings more work on inherited family trauma. I fly with my mother to Rhode Island for a reunion with her two sisters, during which I chauffeur them in a rental car, cook and sing, and love listening to the three of them talk about their experiences growing up together. I sing and share a reading at the wedding of my friend Eddie's son Alexi. On the Spring Equinox, I drive with my mother to San Francisco for the wedding of Thea and her beloved e, after a lovely weekend getting to know e's mother, father, and brother from the Midwest.

In the Mars year of my Uranus cycle, wildfire burns the family land and the house I helped to build in 1963. My father, brother and I had gone back through the wildfire of 1964 to save the house. This time my family is lucky to get out alive. My mother and two brothers lose their homes. The extended family gathers on Thanksgiving Day to absorb the shock of seeing the remains of the house that began in my father's imagination. We make a circle around the harp of his baby grand piano and tell stories about him. The ashes of his body were in the house when it burned, along with his clothes and his musical instruments, recordings and memorabilia. A second cremation, a spectacular release, which we celebrate with a four generation Thanksgiving feast at a hall in Calistoga.

Right now, I am two years younger than my father was when he died at the age of 75. I cared for my father at home during the last three weeks of his life. I was amazed to experience the breaking apart of the boundaries of his personality, like ice breaking in the spring thaw on Lake Champlain. I witnessed the immense energy that had engaged with the world through the aperture created by the limitations of his personality. He looks at me with awe and wonder and asks, "Who are you?" I imagine he is seeing the immensity that is the source of my life energy. I literally watch his spirit expand out of his body. He tells me he knows what everyone is thinking, and demonstrates this. He is no longer bound in the same way by time and space. When he stops breathing, my mother is on the phone. I call out to her. She is devastated. He begins breathing again. She comes to his bedside and says, "I love you very much." My father says, "I know you do," and releases his final breath, a single golden leaf, spiraling gently to the ground.

My father leaves me with a koan. From his expanded state he observes, "It is wonderful how you can be so unforgiving." I tell him I forgive him, that no parent can be everyone to a child. I thank him for all he has given to me and for the challenge of searching for, or cultivating in myself, whatever he is unable to give me. Keeping vigil at his bedside, day and night, I realize I have been looking for him in all the men I have loved. I look at all the ways I am unforgiving— toward these men, toward my mother, toward people who have hurt me, toward myself. What is wonderful about this, I wonder?

I am dreaming and, in my dream, I am on an alpine meadow, surrounded by mountains with snow covered peaks. Women, men and children of all ages are gathered here, wearing the costumes of their homelands and cultures. In their midst, I see a rusty metal statue of an orchestra conductor with a baton in his hand. I look at his face and recognize my father, who steps out of the statue and walks toward me. He is filled with life. He does not speak, but I know he has come to show me who he really is and who I really am. He reaches out his right arm and touches my left shoulder. As we stand facing one another, I see a golden glow, beginning in his heart, radiating from the inside out until it fills his entire body. The golden light pours out beyond the boundary of his body into the meadow, the mountains, the sky, until all I can see is golden light. As the light continues to intensify, it permeates the landscape, and I begin to see the outlines of the meadow and the mountains. The intensification continues until I can no longer see the light. My father, the statue, and the people have disappeared. I stand alone in the meadow, and the radiance that enlivens everything is everywhere.

My father's death is followed by a series of cancer deaths of friends and colleagues in their fifties. After one of those deaths, I make a drawing of my body filled with open windows. Underneath I write: Every death opens another window onto eternity.

Ten years after Ellen's death, my daughters and I are back in Wenatchee, this time for the burial of the remains of the body of their father, next to the graves of his parents. His third wife fills the box with mementoes of their life together. My contribution is to rearrange the contents so the cover of the box will fit before lowering it into the ground. I am 73 now. In the following months, I talk to him, recognizing all the ways in which I was unable to show up fully for our marriage. I pray for my blind spots to be revealed to me, a painful and surprisingly liberating process. I can see now what I could not see then. I accept that I could not see it then, and I am grateful that I am able to see it now.

I want to communicate how intensely and expansively alive I feel at the age of 73, in the Sun year of my Neptune cycle and at the center of the three seven-year cycles from 63 to 84. I am at home in myself in ways I never thought would be possible. I am aware of the immense energy that animates my personality, and I am in communion with the child I was, who experiences all of the world as alive and radiant. This reversal comes out of an initiation that began with caring for my mother after a serious automobile accident in November 2019. I am 69, in the Saturn year of my Uranus cycle. After her death in 2021, I begin manifesting some of her symptoms and know I must consciously connect with my own will to live. I am in a new life now. I take nothing for granted. I want to sing and play instruments and dance and run and walk and write and draw and paint for as long as I am able to, knowing that I will not have this kind of access to the vehicle of my body forever. I am grateful for every minute, the shimmering of raindrops in sunshine on the tree outside my window, the brilliant green of the needles, the motion of clouds across the sky.

This initiation is informed by my second experience of Biography and Social Art at a Biodynamic Association conference in Santa Fe in 2016, the Sun year of my Uranus cycle. Cards are face down in the center of our circle. I draw a card depicting seven figures that look like elongated figure eights, standing on what appears to me to be a stage with curtains on either side. Two figures stand close together on what would be their stage right, with the other five figures standing in a row to the left of them. I see my family: two parents and five children. My family is in trouble, and I am sick and tired of feeling responsible for carrying them all. I do not want this card! But then I notice that above each figure there is something that looks like a lantern. In that moment I know we are on the same stage as a family, each of us with our own destiny and our own light. We are all on the same level. None of us is higher or lower, better or worse. There is no basis of comparison. Trying to fix or save my family members puts me above them, a precarious and false position that prevents me from receiving the gift of standing on this stage together, each of us a miracle, each of us whole and wounded in our own unique ways, with prismatic qualities because of our flaws.

My mother's mother used to say, "Your husband is your destiny." For women of her generation, this was often true. But nobody can be anyone else's destiny. As I continued to experience the tension between care giving and being a responsible steward of my own creativity, I watched myself crossing the line from self-reliance to piggy backing on the lives of others, serving them out of wanting to be a good person and avoiding the hard work of collaborating with the destiny seeking to express itself through me. Being able to see and own this heals the guilt and regret. What did I set out to learn by compulsively abandoning myself over and over again? Giving my power away by prioritizing my perception of the needs of others over my own needs. Feeling cheated, ripped off, resentful, angry, suppressing these unacceptable emotions until the volcano erupts again.

At 69, the Saturn year of my Uranus cycle, I travel with my mother to visit family and friends in Rhode Island and Massachusetts. We return to California on the 4th of July. I search for my car in the long-term parking lot of the Oakland Airport with fireworks all around. I attend a bird workshop at the camp my father directed in the Sierra Nevada when I was a child. I fly to Spring Valley, New York, for the first two-week summer session of the three-year training in Biography and Social Art. I visit my college roommate in Bethesda, Maryland and my dance teacher in Berlin. I feel an urgency to do all these things before my 93-year-old mother can no longer live alone. A golden summer, filled with music and friends old and new.

In November, I travel to Spring Valley, New York, for my second Biography and Social Art session, with a focus on gender. I am grateful for the gift of my female body, for the wonder of conception, pregnancy, home birth and breast feeding, the bliss of bonding with my newborn babies, now young women actively engaged in their own adult lives.

In the airport I accidentally put myself on a later flight. Waiting at the gate I converse with a woman who is flying home from her mother's memorial. She urges me to do whatever I can to prepare for my mother's passing while my mother is still alive. Looking for a will in their mother's safe deposit box, she and her sister find macaroni necklaces they made when they were children. Clearly of value to their mother, but not what they needed to settle her estate.

I return home in the early morning of November 12, 2019. Later in the day, I think of calling my mother to let her know I am home, but I do not pick up the phone. Exactly 24 hours after my arrival at 1 am, I am awakened by a phone call from my daughter Zoe in Santa Barbara. My mother was in an accident after dark on November 12. She is on life support in the ICU with internal bleeding and multiple fractures. I grab a bottle of rescue remedy and my toothbrush and drive north to Santa Rosa.

After twelve days in ICU and three months in rehab, I bring my mother back to the mobile home she purchased after her house and land burned down in 2017. I have a new job teaching K–5 music at an elementary school, am playing oboe and English horn in four orchestras, teaching private students and making the six-hour commute to Calistoga to care for my mother on the weekends. I feel stretched to the limit. I want my life back!

On March 6, 2020, I drive to my mother's mobile home with a tiny suitcase containing my oboe, Bach excerpts, and clothes for five days in New York. On March 8, I cancel my flight to the third Biography and Social Art session, yet another of the many sacrifices I make to care for my mother. That night, after singing her to sleep, I see angelic beings surrounding my mother's bed, silvery presences, weaving beams of golden light through and over her body, healing her. I feel completely peaceful in their presence. I know they are always there. They allow me to see them now to let me know I have made the right decision. My mother is still very fragile.

I miss the session on the twelve senses and fairytales. The following Monday, my livelihood as a musician and music teacher vanishes overnight. I stay with my mother for three months before driving back to my home for clothes and books, English horn and guitar. I ride my mother's tricycle to the grocery store, pharmacy, hardware, library, bank, and bookstore. I write this poem, inspired by an online Biography and Social Art workshop exploring Uncertainty, in June, 2020:

O blessed Uncertainty
as long as I choose to meet you
you are my friend.
You offer close encounters
with the destiny that I chose
before I came into this life
and try to avoid at all costs.
You take away my false sense of self.
You remind me to embrace the world
as it is unfolding all around me.

This morning I pedal my mother's tricycle
through the empty streets of the town
where I went to high school,
with the five-gallon water jug
in the wire basket
between the two back wheels
of a vehicle that invokes
images of early childhood
and old age.

O blessed Uncertainty
somehow you convinced me
that the seniors only hour
at the grocery store was
seven to eight instead of
eight to nine. I feel your delight
as I turn left, cross the street,

and park the trike just in time
to sing up the sun, crowning
the peaks that ring this valley
with luminous golden light.

I begin giving online music lessons, which delights my mother, who is able to see and hear how I interact with my students. After the fire, my brother Rod and his dog Terabyte find a home in a ground floor apartment in Calistoga. Rod is my back up when I leave my mother for one night a week in order to drive to my home in the coastal range near Monterey Bay to teach students who prefer in person outdoor lessons.

Thea and e live, and their beloved cat and goats live, in an intentional community on land high above Saint Helena Road. This community shelters me while my mother is in hospitals in Santa Rosa and Sebastopol and hosts my 70th birthday party at the beginning of my Neptune cycle. My mother impresses everyone by walking with no assistance after coming home from rehab in a wheelchair. Their land burns in the Glass Fire at the end of September 2020. They lose 12 out of 13 co-owned houses. I drive to their land for Saturday work parties to help with post fire clean up and restoration.

Days before the fire, I invite Rod and his son Ryan to celebrate Rod's 69th birthday on the deck of our mother's mobile home. Rod and Ryan bring their keyboards and play music for us. I serve lunch with sweet potato fries and birthday cake.

In November I fly with my mother and brother Brad to Atlanta to visit my mother's sister Auntie Zel, her husband, Uncle Joe, and their family. Auntie Zel is my godmother. She and my Uncle Joe provided comfort, delight and support to me during the years they lived in southern California. I had planned to visit them on Thanksgiving of 2019, but my mother was still in ICU, and I canceled the trip.

In January, Rod and Terabyte appear at the kitchen door of the mobile home at dusk. Neither of them are feeling well. I make them as comfortable as I can and stay up all night with my hands on their bodies, channeling healing energy down through my crown chakra and praying for whatever is best for each of them. They leave in the morning. I know both of them are on the edge, but I do not suspect this will be the last time I am with them.

I drive to my home on Tuesday, February 2, 2021, after confirming with Rod that he will drive my mother to a Wednesday appointment in Saint Helena. I set up a back-up plan with a friend from high school in case Rod does not show up. I am in a meeting on Wednesday morning when Ryan calls to tell me his father is dead and would I please come back as soon as possible to be the one to break the news to my mother. I do get there in time. My mother enjoyed being with my friend. She wonders what happened to Rod. I take time to connect with her before telling her as gently as possible this completely unacceptable news.

Later she tells me that she did not think she would die, but now that Rod is dead, she knows she will. She has recovered completely from the accident. Now she begins to prepare for her own death. More and more I am holding her relationship to time and space as she dances on the edge of the threshold between worlds. We sit at the table after meals while she talks for hours about unresolved issues with my father, who died 24 years previously, when my mother was 71, younger than I am now. We meditate in the mornings and do a therapeutic eurythmy practice facing each other before going to bed. Our hands always tingle when we do this and our hearts connect, regardless of any conflict we may have experienced during the day.

Seeing me cry after Rod's death, she asks if it helps me to cry? She confides her inability to cry after the deaths of her husband, her parents, and now, her beloved son. I remember his devotion to her when he was a child, concerned about whatever was troubling her, wanting to make her happy.

In my heart I hear my brother's voice, speaking these words:

"There is nothing we need to do to be good enough.
Trying to be good enough only reinforces the delusion
    that we are not.
When we know we are already good enough
we stop the war against ourselves."

"Socrates said something similar," my brother's son responds,
as we drive down the valley
in the heat of the afternoon
to retrieve the ashes of his father's body.

I place the box in the east corner of our mother's mobile home
on the wicker shelf below the six-sided glass tabletop
with the photo of her son's transparent face
framed by a halo of dark curly hair.

Rod's death is followed by the quiet passing of Uncle Joe, who has wheeled himself down the hall to the Memory Care Unit to greet his beloved wife on a Sunday morning. He has been living with congestive heart failure for decades. I speak to him earlier in the week. He is excited about his new portable wheelchair now that he is having so much difficulty breathing and is too weak to walk. In April, my friend Eddie's son calls to break the news of his father's sudden death. I call Eddie's wife, but I cannot speak. All I can do is cry. My mother's lifelong friend Rose departs with her daughter and son at her bedside. Her daughter tells my mother that Rose wanted her body dressed in white for cremation. A few days later, my mother shyly hands me her copy of Cynthia Hoven's eurythmy book, with a slip of paper marking the painting of the colors for the vowel Ah: "I open my heart in awe and wonder." These are the colors and flowing garments she wants her body to be wearing for cremation.

After Uncle Joe dies, I call the Memory Care Unit landline and have two long, amazing conversations with my Auntie Zel. She tells me her children have made a slide show of family photos for her, and that looking at them brings both sorrow and joy. We thank each other for all the joy our relationship has given both of us, from the moment I was born. These conversations are our goodbye. By the time I fly with my mother to Atlanta for the celebration of life for Uncle Joe, Auntie Zel's health has deteriorated drastically. The sisters fall asleep in their chairs while cousins Randy and Judy's daughter Kim and her beloved Josh tell me about their relationship. Born prematurely in August and October of the same year, both lost their sight when their retinas were destroyed by the oxygen supplementing their immature lungs to keep them alive. The sisters celebrate their last Mother's Day in Atlanta. I make a recording of songs Auntie Zel and I loved to sing when my cousins tell me she is on hospice care. They play this recording for her during the last three days of her life.

My mother dies two months later, while I am in Spring Valley for our first in-person Biography and Social Art training after a year of meeting online. I am 71 now, in the Mercury year of my Neptune cycle. This is the longest I have been away from my mother since her accident. She wants me to go. The night before I leave, she keeps saying goodbye. Some part of her must have known this would be the last time we would be together.

She stops breathing the night before I am scheduled to fly home. I am out in the beech forest with the fireflies in the warm August night. At my birth time, 3:34 am, I thank her for giving birth to me and for our amazing adventure as mother and daughter. I invite her to join me for our therapeutic eurythmy practice. My hands tingle. She is with me.

My daughter Thea books me on an early flight and picks me up at the airport, telling me stories about visiting Grand Lydia in the hospital the previous weekend. My absence allowed my mother to connect with other family members, some of whom she had not seen since the beginning of the pandemic. I sit with her body in ICU, a silent vigil, until her surviving children gather to honor her body as it is taken off life support.

My daughter Zoe spends a week with me while I am raw from the shock of my mother's death and supports me in reconnecting

with my Santa Cruz Mountain home. I connect with my friends
Stephen and Gloria at the Fall Meeting of the Biodynamic Association of Northern California, hosted at their biodynamic farm.
On September 25, their anniversary and my brother Rod's birthday,
I play guitar and sing with farmers and apprentices on the farmhouse porch. We receive two requests for the song *I'll Fly Away*,
which I once sang in three-part harmony with my brother Rod and
his daughter, Misty Dawn. Stephen has been living with cancer for
three years. I call Gloria when I learn he is in the hospital and drive
to the farm to help care for him and his family during the last three
weeks of his life. I travel to Spring Valley in November and March
to complete my Biography and Social Art training. A novel I began
writing in 2009 after the death of my beloved friend, Ali, is accepted
as my final project. This is the prologue:

MORGAN, FREE, AND THE GOD

"It doesn't feel right to me to call you Chrysalis anymore. You
left that body behind. When I see you in dreams, you are flying
without wings in a place filled with color and light. At least I
know you are not in the underworld. I've thought of calling you
Butterfly or Luna or Mysterious Elegant Moth, but none of those
names seem to fit you. Hummingbird, maybe, or Meadowlark:
even though you were a Chrysalis, you seem more like a bird than
a butterfly or moth to me."

"You could call me Free."

"O Free! There is a hawk circling the meadow as I write. The
sky is mostly filled with soft white clouds with some sunshine
filtering through."

"O Free! I do not know what to hang onto: the story or the dream."

I feel her smiling. "Why not hold onto both, like the two strong
ropes of a swing?"

"I saw the god again on the beach in Santa Monica," I tell her. "I
was running in fog so dense I almost bumped into the pier. He did

his thickening thing, the fog gathering to form his body, clothed in my father's carpenter overalls and blue Sea Bee cap with the yellow emblem. He was wearing the familiar smile: a combination of admiration and amusement, detachment and compassion."

As usual, he is pleased with himself.

"Do you like the outfit?" he asks. "I composed it especially for you."

He looks at the space above and around me.

"I'm amazed you can move, let alone run, with all that baggage," he remarks. There is an edge of contempt in his voice, directed at the baggage. I can only imagine what he is seeing: envy, regret, bitterness, resentment, hatred, rage, shattered hopes and dreams. I see myself as a peddler with broken furniture on my back, drawing the boundaries of my house in the sand, spending hours obsessively rearranging the furniture. South American therapy, Chrysalis used to call it. Life as a rehearsal with the beach as the set: if I put Dad here and Mom there, will there be room for me? How will I make space for the Beloved with Mom and Dad in the house? What will become of them, and me, if I throw them out?

"I can lift that burden from you, if you want," he offers.

What have I got to lose? I think. Now that I see it for what it is, I cannot imagine why I wanted this stuff.

"Sure," I say, smiling. "You can have it. No strings attached."

He does not waste any time with pyrotechnics or snapping his fingers or playing those infernal pipes. He simply vanishes, taking the broken furniture with him. Mission accomplished. As if he couldn't wait to play house in the underworld.

"O Free! Are there stars where you are?"

"Yes, Morgan: galaxies and galaxies of stars. The constellations are different, but familiar. I remember this sky from before I was born."

"I used to feel frightened," I confess, "lying awake under the stars. They are beautiful and close, distant and terrifying. My heart pounds as the brightness presses against my body. I feel myself flying into a million pieces, disappearing into the stars."

"It's like that," she responds, "only you don't disappear. Death is a release, an expansion, a restoration of true identity. At least, that is how it was for me. It's a transition, like birth: not a permanent state. You may be in labor for a long time, but the actual crossing from one world to the other happens in the space of a breath. You cling to the life you are leaving, but the actual letting go is easy. The hardest part was leaving my daughter."

"I loved watching your face light up when she walked into the room."

"Yes. She is my treasure. I wanted to have many more years with her. I did not want to leave her the way my mother left me. I did not want to be the one to inflict that wound. I did not want her to suffer. But no mother can protect her child from suffering. From this side of death, the years don't matter. I have slipped out of the labyrinth of time and space. Love matters: there is nothing else. She knows that I love her. I wrap my love around her, like a cloak, woven of all the phases of the moon and all the seasons of the year. I cover her with love as she scatters my ashes on the dawn shining river and walks through the fire of her grief."

"When you were dying, your daughter said, 'At least, when I talk to my mother, I will not have to use the telephone.' You are like the stars, closer and farther away. I cannot touch you and there is no separation between us."

≈

We sell my mother's mobile home to friends in February 2022. In March I miss being with my father's side of the family for the wedding of cousin Valerie's son Jordan in Virginia, the same weekend as the celebration of life for Stephen at the farm, where he worked on the land with draft horses for forty-five years. In May I gather in Santa Monica with friends from the dance community to celebrate the life of our friend Eddie with his family.

I looked forward to my 72nd birthday, another Jupiter return, and the beginning of the Venus year of my Neptune cycle. I was excited about presenting an in-person biography workshop at the

Summer Meeting of the Biodynamic Association of Northern California on my birthday, but was forced by illness to cancel my plans. I recovered quickly, but felt exhausted and depressed for a month afterward. Caring for Thea and e's cat, revising the manuscript of my novel, and composing a song for Kim and Josh's wedding in Salem, Oregon in July bring me back to life. In September, Thea and Zoe and I fly to Washington for the forest wedding of their cousin Rachel. We look forward to being with their father, who cannot come because of illness. In late October, I attend the back-to-back weddings of sons of Eddie and Stephen in Berkeley and Mendocino, feeling the presence of their fathers and enjoying getting to know their extended families. In April, my cousin Christopher dies after decades of living with multiple sclerosis.

In May, I compose a song for the Sierra Nevada wedding of my sister's daughter Kia. My daughters are unable to be at the wedding. They are in Denver while their father's body is on life support after a fall down the basement stairs of his home in Colorado. They are waiting for his brain to be declared dead in order to fulfill his desire to be an organ donor. When I choke on my first bite of the wedding dinner, I connect with this man who was my husband in the timeless seconds when I cannot breathe, knowing I do not want to die at my niece's wedding, or deprive my daughters of both parents in two bizarre twists of fate. A nurse vigorously applies the Heimlich maneuver. I leave the dinner to change my clothes in the cabin I am sharing with my cousin Glenn and Rod's son Ryan. I am able to sing the song I wrote for Kia and Kai that evening. Glenn calls it my Heimlich performance.

Glenn is the only son of my father's sister Jane. Like my friend Eddie, Glenn is someone who always makes me laugh, and with whom I share a love of family and singing and playing music. He has undergone heart surgery and slowed down since the last time I saw him. When he goes to sleep, I listen to the gaps in his labored breathing, as I did every night while caring for my mother, relieved when I hear him breathe again. The day of the wedding is Glenn's birthday.

I make him a birthday card referencing the music and laughter we enjoyed, playing trumpet and guitar for his niece Julie's wedding in an apple orchard in Massachusetts. Sometime in the early morning of January 15, 2024, Glenn stops breathing in his home in Las Vegas. I am filled with gratitude for the grace of being assigned to the same cabin, for our sweet, poignant time together.

I celebrate my 73rd birthday at home by myself, with loving messages and phone calls from my loved ones. I am beginning the year I am living now, the Sun year of my Neptune cycle. Growing older changes my relationship to time. While I have less time each minute before my inevitable passage through the portal we call death, time has become circular, rather than linear, and remarkably malleable. The more I am able to heal the divide within myself, the more present and congruent I am able to be. Looking back over my life, I see all the ways I was at war with myself and, therefore, unable to stand fully in the truth I was born to embrace. I felt I was fighting for the right to live and believed I would never be good enough no matter how hard I tried. I confused trying to be a good person or a nice person with the practical deed of doing the work. Having been told as a child that I was intelligent and talented and could do anything I wanted to do, I lost faith in my potential when I failed to build competence by doing the work.

Years ago, my oboe teacher said my reed making was holding back my playing. He told me I was playing on unfinished reeds. I continued to play on reeds I thought were finished that would not do what I needed them to do. I thought I was done with playing in orchestras until the Sun year of my Neptune cycle, when I accepted invitations to play in a Halloween concert, another season of Nutcracker, and, most recently, 2nd oboe in Dvorak Symphony Number 7. Initially I was ecstatic to be playing again. Then the reeds started holding me back. Oboe bliss is playing on a reed that sings. Oboe hell is fighting a reed that does not receive and transfer my breath through the instrument in a way that allows me to play what and how I want to play.

The second movement of Dvorak 7 opens with an exposed woodwind choir, with the 2nd oboe playing very soft, sustained low notes that must blend with the other instruments. Playing soft low notes on a clarinet is easy. Playing soft low notes on a double reed instrument is extraordinarily difficult. I was not able to do this at the dress rehearsal. But rather than plunging into self-hatred, I asked myself: How can we solve this problem?

I had accepted a ride to a meeting of an organization supporting women in the arts on the day of the concert. I called my friend in the morning and told her that I would not be coming to the meeting, that I needed to spend the entire day working on reeds. This was a huge step for me. I have abandoned myself countless times out of loyalty to others. This time I chose to take care of myself.

I literally worked on one reed that I thought I had finished for the entire day. I played, assessed, sharpened my reed knife, and made minuscule adjustments to the tip, heart and back of the reed, careful not to obliterate the spine that provides structure and stability, balancing resistance and response, over and over again, until all of these parts of the anatomy of the reed vibrate together, play in tune, and take the wind. By the end of the day, I was able to play the second movement low notes much more softly and consistently.

Fighting the reed means I cannot be fully present for the music. That night I played my part and thoroughly enjoyed hearing how all the other parts weave together to create the fabric of this symphony. Playing on unfinished reeds made me defensive and isolated, thinking there was something wrong with me, rather than taking care of the problem with my reeds. There is no substitute for doing the work!

I have been playing oboe for 52 years, mostly on unfinished reeds. I am profoundly grateful to have lived long enough to experience this breakthrough. My oboe is my teacher. The scales and arpeggios I practice every day ground me, bring me into my body, into my breath, into my love of the language of music and harmonic syntax and the relationship of parallel and relative minor and major scales to one another. I am no longer playing in a doomed attempt to be good enough. I am playing because I love to play. I am teaching because I love to teach. I am writing because I love to write. How amazing to return to these forms from a place of wholeness, knowing that I am already the only person on this planet who is good enough to be the whole and miraculous being I already am. Stopping the war against myself changes everything, allows me to live fully as the only being I am able to be.

Stepping away from the computer to sit in sunshine and eat the lunch I have prepared, I reflect on how I am like an oboe reed. My spine provides structure and stability, the core of my essential being, while tip, heart, and back express thinking, feeling, and willing. I am fine tuning my instrument through meditation and oboe practice and writing and teaching and walking in the redwood forest and remembering, recording, and reflecting on my dreams.

What I have danced around, but not yet explicitly articulated, is the alchemy of recognizing that what I judge in others is what I disown in myself. As I recognize and honor what I have disowned in myself, I heal the divide between myself and others and the divide within myself. Paradoxically, I am no longer looking to others for validation. I reside in my wholeness, honoring their wholeness, knowing all of us are connected and reflecting facets of the mystery that is our origin and destiny.

I am dreaming and, in my dream, I am living in a house with my mother. Without asking me she has been taking things out of my room and filling it with her stuff. She has decided that she needs more space and I do not need as much space. I am busy practicing my instruments, playing music, cooking, and cleaning the common space. I do not notice what she is doing. But then, in the lamp light of evening, I put my instruments in their cases, stop playing the piano. The kitchen is clean. The living room warm and inviting, but when I walk to the door of my room the doorway is filled with my neatly arranged bookshelves and I cannot go in. The shock of seeing this wakes me up.

I am dreaming and, in my dream, I am with my mother. She is vibrant, alive, living in a large luxurious home near my piano teacher's flat, close to the Golden Gate Bridge and the outlet of San Francisco Bay. Her home is being renovated, workers and equipment spilling out into the street. She is on her way to a study retreat in Asia. We stand on the street and talk. I am excited to see her fully engaged in passionate inquiry, in the company of teachers and colleagues she loves and respects. She does not invite me into her house, does not know if she can enter in its current state of tear down that precedes reconstruction.

I am dreaming and, in my dream, I am walking on a precipice with my mother. I decide the light is too dim to do this now. Very steep, sheer drop. I cannot see the bottom. The path along the edge is wide enough, but a fall would be fatal. We go back to a rambling house, one story with many rooms. I lose my mother. I have a feeling she is safe and well, but I don't know where she is. Color here is muted by twilight to shades of white, black and gray. I wander in and out of rooms and courtyards, completely still. No celestial bodies or sounds of night creatures calling, rustling, singing. A white lion. A white elk. Completely motionless, smooth. Elk is my mother's birth animal on Sun Bear's medicine wheel. She died while the sun was in Leo.

I find her in a room with two beds and a bathroom, like the hotel room in Atlanta, where I talked her through one of her many respiratory arrests. She is sleeping peacefully in the bed closest to the bathroom. I get into the other bed. There is no wall between me and the night. I fall asleep in the dream and wake up into my body.

The incessant winds of the last two nights are still now. I see stars and hear the voices of frogs. I see us starting to walk on the path around the precipice. I hear myself saying to my mother, gently and with no fear, "There is not enough light now. Let's turn around."

This sequence of dreams tells me I am returning to life after walking with my mother and all these other loved ones in the twilight of the valley of the shadow of death. I have learned so much by being there, but I cannot live there. It is not my time to make that transition.

As I rejoice in the sincere, heartfelt weddings of the younger generation, I welcome the presence of the Beloved in my own life. He has always been there, but I needed to learn how to love myself before I could be open to the mystery of this inner marriage.

I am dreaming and, in my dream, I am walking out of doors, in a vast open space above the ocean. Someone is talking with me in a constant ongoing conversation, but I cannot see who this is.

"Who are you?" I ask.

The voice answers: "I am the path beneath your feet. I am always here, and the only time you cannot see me is when you compare yourself to others."

Throughout my life I have been blessed with moments of grace, when all comparisons fall away. Once when my two daughters were young, I found a silver feather from an earring on the ground outside my parked car. I kept it as a reminder that on the path beneath my feet every step had been necessary to bring me to this moment.

> Nothing is wasted
> Nothing is lost
> Everything furthers

I am shedding the membrane of shame I inherited from previous generations. I am thinking about how cultures use shame to control behavior. "You should be ashamed of yourself," the child is admonished. One may feel shame over an action one regrets, a thought, word, or deed or from being shamed by another. But to be ashamed of oneself? To be covered by shame? Enveloped by shame? To have shame as one's identity?

Through all the different flavors of the seasons of my life, my connection with the natural world has been a constant foundation, literally the ground beneath my feet.

Two women who continue to inspire me are my piano teacher and my father's mother. To me, they were trees with many rings, with full recall of all the ages of their lives and a radiance that made me excited to experience who I might be when I had lived as long as they had. They died at the ages of 84 and 72 when I was 22. I have already outlived my grandmother, and the two of them came to me in a dream after their deaths to tell me that they would always be with me, as indeed they have. Both of them loved music, were visibly transformed when playing the piano or singing. Each of their lives included tragic events, breakdowns, suffering, about which they spoke openly. Both lived lives illuminated by love and wonder.

During the Moon cycle of my life, I loved helping my grandmother trim the wicks, wash the chimneys and fill the lamps with kerosine at the family cabin in Massachusetts. I loved walking with her to the outhouse after dark, with the light of the kerosine lantern dancing with the shadows of the pines all around us. Coming back to the cabin, she would say, "I wonder who lives here?"

> Wind in the pines
> Moon on the water
> My grandmother's voice soars as high as the stars
> While mother and father
> Uncle and aunt
> Weave a fabric of harmony in the pine scented night
> And the light of the kerosine lantern
> Slants under the blanket that darkens the door
> My brother and cousin breathe gently beneath me
> While I lie awake in the spell of the song
> I am worthy of love, hear my heart sing
> I will treasure the trust of the ancestors
> I am worthy of love

I loved threading needles and snapping beans with my mother's mother in Rhode Island, where my grandfather grew greens for soup and the best tomatoes I have ever eaten in the garden behind the house. This grandmother told me how much I reminded her of her mother, who died in Portugal when my grandmother was ten years old.

After my family moved to Calistoga, I sat on buses for hours to and from my piano teacher's flat in San Francisco. After my lesson, we sat together eating lunch on the carved wooden table with the three-legged chairs from her native Norway. In the dim light of the dining room, she told me stories about her life, while her yellow canary, Pretty Boy, sang in his cage by the window in the bright light of the kitchen.

As I see it now, my primary responsibility is to care for my own light, to trim my own wick, to adjust my own reed, so I can show up fully for whatever part the symphony of life calls me to play. Life that includes birth and death, darkness and light, sadness and joy. How freeing it is to be able to see my blind spots, to embrace the flaws in the gifts and the gifts in the flaws. To rejoice in the miracle of my own precious life as it unfolds within and all around me. To be a source of delight and inspiration, as these beloved elders were to me.

Lorna Kohler is a singer songwriter, musician, writer, dancer and dreamer living at the top of a ridge in the coastal range of California near Monterey Bay, where she teaches music lessons in a renovated redwood chicken barn and sings to the trees in the redwood forest on both sides of the ridge. She completed the training in Biography and Social Art in 2022, with gratitude for the exponential growth in the crucible of community she experienced on this remarkable, life changing journey. She gives thanks to the family and friends who appear in these pages, named and unnamed, for the priceless gift of our interwoven lives.

WAYS OF WORKING:
ONGOING REFLECTION

Researching the Later Years

Betty Staley

Biographers focus our interest on the human life cycle. We work with groups and individuals, offer exercises, and support people as they try to understand something of their own life journey. There are other times when we do research into our own lives as well. Recently, a question was posed to some of us who work in this way. Was there a time when you were no longer experiencing karmic challenges, but felt free? Was there a decade or a stage in the life cycle where you felt such a difference, and if so, how?

We were specifically challenged to do the research based on our own life. I found the question intriguing. I pondered how the aging process changed my understanding of my life's path. Was there any sense of being free of karma? In what way did I experience that I had resolved difficult situations with others?

As I tried to answer these questions, I decided to approach the question in two ways: by digging into my own biography, and also by discussing it with others in their early eighties.

At my present age of 85, much of the past seems to blur from one decade to another. In order to become clearer, my first task was to grasp the differences between my sixties and seventies. In a traditional way, I listed events in each decade. What happened, where, when, how, with whom, and why. As I contemplated these, I asked whether there was a question in each decade? Did themes emerge?

As I looked at my sixties, I was surprised by how busy I was in so many different directions. The key question that arose was, what was essential and non-essential as I tried to simplify my life?

In my seventies, I asked, what did I learn from the major events?

Now that I had key questions, I looked at each decade and made a line picture of the significant events, meetings, and challenges. This was interesting because it simplified the picture. I noticed that the line picture of my sixties was curved, and yet the essential situations stood out.

The line drawing of my seventies was angular and dramatic, which I could focus on to see what I learned from this decade.

Next, I stepped back and contemplated the two lined pictures and asked the question, what kind of weather does each represent? When we form an image, we are able to step out of the physical focus and move into the etheric realm, just as when we write poetry. When I thought about the weather, I described my sixties as changeable weather, sometimes cloudy, sometimes sunny, whereas I described my seventies as storms with the sun occasionally breaking through.

Having created images, I could now ask: what did I learn, what did I discover when I felt overwhelmed by what was coming at me, and when did I feel I had reached a stage of balance and freedom?

When I spoke with people who had reached their eighties, I learned that not everyone is keen to reflect on their biography. Perhaps painful memories were uncomfortable. While some people were keen to engage and found the experience very worthwhile, others thought it strange to dig into their past and try to learn from it. Those people were more comfortable looking at other people's lives than their own.

For a year, I visited an eighty-two-year-old friend, let's call him Arthur, who was on hospice. When I shared what I was doing with biography, he thought it odd to encourage people to look back into their past. In fact, he thought I was invasive by doing biography exercises even though I explained that the person doing them did not have to share the results with others. The mood changed when I read chapters out loud from David Brooks' book *How to Know a Person*, and Arthur's interest was piqued. As David Brooks observes, "There is one skill that lies at the heart of any healthy person, family,

school, community organization, or society: the ability to see someone else deeply and make them feel seen—to accurately know
another person, to let them feel valued, heard, and understood."

When we work with biography exercises, we try to help the person see themselves more clearly. Brooks asks a specific question,
What kind of conversations should you have? What parts of a person's story should you pay attention to?

Whereas Arthur was shy about his own life, he enjoyed describing the lives of others, and he shared the stories of friends he had
at the gym or at Rotary. That gave me a lead in to occasionally ask,
how was this in your own life? It was as if by describing someone
else's life, he was more comfortable moving over to his own. Then
I would hear him exclaim, *"Oh, I never thought about that."* It
was helpful for me to understand that there are various kinds of
approaches in doing biography work.

Another person who is 87 resents the subject of the past being
raised. She becomes defensive and attacks. It is hard for her to hear
that when her daughter asks a question, it is coming out of love.
Instead, she doesn't want to confront the limitations of her age. She
hides her fear with belligerence. However, when her young granddaughter asks a question about earlier times in her life, she smiles
and enjoys sharing. She is happy to describe events, but she doesn't
want to go deeper.

Another elder, Fred, tells me, "The past is the past. I'm not going
there. But I'll tell you one thing I've learned and that is that I don't
have all the answers." Even though he does not want to confront his
past directly, he has thought about it and gained some wisdom.

At a conference auction, I offered a biography session. Linda purchased it, and we began a conversation. Since she lived in another
area of the country, I sent her questions she could use to fill out her
life phases "U chart." After some months, she visited me, and we
spent the day discussing what she had written. She was enthusiastic
to look back at her past, and enjoyed the revelations that were occurring. In her case, Linda was excited to see certain patterns emerge

and considered different ways she could now deal with life issues. Reflecting on what David Brooks asked, I could see that Linda felt seen and understood by asking her own questions regarding her life.

It was helpful in my research to find that some people enjoy sharing a biography exercise, while others do not. However, there were other ways to help them recognize what significance lay in their biographies, as Arthur was able to achieve. I also found that being able to come up with an image was more comfortable than reliving the emotions of that period. I realized that when I made the line drawings of my sixties and seventies, I was creating some distance and was objectifying my experiences. When I created the image of weather, I was even more distant from the experiences. Rather than revisiting the emotions, I felt curiosity and interest in those decades, and I was able to see things in a new way.

Although my conversations with others did not lead to any clear answers, I was inspired to go more deeply into my own life.

When I look at the years, I see the period after 80 as being very different from earlier decades. I experienced the illness and death of my daughter Andrea when I was 83. It was a shocking, painful time as parents don't expect to have their children die before them. Because I was at an age when some friends had died, and I was already thinking about death and dying, I had a different reaction than if I had been younger. I felt that she was going first, and I would be joining her at some time in the future. Since then, I have read to her and others every Sunday, mainly from Rudolf Steiner's works on death and dying.

At the same time, I feel inwardly freer than any other time of my life. I am less emotionally attached. I respond rather than react. I'm probably a nicer person than I was earlier, less choleric, less attached to fulfilling goals, and more able to listen to others. I wonder if this is what Rudolf Steiner meant when he said after a time we feel free of our karma. I feel I have choices of how to respond to what comes to me. I consider what questions come, what people I meet, and I am grateful for these encounters. I am quicker to notice when I am losing my balance, and I work with it inwardly.

One area where I experience the freedom in my eighties is looking at my present connections with people who have been either unpleasant or challenging. I ask myself, what is the reality there? What is my role in the dysfunction of this relationship? Am I missing something? I've realized that once I have created a fixed picture of a person, the relationship becomes cold or even problematic. Once I make a concerted effort to connect with the person out of interest, something changes within me. Here are some examples:

This person, let's call her Anna, was a colleague for many years. I found her negative bombastic way of speaking difficult to deal with. She expressed her views about people without regard to those listening or even the appropriateness of the situation. At the same time, she had a sunny nature and could be great fun. I had made a point of getting to know her, occasionally going out socially. Everything changed when I was no longer a colleague, but in a position of authority and responsibility. She targeted me behind my back. When I was no longer working with her, I avoided her when I could. Some years later, a situation occurred when I could do something helpful for her, and I did. We had a conversation that did not touch on the past, but on how we were now. We shared our current health issues, our interests, and our challenges. It was filled with warmth and humor. Something cracked, and from then on, we greeted each other warmly, and I experienced something had healed.

Another person, Rena, had also been a colleague. She is a very reserved person, and it sometimes comes across as coldness. I found it very off-putting. I respected her intellectual strengths and energetic contributions to the community I live in, but there was a coolness between us. Although I wasn't the only one who saw her in that way, it was troubling to me. I couldn't figure out whether she just didn't like me or what was going on. A situation occurred when she wanted to speak to me about something professional. Instead of speaking on the phone, I invited her to my house. As we spoke about her request, we exchanged perspectives about our mutual interests, and our enthusiasm opened up our relationship. I realized that what I had perceived as coldness was actually shyness. I was able to delicately ask a question about the way I had felt she had treated me in a particular situation, and she clarified it. There was no defensiveness, but only explanation. The new warmth between us has led to working together on a project. I feel excited and happy to see her and to feel the change in our relationship.

The third person I will mention, Marilyn, is a very emotional person. She is very outgoing and speaks her mind openly, sometimes telling personal things about other people that seems very inappropriate. When I would have a conversation with Marilyn, it would go on and on, and it was difficult to limit her. If I tried to end it, she took it as criticism. That led me to avoid contact until I tried to put myself in her shoes. I felt her loneliness and her need to feel other people's appreciation of her. I was able to reframe our phone calls. Instead of resenting how long she would speak and how she would tell personal things about other people, I told myself that I was going to have a visit that evening with Marilyn. I was setting aside time to speak together, and I wasn't going to be in a hurry. This changed the whole mood. I don't speak to her often, but when I do now, I am patient and interested, and I also feel comfortable telling her that I don't need to know those things about someone else. Instead of feeling frustrated and impatient, I feel the warmth of our sharing.

Of course, there are a few other relationships that I still need to transform. As I have more control over how I use my time, I feel very good that I can pay attention to the quality of my relationships. I am also less defensive and more ready to recognize my role in a relationship.

There are also other ways I have tried to work on relationships, and the one I find most helpful is a variation of the Equanimity exercise given by Rudolf Steiner in the Six Basic Exercises. I have shared this many times, and others also find it helpful. I don't remember where I first read this particular version of the exercise, but since then, it has become my number one tool.

I choose a problem, whether it is a situation or a person as the cause. I then go through the following steps:

1. State the problem. What happened? What is the issue?
2. What is my role in this situation?
3. How do I feel about it?
4. What is my intention in this situation?
5. What would my higher self or angel say about this?
6. What does this situation tell me about human life?
7. Now, what am I going to do about it?

Although I have used this exercise for many decades, I have noticed in the past five years that I am quicker to use it and quicker to find resolution within my own mind and heart.

I also found that some older people were more interested in working with the equanimity exercise than in responding to a specific biography exercise that required them to focus on a particular time or event. They found this practical and helpful. Whether it helps others or myself to feel free of our karma, I don't know; I can say that it is a helpful tool to address a sticky situation more effectively so that I do not continue to harbor ill will. I take responsibility more quickly for my role in a situation. That brings a sense of peace, and often of humor.

That is surely a good thing!

Betty Staley, long time Waldorf teacher, teacher trainer, writer, and mentor, has also worked with biography for decades. Her book *Tapestries: Weaving Life's Journey* is based on birth order and life cycles.

BIOGRAPHICAL QUESTIONS: SHARING OUR STORIES

SIGNE EKLUND SCHAEFER

I have been busy with biography and social art activities for many years, and in the last two decades I have been especially interested in the years beyond 60. I know that sharing with others about the process of aging—the questions, challenges, and personal journey—can be both supportive and enlivening. Some years ago I gathered a research group of people in my community who were over 70 to see what we could discover about the later decades of life. I have also led several biography and writing groups at local retirement homes. In addition, I have been a grateful participant in self-organizing groups with other elders seeking connection and a deepening knowledge of ourselves and others. Examples of this latter include a grandmothers' group that has been meeting for several years, and a monthly zoom meeting with women friends from high school.

I have worked with biography exercises for many decades, with adults of all ages. In the more recent groups, since my retirement from full-time teaching, I have been able to explore what kinds of exercises are particularly meaningful for older people, and I have also learned so much from the suggestions of others in the different groups. In this chapter I will share some of the exercises with which we have worked, and I will consider various approaches that have been useful in deepening an understanding and appreciation for the later years of life.

Because we form mental pictures without always realizing how they work on in us, I have sometimes found the following exercise to be a helpful beginning for groups exploring aging:

- Find an example of an older person in your life who inspired you about aging—by their attitudes, behavior, ways of relating, etc.
- Find another example of someone whose way of aging was distressing for you. (In an exercise like this, it is always important to bring compassion, not critique toward the person who exhibited the distressing behavior.)
- In small groups, introduce these people to the others, sharing what it was about their ways of being that affected you.

This kind of exercise can be used with people of any age as a way of looking toward the later years of life. With a group of elders, further questions can be added:

- At what age did you form these particular pictures, and how do they resonate in you now?
- Do you see any of these qualities playing out now in your own ways of being?

While much biography work centers around the seven-year phases leading up to 63, and some chapters in this book address experiences with further phases into the seventies and eighties, it has been my experience that many older people are less interested in reviewing their lives phase by phase than they are in finding themes that have lasting resonance or working with prompts that ground them in the present or take them forward. Many years ago, when I was much too young to be working with questions of aging, I was invited to bring some biography questions to a group of older women at a nearby retirement community. Before we got started, a woman in her late eighties pulled me aside to say, "We're not interested in just looking back at our lives. We've been telling the same old stories long enough. We are now fairly new friends with each other, and we want to share about experiences we have all had or may be having now; we want to look at things from this present point in our lives." I found this comment very interesting in light of what Rudolf Steiner said about experiences after age 63, and particularly after 70. He suggested that some of what we meet in our later years (new interests, experiences, even people) may have more of a connection to a future life than to the biography we have lived so far. Of course, such a statement needs to be taken broadly, not as a simplistic picture of "this experience will obviously lead to that." So, with that group of older friends we explored together themes that interested them—like bridges or landscapes or transitions in their lives, and also how they were experiencing being older.

Many people do have particularly important experiences around age 63. Some describe the years between 62 and 64 as bringing a kind of new birth, often after hard labor, such as illness, loss of loved ones, relationship challenges, moving house, or work changes. Then there can be a new feeling of openness moving toward 70, more inner spaciousness and a sense of going forward in unexpected ways. Connecting the earlier phases in life to different planetary influences before we were born, Steiner suggested that by 63 we have met the major pre-birth intentions with which we came into this life.[1] I have never been convinced that we are then "free of karma," as some would suggest; for, of course, there are ongoing consequences from how we have met everything we encountered pre-63. But we may feel less bound by some of the life intentions or themes that have held and guided us through our lives. As the years go by, we may experience an inner attitudinal shift in the why and how of what we do with our time and energy. One friend summed up this time of transition with a grateful sigh: "I'm now less in my own way."

---

1 For an overview of life phases and other aspects of human development, see my book *Why on Earth? Biography and the Practice of Human Becoming*, SteinerBooks, 2013.

This is not a given, but rather the result of taking our own development seriously, both when we were younger and ongoingly. Certainly many, perhaps all of us to some extent, can be caught in long-established ways of reacting to life's challenges. In any case, as stated above, Steiner does suggest that some of the major themes that meet us after 63 may have more to do with laying seeds for a future life than with what we are carrying over from the past.

It is certainly a useful exercise to reflect on what happened in our own lives around, and then after 63. Were there aspects of my life with which I felt finished? Or others that remained painfully unresolved? Did new interests begin to stir in me, or quite new experiences present themselves? Were there significant endings or beginnings? Surprises or realizations? It is generally deepening and encouraging to share one's reflections in a small group or even with one other person. An open listening heart can help us to see ourselves in new ways, and listening to another's story invites not only resonance but growing interest.

At any age it is important to consider the threefold human being—body, soul, and spirit—and for older people it can be useful to reflect on the changes that aging brings to each of these aspects of life, interwoven as they of course are. However people might want to resist it, the changes that happen in the physical body as we age cannot be ignored. They are obvious. Life begins to ebb, the body gradually becomes weaker with less energy and stamina. Sense organs become less acute, arthritis brings attention to previously unattended body parts, and people even grow shorter as the years go by. The wonderful physical vessel that has made possible our life on earth is in a process of slow contraction and decline. Frailty, balance, and the possibility of falling become part of daily reality as we grow older.

The soul, in its mediating role between body and spirit, also undergoes changes with aging. As life forces withdraw, the habits that we have built over the years can become somewhat fixed.

Where people have avoided the invitations for self-development, certain habits may have become so automatic that they appear like a caricature of earlier ways of doing things. Those who have attended to working on their habitual reactions or less than worthy traits may find growing inner flexibility and be able to ray out more open interest, spontaneity, and true kindness. As sense impressions weaken, the recall of what just occurred has less to call upon. Short term memory can be an ever-greater challenge even as long-forgotten images from decades earlier may arise with surprising clarity. Over time our soul activities of thinking, feeling, and willing may have less focus and follow through, leading to disengagement or confusion. On the other hand, the present moment can offer an experience of unparalleled beauty and worth. And further, there are those elders who manifest a spaciousness of soul in which ever renewing creativity can flourish.

As the body and the soul begin to decline in vitality, they are ever less able to serve the spirit as they once did. The declining body has less to offer to spirit-inspired activity, and the soul no longer perceives the sense world as clearly; nor does it as readily offer living memories born of our previous thoughts, feelings, or deeds. The "I" is slowly excarnating from the vessel of our aging body and soul, but as long as we are alive it accompanies us in its wholeness, learning from life's gifts, even when this can seem imperceptible to the senses. It is our "I" that can discern the essential from the inessential, that can experience how daily life becomes our spiritual practice. If we are fortunate, gratitude becomes a way of being. As the years go by, experiences of past, present and future may begin to intermingle. Even the living and the dead may no longer reside in isolated worlds for us. Beyond any spiritual or religious beliefs, the threshold between spirit and matter can feel more permeable, the experiences of inter-being or inter-connection more real.

To make time to appreciate the real changes taking place in our body, soul and spirit, for example by listing out or sketching what we experience from these different interweaving realms, can invite important self-knowledge. Asking ourselves and sharing with others about what we see changing can lift what could feel like loss into a perception of unexpected opportunity. As the poet W. S. Merwin said in an interview in 2014, when he was 86: "I think of old age as being a time like the others. It has its revelations of its own that you can't come to any other way.... I accept it with a certain amount of curiosity."

A shared teaching along many paths of inner schooling is the encouragement to bring one's consciousness to the present moment, to let go of lingering attachments from the past, to avoid being drawn into fantasies of the future. The process of aging makes these practices ever more real, whether one has sought to develop them or not. Questions such as the following can aid in looking at how this is occurring in oneself:

- What do I find I have let go of lately? (i.e., skiing, hosting large Thanksgiving meals, the idea of running a marathon, a trip to Antarctica, being right...) How has this letting go been for me? Was I relieved, resentful, angry, or did I perhaps hardly notice that I no longer have the desire for what has been let go of? How is letting go related to my sense of being in control?

- What am I now able to let be?—with a nod to that Beatles song of our youth! What can I now freely accept, with a knowledge that I cannot change the situation but that it also does not need to go on bothering me? (i.e., the open jam jar left on the table, the fact that loved ones live far away, a brother's politics, flabby arms...) What keeps me from letting things be? Does it feel like a loss or a gain when I do? Within echoes of that old song, am I aware of a larger presence of acceptance helping me to "let it be"?

- What do I freely give my full heart to now? (i.e., events, people, ideas, loving...) Does this have anything to do with living more attentively in the present?

Living in the present moment can be especially challenging in the busy, multi-tasking years of early and middle adulthood, but it is a gift that arrives with old age. We may resist this, of course, trying to carry on in the ways we have for years, or still caught in resentments from the past or complaints about the present or the future. But as the years go by, each day, each moment invites our attention. As old age advances, the past and future begin to hold ever less significance. With grace, gratitude can awaken in the (eternal) present: beyond any sense of odious comparison, that autumn tree in the field really is the most beautiful ever, this baby is the most adorable, today's sunset is unparalleled, and a loved-one's visit is enough.

Members of an ongoing group can also bring attention to their own and each other's present lives with exercises like these:

- Share three images of where we might have seen you in the last few days (such as: weeding a flower bed, reading by the fire, talking on the phone to an old friend, cooking a stew, or writing a poem on the computer). These memories could be evoked and shared with simple drawings or in word pictures.
- Share about some object in your living room that is particularly meaningful to you these days. What is it that makes it feel special to you?

I did not mean to suggest earlier that there is no value in looking back at the different phases of our lives; this depends very much on the group. I mentioned my recent meetings with high school friends, in fact with nine women from our teenage "potluck group" when we were students at our large public school. During Covid we began monthly meetings on zoom; we were all 75 at the time, and since we now live in nine different states, we had not been in touch as a group for many years. We decided to share from the decades of our lives, taking one decade each month. Some had known each other since early childhood, others of us came along as teenagers. There were different groupings of two or three who had stayed in touch over the years, but as a totality we had not had much contact through the many decades of adulthood—as we built our families and careers. Among us all there was a deep foundation of caring from our shared years discovering ourselves as young women. To re-meet and be able to explore together the arc of our lives was an unexpected joy of the pandemic years. We still continue to meet, ending each time finding a theme to ponder as a focus for our next sharing. A few recent themes have been: friendship, balance, decluttering, celebrating festivals, and how our adult children—and we—are approaching our aging.

I want to say something about different ways of working with exercises. Of course, there is always quiet self-reflection in relation to a question or prompt, but there are so many other ways as well. A much-appreciated tool in biography and social art activities is the use of postcards. The images, spread out on a table, can touch deeper levels of memory or attention than simply pondering a question. People often describe that a particular card jumped up to meet them, for example a card that captures something of the young child they once were, or one that represents in some way a significant turning point in life, or one that encompasses a particular phase of life, or a quality one appreciates developing as a grandparent. Needless to say, when later sharing in groups, it is what the person sees in the card they chose that is important, not how differently someone else might have reacted to the same image. It is important to begin with a description of what one sees in the image, and then move on to why this was selected, what it is saying to the person who chose it.

Writing is also a very useful way of working. For example, spontaneous writing in response to a reflection prompt—i.e., when I was 21...or when I was 63...or a memory of my mother...or a moment in nature. It is also possible to bring single words, each on a small slip of paper, to be spread around upside down, and have people choose two or three, from which they will then select one to write about, reflecting on their changing relationship over the years to the chosen concept, and especially how it lives in them now. Words I have used include: resilience, loneliness, wonder, balance, connection, memory, hope, love, anger, fear, forgiveness, health, friends, self-acceptance, time, freedom, courage, death, family, trust, and the list goes on. When individuals then read what they have written into the group, everyone is touched by the different themes. And the writer has usually gone to unexpected places of attention. Obviously, no one has to share if they don't want to. Here is an unedited example of one such exercise, from less than ten minutes of writing:

> Illness—I tried to reject this but chose it twice—probably a clue to how I feel about illness. When young, I avoided giving it attention—I had a strong healthy body. But when I got sick, I got very sick—most obviously when I ended up on a respirator for 3 days with a closed throat. I couldn't swallow anymore—literally and figuratively. That metaphoric aspect to illness has always interested me—what is the learning, the opportunity?
>
> Now the illnesses of old age are hitting people I love—maybe me too, but I avoid doctors if I can. The body begins its decline—some aches are not illness, but where is the line with something like arthritis? What is it about older bodies that gives cancer room to grow—less vitality, depleted immune system, longer time in the pollutions of our age?
>
> The "I" (the true self) is not ill. I know this more deeply than I did when I was young. It is gaining experiences from the illness the body suffers. The soul too I guess. How much was intended? and when along the way?
>
> The question I don't really understand is—why must so much suffering accompany illnesses?

With spontaneous writing it is important to remember that many older people have pain in their hands. In one writing group I did at a retirement community, there were three people in their 90s, and the rest were in their 80s. I suggested writing for ten minutes, but I found that this was too long. Five minutes was more realistic. Some wrote short essays, while others simply noted down what felt important to them and then later shared from their notes. I want to emphasize here how important the sharing was. As the group went on over the weeks, in a moment of review, they all agreed that hearing the others share something meaningful had become a highpoint of their week. With that group I also had another important learning: older people don't really care about the details of instruction. As we moved around the table hearing remembrances of being 21, we came to the woman who said, "I wasn't interested in 21, so I wrote about 30." And why not?! As we get older, it is a relief to care ever less about doing things to fit someone else's liking, but instead to listen in the moment to what feels right for us.

Reading a poem can provide enlivening images to then be discussed or also worked on individually. One example of this is to write from the last line in Stanley Kunitz's very evocative poem "The Layers": "I am not done with my changes..." (I will share a list of poems I have found helpful for working with groups at the end of this chapter.) Writing poems can also be very meaningful—wording a memory or an insight, and as an exercise of creativity. Even a simple haiku (5–7–5 syllables) can be a way for group members to bring individual attention to something that has been shared. Or people can write a poem after selecting a word to work with. Here is one I wrote in my early 70s, using the word *spaciousness*. I find it interesting to discover within it a foreshadowing of the title for this book:

> Spaciousness—
> I feel it growing
> within me and around me.
> After years of busy fullness
> I am quieter now
> watching more and waiting
> against old habits of direction.
> This is an opening I cherish,
> the inner space
> to see what comes,
> to listen into layers,
> to let what is reveal itself—

bird, tree, new idea
or old friend come again.
Even familiar hurts
have room to heal.

Today I choose to call this spacious
    possibility
"elder flowering."
Gratefully I gather white blooms
and taste sweet tonic.

Still another possibility for writing in groups is to work with metaphor. After group members share what they have written, there are inevitably images that can lead to further conversation. Here are some mini pictures that appeared in response to the prompt "Aging is…"

Aging is a waiting game
    not sure what strategies will win
Aging is a book shelf
    stuffed with old friends and their neighbors
Aging is an old painted trunk
    full of priceless treasures
    some moth-eaten beyond repair
Aging is a fat pre-internet encyclopedia
    facts galore but none quite up to date
Aging is a memory of scattered friends
    waving warmly from afar
Aging is a trek across the ice of winter
    and seeing sun sparkles if you look
Aging is a grand old hotel with rooms to spare
    and very little staff
Aging is a crowded bus with memories entering and exiting
    all pushing in different directions
    until you reach your final stop

Exercises that use drawing can also be very meaningful. For example, residents in a retirement community can draw an experience map of how they have come to be at this place, finding simple ways to represent important steps on their journey—people, events, questions, whatever acted as a milestone along the landscape of their lives, leading to this present moment of meeting each other in this shared space. This could be done by working backward from where they are living now. Colored pencils work well for this kind of exercise, and a large piece of paper. It is probably best offered as homework for an ongoing group, so that individuals can let the story grow over a few days. This is a way of following one perspective on a life review that includes the present. It is less about all the details and more about the movement, the encounters, the decisions and turning points that threaded their way to the current circumstances. Sharing each one's drawing deepens connections between group members, and similarities and differences show up as objective parts of each other's journey.

Another kind of exercise, with or without the use of postcards, is to consider these questions:

- What is something you value about your aging?
- What is something that is challenging for you about aging?
- What is something you see developing in you that would not have been possible without getting older?

These kinds of questions are often not addressed with family members, but they may be quietly active within, longing for a sharing, and interest from others, that can evoke added clarity.

Such an exercise can lead into a conversation about what I call the "bifocalism" of aging. Many older people need to wear bifocals, which give different support for near and far vision. Within the lenses are two distinct perspectives, simultaneously available. This gives us an experience of paradox—both views are significant, neither rules out the other in spite of any apparent contradiction. And so it is with old age: we may be lonely and also value our solitude;

we may remember long ago events even as we live largely in the present moment; we may feel both capable and lost; or feel less able but more responsible; we may be kind and also have our own boundaries and commitment to truthfulness; we can feel ourselves slowing down physically even as we experience an inner quickening; we may feel objectively detached but also compassionate toward others; even as we experience greater limitations of body and soul, we may also feel our heart expanding and our inner life deepening.

To be able to live with paradox becomes increasingly important in the times we live in, and it seems to me that older people can lead the way through our own lived experiences. We have the possibility of stepping beyond the right/wrong, good/bad, spirit/matter polarized ways of thinking and acting that are so prevalent today. We can embrace with inner calm what others see as irreconcilable contradictions and thereby represent a greater wholeness encompassing our human development.

Creating situations to discuss ideas like these can be very enlivening for people who may feel isolated and unsure of how to initiate meaningful conversations. At the last session of the writing group at the retirement home referred to above, one woman thanked the group and me for all the sharing and for helping her to keep thinking; then turning to me she added, "Believe me, we don't have conversations like these at dinner."

In whatever ways we can, I find it so important to continue encouraging each other to know that there is meaning in life, in each of our unique lives—to find ways to reflect on the long arc of our life, and to be interested in the journeys of others. An enjoyable exercise is to write a five-sentence autobiography. Of course, this can be done at any age, when different aspects of our life will stand out; but when older people do it, there is more of a sense of lifelong threads being sounded. People can do this is many different ways: following chronological events, picking out central themes, focusing on important people, telling a fairytale, writing newspaper headlines, or even writing spontaneously. There is no one format, only the limitation of five sentences that are not too run-on, with not too many dashes and semicolons! I have done this exercise many times over the years; here is an example of one I wrote when well along in my 70s:

1. Born into a loving family and as the daughter of an explorer, the world opened early—geographically, relationally, and spiritually.
2. Being a woman was a central intention guiding my way young into a long, learning-rich marriage, into the joys and challenges of being a mother and grandmother, and providing a clear focus for a lifetime of developing consciousness, social action, and gratitude.
3. I recognized Anthroposophy at 20 and the path it offered strengthened my being, anchored my work in the world, and helped me weave together the pleasures of learning, teaching and writing.
4. Friends were essential all along the way.
5. It has all been about learning to love.

Particularly for those who are interested in karma, being able to look at the arc of one's life can reveal threads of destiny that have been weaving through us since childhood. Finding a postcard that captures something important we remember about ourselves as a young child can be a mirror to ways of being whose lifelong significance we had not necessarily noticed: that feisty little girl who became a warrior for truth, the quietly observing young boy who became a writer of deep character studies, the diligent bug collector who went on to do careful research into interest after interest.

There are many questions that can prompt realizations about the working of destiny:

- Find a turning point in your life. Was this something expected, wished for, dreaded, or did it happen seemingly out of nowhere? Who else was involved in what happened? Look at who and how you were before this happened, and then also afterward. What were some lasting consequences from this time of change?

- Try to identify experiences or episodes in your life without which you could not have become the person you know yourself to be. "I would not be me without…" Some of these experiences might have been difficult when they occurred, yet led to later, unexpected gifts in your biography.

- Find a memory of someone who metaphorically opened a door or window for you. This could have been a stranger who looked at you on the street in a way that let you see yourself in a new way, or someone who offered you an unexpected job or other opportunity. It could have been a teacher who opened the world of art, or architecture, or chemistry to you. Such experiences have been happening throughout our lives. Postcards can be helpful in prompting memories. Have everyone share something about this person who was the door opener, what happened, and also images of who and how they themselves were, both before and after this opening.

Creating situations where people can bring to consciousness how important others have been in our lives, in our very becoming, and still ongoingly, is especially important for people who may feel isolated and cut off from busy or distant loved ones. Creating small groups in which to share significant life threads or the people who shaped us in some way, is both enlivening and it offers concrete review experiences from other, perhaps forgotten, times in our life. It can also invoke lasting gratitude.

Other kinds of questions that are difficult for many to raise with family and friends have to do with death—the process toward it, our thoughts on where it may lead, our fears, and also the grief we may feel as people who matter to us die. Or perhaps it is not only sadness we feel when someone we love dies, but more of a sense of "bon voyage!" or "see you later," and a feeling of celebration for a life well done. Are we able to share such feelings with others?

Finding supportive ways to open up the subject of death and dying is important, especially in our times when ever-more people experience neither the guidance they seek nor real comfort in traditional religious forms. It can be a great benefit to look at the process of excarnation, at the gradual release of the individuality from the holds of the physical earth. In our materialistic times it is often difficult to let go, to trust that death is not an end but a return to the reality of spirit. Rudolf Steiner offered much about what lies beyond the threshold of death and about the journey between death and a new birth.[2] Sharing with others one's own questions and exploring different imaginations can be clarifying and supportive.

The work of reviewing one's life, in all the many ways that this can be done, serves our ongoing daily life; and it also can serve as a preparation for facing death, for bidding farewell to this life on earth. I have already shared several kinds of review activities, and other chapters in this book also address this theme. Here are a few more prompts to deepening conversations:

- What did you bring with you into this life by way of pre-birth intentions, or endowment—such as family, gender, temperament, gifts, challenges? Try also to identify some difficulties that you feel you intentionally brought with you into this life and that you recognized as yours for learning and growing.
- What did you do with this endowment? How are the consequences of these encounters with your pre-birth intentions still working on in you? What have been some of your life learnings?
- What will you take away from this life as new learning, perhaps from experiences that felt quite unimagined, even unintended, in this lifetime?
- Are there themes/experiences that presented themselves in your childhood that have reappeared in a new form in old age, though they may have been fairly dormant

---

2   Rudolf Steiner, *Life between Death and Rebirth,* Anthroposophic Press, 1968; *Staying Connected: How to Continue Your Relationships with Those Who Have Died,* Anthroposophic Press, 1999.

throughout most of your adult life? Do you experience
new steps, resolution, or even seeds toward the future?

- Can you perceive a "greater will" at work throughout
  your life, like a thread of destiny that never left you,
  though it may have burned or grown slack at times?

Quite another way of looking at our life on earth is in relation to
the cycle of the year. The four seasons—at least as they occur in
parts of the earth not too close to the equator—offer a living anal-
ogy for reflecting on an average span of life in twenty-one-year
segments: spring—birth to 21; summer—21 to 42; autumn—42
to 63; winter—63 to 84 and beyond.[3] It is not hard to see the
delicacy, opening, and vulnerability of springtime and childhood.
Or the fullness, lushness, and heat of summer in the 20s and 30s.
Or the sense of harvest in the autumn and the colorful fruiting of
midlife. And then winter brings a gathering in, cold and a growing outer darkness, with seeds going underground for some distant future, while storytellers warm each other around the embers
of life's gifts.

Postcards or simple sketching can help in remembering the
springtime, the summer, and the fall of our lives and what was
offered to us through these different seasons of our becoming. But
it is especially the experience of winter that can speak to our later
years. Of course, no season arrives fully developed on one day; there
is a gradual approach to the richness of its particular offering and
then a retreat so that a new cycle can begin.

In nature, winter is a time of contraction. The trees become
bare of leaves and show their skeletal essence. We go in from the
cold, as older people go more into themselves and their memories.
The landscape is more visible in winter, we can see farther; and so
too can we look back more clearly on the wholeness of our life journey. We may find a different perspective on the mysterious working
of the greater will that has been threading through our days. Time

---

3 Op cit. *Why on Earth?* chapters 4–8.

opens up in new ways, such as with the ability to experience the passage of a century. We can often take a longer, larger view on world happenings.

With less obligations than before to the outer responsibilities of work or family, different ways of being old begin to show themselves, and this is often related to how we took up the calls for self-development in earlier phases of our life. The release from outer commitments can offer an inner spaciousness or a feeling of emptiness. Some older people become ever more contracted, pinched in soul, fearing aging, threatened by and critical of the young. Others become more inwardly alive as they experience ever more what is essential in life. They want to share their own life wisdom, even as they remain interested in the young and open to the future, however strange it can seem.

Winter comes gradually through the sixties, arrives more fully in the seventies, and then settles into the eighties and beyond; of course, the process is different for each person. Winter can bring us images of ice and snow, both sparkling and treacherous; we can also feel the renewing sunshine that snowbirds seek, and after a long night of darkness a clear morning sky. Being able to entertain with others the metaphors of wintering fosters interest, offers examples of different ways of being than our own, and invites deepened self-knowledge and self-acceptance.

One last way of exercising our way into our biography is to make space for gratitude. This might be within a meaningful exchange between friends, such as when a friend in her late 80s said to me, "I felt old today, but now I feel bathing in life. Life has been such a gift. I can finish now with a smile on my face." To be really present for such sharing with a friend or family member is a blessing for all.

It is also possible for each member of a group to write a gratitude poem like the following one, which was inspired by the reading of W. S. Merwin's "Variation on a Theme":

Thank you for beloved people
without whom I could not have become
for my lifelong partner who keeps me growing
and my children who ever open my heart
for their partners too and the next generations
thank you for parents who valued my chatter and
    my possibilities
and for my sister whose sorrows deepened us both
thank you for friends who hold and lead and love me
across distances and thresholds
thank you for work that was an honor and a joy
for the encouragement I received and strove to give
thank you for ideas that fire my heart with recognition
with inspiration, purpose and hope
thank you also for the heartaches that stretched me
    beyond imagination
pushing me onward and deeper
and thank you earth that held my wanderings
and trees and flowers that slowly I could see
thank you for the questions that have ever guided me
and for my trust in going my own way

If a long poem feels too much, having groups write a gratitude haiku can also be meaningful, for the individuals and the group. Here are two examples that somehow ended up in my notes:

> Thank you, dear people
> dear earth you have held me strong
> I feel such blessing

> Thank you beloveds
> Joys and pains have stretched me wide
> Sunshine in my heart

Most of the activities I have presented here assume a level of self-knowledge and responsiveness, as well as a conscious interest in others, that might not be possible for older people experiencing some form of dementia. Yet even those with impaired memory or attention can benefit from small groups where real sharing takes place. For example, choosing a postcard (i.e. of children, or a landscape, or a seasonal image) that appeals to one and speaking about what one sees there can be enlivening for all. It does not matter that this experience may soon be forgotten; the moment itself offers life and a connection with others. For someone leading such a group the challenge is to find questions or prompts that can resound in the present moment.

Many of the exercises described in this chapter can be done not only in groups, but also on one's own. Nevertheless, when it is possible, a social context for this kind of working is so beneficial. Witnessing another person matters, as does being openly, lovingly witnessed by others. Older people know this, yet may need encouragement to do it. When others truly listen, the speaker can experience a confirmation of their growth, struggle, and life learnings—a blessing of meaning on the unique and winding journey of their life. And the listeners step away from self-concerns and grow in interest and empathy. The spiritual magic that can visit our sharings is greatly aided when this work can be facilitated by a trained biography and social art worker. Even when this is not possible, group members can call upon themselves to practice, ever and again, open-hearted listening and the holding of a "space between"; into this spirit-filled space can come healing, inspiration, and grace.

≈

A random selection of poems about aging that are useful for working with groups:

> Wendell Berry, 1916, V ("Some Sunday afternoon, it may be")
> Raymond Burns, "Personal Effects"
> Billy Collins, "Forgetfulness"
> Judith Heron, "Words to Say on Nearing Seventy"
> Maxine Kumin, "Looking Back on my Eighty-first Year"
> Stanley Kunitz, "The Layers"
> Stephen Levine, "Millennium Blessing"
> W. S. Merwin, "Variation on a Theme"
> Mary Oliver, "I Worried"
> Parker Palmer, "Everything Falls Away"
> Samantha Reynolds, "I Am Not Old"
> Jan Richardson, "For Those Who Have Far to Travel"
> Pat Schneider, "Instructions for the Journey"
> William Stafford, "The Way It Is"
> Joyce Sutphen, "This Body"
> Tomas Transtromer, "Romanesque Arches"
> Rosemerry Wahtola Trommer,
>   "Though I Respond to my Name, I am Aware"
> Alice Walker, "What Do I Get for Getting Old?"
> Sheila Willson, "After All"
> and other poems by all these poets and many others...

Signe Schaefer directed Foundation Studies at Sunbridge College and founded a training in Biography and Social Art. Recent books include: *She was Always There: Sophia as a Story for Our Time* (2023); *Why on Earth? Biography and the Practice of Human Becoming* (2013); and *I Give you My Word: Women's Letters as Life Support* (2019). A mother, grandmother, and great-grandmother, she lives in Great Barrington, Massachusetts, with her husband Christopher.

Why Not (a) Play?

Heart and Soul: A One-Act Play

Kathi Ciskowski

Characters:

Rose: 71-year-old woman who is Roger's mother
Roger: 50-year-old son of Rose
Setting: Rose's childhood home

At rise:

Roger and Rose are standing at the front door. Rose is fumbling in her purse mumbling to herself (things like: I'm sure I put it in here) and pulls out the key. Roger is fidgeting in controlled impatience.

Roger:

Well, mom, now that you're actually standing here, getting ready to head back into your childhood home, are you ready for this?

Rose:

Still fiddling with the key:

Grrr, what is wrong with this lock? I don't think we even had a lock on the door when I was growing up!

Roger:

Waiting for her to get the door open.
Steps back when she succeeds and there is
a loud "crrrreeeeeeekkkk" as it slowly opens.

Whoa, we need to put some oil on that screaming hinge.

Rose:

What are you talking about? I didn't hear anything.

ROGER:

How could you not hear that? It was like a screeching raven! Are your hearing aids still in your purse?

ROSE:

Yes, of course. I hate them and I don't really need them. I keep encouraging people to stop mumbling (including you), and I won't have to fix the creaking door if I don't hear the creak.

They enter the living room and carefully look around.

ROGER:

It's strange, really, that I have never seen this house. I guess that after your mom moved into that intentional community it has always been a rental. Now that grandma has passed on I guess we have our work cut out for us getting it ready for the next stage.

ROSE:

A bit overwhelmed as she slowly surveys the room
and then startles Roger who is wandering around.

I can't believe it, look! This small little rocking chair in the corner is the one I had when I was little, my great granddad Robert made this in his furniture factory. I can't believe it survived all of the renters. Here, Roger, take this because we have to keep it. You can have it for your grandkids!

Roger groans but picks it up
and puts it by the front door.

ROSE:

Oh, and look, I can't believe this either, but here is the piano I got after years of begging for one. I love this piano so much. We have to take this, too. It's not too late for you to take up the piano. Or give it to one of your kids. They will love it so much, too!

Roger takes a very deep breath.

ROSE:

So what will we do with everything else? Luckily, you are a very smart man, so I'll leave this problem for you to solve. Just don't get rid of anything that you think I might still want to keep or that could still be useful!

ROGER:

Mom, I'll hire someone. There are people who do this for a living.

ROSE:

Hmmm, that seems like a waste of money. We'll talk about this later!

Okay then, let's go upstairs and take a look there. That's where my bedroom was. Wow, I don't remember these steps being so steep and hard to climb. They must have replaced them at some point.

> She starts climbing the stairs and makes a small breathy
> noise with every step using the banister to help herself
> move from one stair to the next.
> Arrives at bedroom and opens the door.

ROGER:

This room has seen better days, but what a great view. It definitely cries out for a paint job.

ROSE:

You know, I painted this room myself one time. Back when I thought that barn red was the perfect color for a bedroom. I used to love to paint rooms. There was something about the stroke of the brush laden with vibrant color. The next thing you know, everything around you is transformed. It surprises me that I don't want to do this room myself, but my passion for that kind of project appears to have completely disappeared.

ROGER:

Well, I guess we'll hire someone for that, too.

Rose walks to the closet, opens the door and slowly
crawls inside. She is remembering something. In the
back corner of the closet is a small nail head rising
slightly above a corner floorboard. Rose pulls the
nail up and the board comes up, too. She reaches
in and pulls out a small box.

Rose:

Roger, will you please help me up?

He takes the box in one hand and then takes her other
hand as she stands. They go sit on the bed where
she opens the box and removes a small mirror.

Rose:

*This hand mirror belonged to my great-grandmother (your
great-great-grandmother!). Wow, the mirror must be shocked
to see my face after all of these years. And maybe shocked that
it is not my great-grandma's young, then old, face. And next
my grandmother's young, then old, face. And then my mother's
young, then old, face. And now MY old face is what is left. Oh,
wait, here, you look in it so it can see you, too. Now you're part
of the mirror world, too!*

*I remember when my mother gave this to me and told me
the story of some of our family women who came before. The
first to come to the United States was a German immigrant
who went to the California gold rush along with her brothers.
On the ship over, she dressed as a man to disguise and protect herself. She met her future husband in a town near Sacramento, they made money, moved to Iowa, and the next thing
you know, here you and I are, due to the chance that two German immigrants, Gesche and Paul, would meet across the sea
in a dusty mining camp. That gold rush money was used to
buy a farm and then that led to a small inheritance, and that
inheritance eventually led to the purchase of this house. Had
that never happened we wouldn't be here today looking at her*

old hand mirror. Neither of us would have been born, and I am
very happy that I got to know you!

> Hands the mirror to Roger who looks at himself,
> pats down a little patch of hair that is sticking out
> over his ear and puts the mirror back in the box.

ROSE:

*And here is my secret tube of red Tabu lipstick. I don't know
where I got this in the first place, but I was so anxious to be
grown up and to wear it. Obviously, I never did wear it because
it's still in the box. Maybe I'll put it on now!*

> She takes out the mirror, puts on the lipstick and turns to
> Roger, who responds by involuntarily closing his eyes.

ROGER:

*That is not your style! I don't really remember seeing you wear
makeup at all when I was growing up. Is that true or did I just
forget?*

ROSE:

*I enthusiastically did wear makeup when I was in college, so I
guess I got to fulfill some sort of childhood dream and expectation. But after a while I found the whole concept of makeup
confusing. It seemed to be presenting me as someone different
than who I was, and it seemed odd and weird to do that. You're
right. I stopped wearing it and basically lived my life as "what
you see is what you get." From your reaction, I'm getting the
sense that you don't think I should take it up at this point in my
life. Okay, Tabu, you stay in the box!*

> Rose puts the lipstick back in the box, takes out a diary,
> flips to a random page and then reads out loud:

ROSE:

*"Today, Mom drove me to the mall. I had a haircut appoint-
ment and was going to meet Jane to shop for some new shoes.
I couldn't believe how annoying Mom was. It took her forever*

to get to the car. Her hip is bothering her again. I don't know why she doesn't just exercise more, or why she lets the pain get in the way of getting me where I need to be. I can't wait until I can get my own car. She is so frustrating."

ROGER:

Did she have some kind of injury? I suppose back then they weren't doing hip replacements the way they are now. I'm guessing that, since I'm in such good shape and take good care of myself, I won't ever end up dealing with body pains.

ROSE:

Who knows? I hope you're right. I was surprised when I had a skiing accident that messed up my ankle, and it has never really healed. I wasn't expecting that! That old song about the ankle bone connected to the knee bone, connected to the hip bone, etc. One thing affects the other...and then arthritis sets in. And then you find you can't really see where the little arrows are on the childproof caps of the pill bottles to quell the arthritis. And as your eyesight gets worse it makes driving more stressful, even when you do get glasses. Then you hear you need cataract surgery but who wants that? And when driving becomes more stressful, you don't want to go anywhere. And when you don't want to go anywhere that brings a whole new set of challenges! Luckily, in the midst of all of these physical inconveniences, I still have a sense of humor. And that is something I will do my best to hold on to! Keep reminding me!

ROGER:

Is there anything else in that diary that jumps out at you?

ROSE:

Here is a folded-up newspaper article about my parents' anniversary celebration. They were married in 1946 and had gone through a lot to stay connected during World War II. It must have been so strange not to know if Dad would actually make it back home from overseas or if every time they saw each other it might be the last time. They ended up being married for a long time, and each one of them helped the other through significant illnesses.

ROGER:

It makes me think of that famous Ram Dass quote: "We're all just walking each other home." So, even though there were struggles, they were lucky to have each other.

ROSE:

When my dad died at 61 I had so much grief at his loss that I hardly thought about my mom. When she would express fear or loneliness, I just shut it out and felt angry at her for being so selfish. I sure understand her struggles now. She spent 30 aging years of her life without him.

ROGER:

Well, I guess when he died you were busy raising us kids and working at your job and didn't really know what to do to help Grandma.

ROSE:

Now I wish I could reassure her and tell her I would be there to help her. Let her know that I understood her pain and wouldn't be so impatient. I wouldn't get so annoyed when she periodically lost her words. Some of those words turned out to have wisdom and humor and were stories I wish I could remember today. I must say that one advantage of her final years of dementia was that she repeated the same things over and over again, and those are the stories I remember! It has taken me a long time to develop compassion for her, but now (and maybe it took her death to open the door) I am often overwhelmed with compassion and gratitude for her life.

ROGER:

Well, here Mom, hand me the box and I will help you up. We can go through the rest later.

Are there any other hidden things in this house you want to find before we go? Let's walk through all of the rooms and see if there's anything else you want to keep before we get the house ready to put on the market. We haven't really talked about this, but have you considered that you might want to move back here?

ROSE:

I had a moment of thinking about moving back but that quickly passed. I love where I am now. I seldom like to leave home; it seems to have everything I want anymore. I watch the sea, the birds, the clouds, the boats. The sky changes color all day long, and the evolution of the sunset from winter to summer keeps me engaged. Who would have guessed—after all of my travels and longing for more? I have enough…

ROGER:

You know, though, I can't help worrying about you living by yourself and watching you become a bit more forgetful and unsteady. Sometimes I wonder if you might actually want to go to an assisted-living place. They always have lots of activities and company and extra help. What do you do with yourself every day now?

ROSE:

You're certainly hitting on the challenges of aging! Forgetfulness, sometimes loneliness, unsteadiness, and even pain. So many unexpected situations. And I can't minimize the decrease in sensory abilities. Luckily, I, like a lot of my friends, seem to have unleashed this odd little reservoir of creativity! I have friends who paint, do woodworking, dance, sing, and act.

In my case, it turns out that it is writing that inspires and energizes me. I write history and family stories, but mostly I like to write one act plays. I have even had the good fortune to have them produced sometimes. I guess you know about that.

ROGER:

Yes, of course, I've attended those plays, remember?

ROSE:

Yes, and I appreciate that you did! Oh, and that reminds me. I have tickets for us to go to a play tonight. My walking partner has the lead role, and I have helped her to rehearse.

It is called "Whose Turn Is It Now?" and it revolves around an elderly couple going on vacation. At the beginning, the wife is having trouble walking and can't keep up with her husband at all. She is very discouraged and embarrassed. During the second half, the husband contracts pneumonia, and the wife becomes the strong one and gets him home.

Hopefully, the seats won't be uncomfortable, and we will be sitting close enough to see the faces. Hopefully, the actors will have good clear voices so I can hear what they say. Hopefully, the play won't be too long. And hopefully, it will inspire me to write my next play!

ROGER:

Well, Mom, hopefully it won't put me to sleep!

> Smiling on her way out she stops at the piano and, thanks to muscle memory, plays "Heart and Soul" very loudly. She motions Roger over, hoping he knows how to play the bass part with her.

Kathi Ciskowski, along with her husband and (now grown) two sons, has lived on a small island in the Salish Sea in Washington State for 40 years. She is now 74. When she was 20, she made a decision to dedicate her life to nature, music, children, and the joys of reading and writing. That is pretty much how things unfolded. Waldorf education and the works of Rudolf Steiner inspired her to become a Parent/Toddler group leader; remedial educator; biography student and teacher; tutor and a founding board member with the Orcas Anthroposophical Trust.

BIBLIOGRAPHY

Barry, Wendell. *The Long-Legged House: Essays.* Berkeley, CA: Counterpoint, 2003.

Bergh, Kirsten Savitri. *She Would Draw Flowers: A Book of Poems.* Galway, Ireland: Parzival Productions, 1997.

Bryant, William. *The Veiled Pulse of Time: An Introduction to Biographical Cycles and Destiny.* Hudson, NY: Anthroposophic, Press 1993.

Burkhard, Gudrun. *Taking Charge: Your Life Patterns and Their Meaning.* Edinburgh: Floris Books, 1998.

———. *Die Freiheit im "Dritten Alter." Biographische Gesetzmäßigkeiten im Leben ab 63.* Stuttgart: Verlag Freies Geistesleben, 2004.

Fuller, Robert. *Somebodies and Nobodies: Overcoming the Abuse of Rank.* Gabriola Island BC, Canada: New Society Publishers, 2003.

Gawande, Atul. *Being Mortal: Medicine and What Matters in the End.* New York: Metropolitan Books, 2017.

Glas, Norbert, MD. *The Fulfilment of Old Age.* New York: Anthroposophic Press, 1970.

Heusser, Peter. *Anthroposophy and Science: An Introduction.* Berlin: Verlag der Wissenschaften, 2016.

Hillesum, Etty. *An Interrupted Life: The Diaries of Etty Hillesum 1941–43.* New York: Henry Holt and Co., 1966.

Hillman, James. *The Force of Character: And the Lasting Life.* New York: Ballantine Books, 1999.

———. *The Soul's Code: In Search of Character and Calling.* New York: Ballantine, 1996.

Husemann, Friedrich, Otto Wolff, et al. *The Anthroposophic Approach to Medicine: An Outline of a Spiritual Scientifically Oriented Medicine* (3 vols.). Steiner Books, 1983.

Jocelyn, Beredene. *Citizens of the Cosmos: Life's Unfolding from Conception through Death to Rebirth.* Great Barrington MA: Steiner Books, 2009.

Lagerlöf, Selma. *Christ Legends.* Edinburgh: Floris Books, 2013.

Lawrence-Lightfoot, Sara. *The Third Chapter: Passion, Risk, and Adventure in the 25 Years after 50.* New York: Sarah Crichton, 2009.

Lievegoed, Bernard. *Phases: The Spiritual Rhythms in Adult Life.* Forest Row, UK: Rudolf Steiner Press, 1998.

Moody, Raymond. *Life after Life: The Investigation of a Phenomenon— Survival of Bodily Death.* San Francisco: Harper, 2001.

Moorjani, Anita. *Dying to Be Me: My Journey from Cancer, to Near Death, to True Healing.* Carlsbad, CA: Hay House Press, 2012.

Nuland, Sherman. *How We Die: Reflections on Life's Final Chapter.* New York: Vintage Books, 1993.

O'Neil, George and Gisela. *The Human Life: Understanding Your Biography* (edited by Florin Lowndes). Spring Valley, NY: Mercury Press, 1990.

Paxino, Iris. *Bridges between Life and Death.* Edinburgh: Floris Books, 2021.

———. *Speaking with Angels. Life Lessons from the Angelic World.* Forest Row, UK: Temple Lodge, 2023.

Ritchie, George. *Return from Tomorrow.* Grand Rapids, MI: Revell Books, 1978.

Roszell, Calvert. *The Near-Death Experience: In the Light of Scientific Research and Rudolf Steiner's Spiritual Science,* 2nd edition. Great Barrington, MA: SteinerBooks, 2018.

Schaefer, Signe Eklund. *Why on Earth? Biography and the Practice of Human Becoming.* Great Barrington, MA: SteinerBooks, 2013.

———. *She Was Always There: Sophia as a Story for Our Time.* Great Barrington, MA: SteinerBooks, 2023.

Scott-Maxwell, Florida. *The Measure of My Days: One Woman's Vivid, Enduring Celebration of Life and Aging.* New York: Penguin, 1979.

Soesman, Albert. *Our Twelve Senses: How Healthy Senses Refresh the Soul.* Gloucestershire, UK: Hawthorn Press, 1990.

Staley, Betty. *Tapestries: Weaving Life's Journey.* Gloucestershire, UK: Hawthorn Press, 1997.

Steiner, Rudolf. *Ancient Myths and the New Isis Mystery* (CW 180). Great Barrington, MA: SteinerBooks, 2018.

———. *At Home in the Universe: Exploring our Suprasensory Nature* (CW 231). Hudson, NY: Anthroposophic Press, 2000.

———. *Becoming the Archangel Michael's Companions: Rudolf Steiner's Challenge to the Younger Generation* (CW 217). Great Barrington, MA: SteinerBooks, 2006.

———. *Biography: Freedom and Destiny: Enlightening the Path of Human Life* (edited by E. Fucke). Forest Row, UK: Rudolf Steiner Press, 2009.

———. *From Comets to Cocaine…: Answers to Questions* (CW 348). Forest Row, UK: Rudolf Steiner Press, 2002.

———. *Getting Old: Excerpts from Rudolf Steiner's Complete Works*, edited by Gisela Gaumnitz. Chestnut Ridge, NY: Mercury Press, 2009.

———. *Growing Old. The Spiritual Dimensions of Ageing*, edited by Franz Ackermann. Forest Row, U K: Rudolf Steiner Press, 2019.

———. *The Healing Process: Spirit, Nature, and Our Bodies* (CW 319). Hudson, NY: Anthroposophic Press, 2000.

———. *Health and Illness*, vol. 1 (CW 348). See *From Comets to Cocaine…: Answers to Questions*.

———. *How to Know Higher Worlds: A Modern Path of Initiation* (CW 10). Hudson, NY: Anthroposophic Press, 1994.

———. *Initiation, Eternity, and the Passing Moment*. Spring Valley, NY: Anthroposophic Press, 1980.

———. *Intuitive Thinking as a Spiritual Path: A Philosophy of Freedom* (CW 4). Hudson, NY: Anthroposophic Press, 1995.

———. *Isis, Mary, Sophia: Her Mission and Ours*, edited by Christopher Bamford. Great Barrington, MA: Steiner Books, 2003.

———. *Life between Death and Rebirth: The Active Connection between the Living and the Dead* (CW 140). Anthroposophic Press, 1968.

———. *Love and Its Meaning in the World*, edited by Christopher Bamford. Hudson, NY: Anthroposophic Press, 1998.

———. *Macrocosm and Microcosm: The Greater and the Lesser World: Questions Concerning the Soul, Life and the Spirit* (CW 119). Forest Row, UK: Rudolf Steiner Press, 2021.

———. *An Outline of Esoteric Science* (CW 13). Hudson, NY: Anthroposophic Press, 1997.

———. *The Presence of the Dead on the Spiritual Path* (CW 154). Hudson, NY: Anthroposophical Press, 1990.

———. *The Spiritual Background to the First World War* (CW 174b). Forest Row, UK: Rudolf Steiner Press, 2024.

———. *Staying Connected. How to Continue Your Relationships with Those Who Have Died* (edited by Christopher Bamford). Hudson, NY: Anthroposophic Press, 1999.

———. *Reincarnation and Karma: Two Fundamental Truths of Human Existence* (CW 135). Hudson, NY: Anthroposophic Press, 2001.

———. *Verses and Meditations*. London: Rudolf Steiner Press, 1979.

———. *World History and the Mysteries: In the Light of Anthroposophy* (CW 233). Forest Row, UK: Rudolf Steiner Press, 2021.

Steiner, Rudolf, and Ita Wegman. *Fundamentals of Therapy: An Extension of the Art of Healing through Spiritual Knowledge* (CW 27). Forest Row, UK: Rudolf Steiner Press, 1983. Current edition: *Extending Practical Medicine: Fundamental Principles Based on the Science of the Spirit*. Rudolf Steiner Press, 1997.

Storr, Anthony. *The Essential Jung*. Boston: MJF Books, 1983.

Sturgeon-Day, Lee. *Biography and Life Cycles Workbook*. Prescott, AZ: LifeWays for Healing Education, 2019.

Tippett, Krista. *Becoming Wise: An Inquiry into the Mystery and Art of Living*. Penguin, 2016.

Wagner, Roger. *The Nearer You Stand: Poems and Images*. Norwich, UK: Canterbury Press Norwich, 2019.

Zeylmans Van Emmichoven, F. W. *The Anthroposophical Understanding of the Soul*. Spring Valley, NY: Anthroposophic Press, 1982.